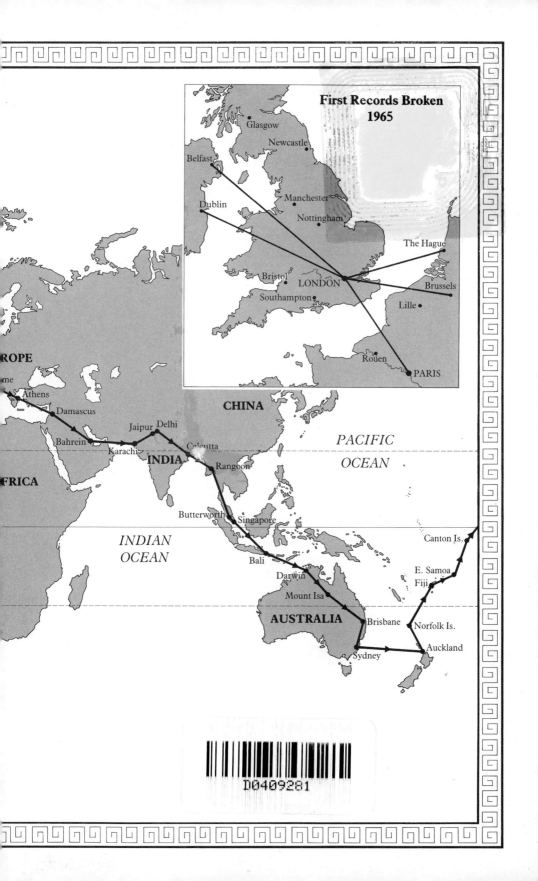

First Records Broken
1965

Glasgow
Newcastle
Belfast
Manchester
Dublin
Nottingham
The Hague
Bristol
LONDON
Brussels
Southampton
Lille
Rouen
PARIS

ROPE
me
Athens
Damascus
Jaipur Delhi
Bahrein
Karachi
INDIA
Calcutta
Rangoon
FRICA
Butterworth
Singapore
INDIAN
OCEAN
Bali
Darwin
Mount Isa
AUSTRALIA
Brisbane
Sydney
Auckland

CHINA

PACIFIC
OCEAN

Canton Is.
E. Samoa
Fiji
Norfolk Is.

D0409281

SHEILA SCOTT

BY THE SAME AUTHOR

Walking in the Clouds
Women of the Air
Hanna Reitsch

SHEILA SCOTT

JUDY LOMAX

HUTCHINSON

London Sydney Auckland Johannesburg

Copyright © Judy Lomax 1990

The right of Judy Lomax to be identified as Author of this
work has been asserted by Judy Lomax in accordance with the
Copyright, Designs and Patent Act, 1988

All rights reserved

This edition first published in 1990 by
Hutchinson

Century Hutchinson Ltd,
20 Vauxhall Bridge Road, London SW1V 2SA

Century Hutchinson Australia
20 Alfred Street, Milsons Point, Sydney NSW 2061, Australia

Century Hutchinson New Zealand Limited
PO Box 40–086, Glenfield, Auckland 10, New Zealand

Century Hutchinson South Africa (Pty) Ltd
PO Box 337, Bergvlei, 2012 South Africa

British Library Cataloguing in Publication Data
Lomax, Judy, *1939–*
    Sheila Scott
    1. Aircraft. Flying. Scott, Sheila
    I. Title
    629.13′092′4

ISBN 0–09–174114–9

Typeset by Speedset Ltd, Ellesmere Port
Printed and bound in Great Britain
by Richard Clay Ltd, Bungay, Suffolk

HERTFORDSHIRE
LIBRARY SERVICE

No.

Class
61SCO/629.13092/sco

| Supplier | Price | Date |
| JMLS | 16.95 | 22/6 |

1 8 JUL 1990

Contents

Acknowledgements	vi
Introduction	1
Chapter One	6
Chapter Two	16
Chapter Three	30
Chapter Four	41
Chapter Five	57
Chapter Six	73
Chapter Seven	89
Chapter Eight	103
Chapter Nine	115
Chapter Ten	127
Chapter Eleven	141
Chapter Twelve	157
Chapter Thirteen	169
Chapter Fourteen	189
Chapter Fifteen	204
Chapter Sixteen	221
Chapter Seventeen	234
Chapter Eighteen	245
Epilogue	255
('Dancing the Skies', by John Gillespie Magee, read at Sheila Scott's funeral and memorial services)

Acknowledgements

Without Sheila's agreement, and her cooperation during the last few months of her life, this book would not have been possible. After her death, her executors carried out her wish that I should be given access to her papers. My thanks go therefore both to them, and in particular to her cousin David Hurlstone, and to those who have granted me interviews, answered letters and telephone calls, and in many cases have gone out of their way to help me. I am also grateful to Sheila's publishers, Hodder and Stoughton, for allowing me to quote from her books, and to Jack Meadows and Doreen Deane, through whom I was granted permission to use the correspondence between Sheila and Kaye Maclean. Last, but not least, I should like to thank my family, for allowing Sheila to become a part of their lives both before and after her death.

My thanks go to all those listed below. I apologise to them for not having the space to go into details of their assistance, and to those whom I have not been able to include but who had the courtesy to answer letters or to return phone calls.

Individuals:

Gerald Abrahams; Jack Allen; Graeme Altern; Helen Anderson; Simon Ames; Sydney Amster; Philip Attenborough; Dennis Bardens; Olivia Barrington-Ward; Betty Bascomb; Robert Batt; Colin Bell; Lady Gwen Bellew; Kay Beng (née Bird); Edna Bianchi; John Blake; Col. John Blashford-Snell; Chay Blyth; Margaret Body; Sheila Bond; Marianne Borman; David Brackley; Lady Bromet; Sir David Brown; Captain Eric Brown; Wendi Brownlie; Betty Burford; Peter Cadbury; Victor Cannock; Tom Carpenter; Phil Chapman; Col. Naomi Christie; Michael Cobham; Hugh Collins; Sandra and Tabitha Collins; Brenda Constable; Chuck Cote; Theo Cowan; Stella Cresswell-Wall; Sir Peter Cunningham; David Davies; Ian David; Wilma Dawes; Robert and Doreen Deane; Jeanette Dexter; Andrew Donelly; Hilary Duke-Woolley; Molly Diamond; Bridget Dobbs; Geoffrey Edwards; June Eggleston; Jack Effner; Lord Erskine of Rerrick; Bob Evans; Tony Everard; Joan Faram; Sheila Farrar; Fleur Ferri; Brian Fields; Captain Delphine Gray Fiske; Lady Sheila Francis-Chichester; Connie Fricker; Paul Garber; Arthur Gibson; Pat Gibson; Fay Gillis Wells; Fred Gooch; Dr Malcolm Green; Ivan Hattingh; Ted Hawkes; Arthur Honeyball; Ann Hegarty; Dr Colin Herridge; Dick Hoagland; Jack Holmes; Brenda Horsfield; Col. Philip Howes; Lady Pamela Huntly; Mrs Ray Hanna; Gloria Hunniford; David and Jean Hurlstone; Paul Huxford; Lana St George Jeffers; Norman Jones; Colonel Trevor Jones; Lord Kimberley; Lord King of Wartnaby; Michael Korda; Alan Lathan; Chery Lea; Lord

Leinster; Ann Lennard; Fred Lewis; Peter Lewis-Crown; Eileen Lindahl; Rosemary Longmere; Norman Lonsdale; Lady Lothian; Dr Paul MacLoughlin; Bella Mackinnon; Squadron Leader Robert Major; Tony Marchant; Ray Marley; Fred Marsh; Sir Peter Masefield; Jack Meadows; June Mendoza; James Molyneux; Bryan Monkton; Princes Helen Montafian; David Morris; Margot Morse; Frank Murphy; T. Murphy; Fran Nolan; Peter Odds; David Ogilivie; Richard Ormsby; Dr Neville Oswald; Captain Elizabeth Overbury; Monti Mackey Parker; Gerald Pawle; R. F. Penney; Sir Ralph Perring; Dr Ian Perry; Jean Ross Howard Phelan; Jim Phelan; John and Paddy Pimley; Gerald Pollinger; Dr Robert Poole; Bob Pooley; Dr Frank Preston; Colonel the Rt. Hon. Lord Pritchard; John Profumo; Hazel Prosper; J. Shirley Rainer; Eve Raphael; Jim Reynolds; Bill (Robbie) Robinson; Sadie Robinson; F. N. L. Rogers; Jill Roper; Marjorie Ryland; Eric Rylands; Vivienne Schuster; Major General Michael Scott; Nicholas Scott; Major Sir James Scott-Hopkins; Bill Seechuck; Freydis Sharland; Biddy Shout; Ellen Sighvatsson; Anthony Smith; Dr Peter Smith; Beverley Snook; Angus Stewart; Fred Stringer; Catherine Sugden; Anne Steventon; Colonel Jocelyn Tatman; Frank Thornton; Charles Thomas; Frank Thomas; Jean Topping; Joan Toulson; Edward Trees; Leslie and Jean Tuck; Muriel Tucker; Joan Turner; Iris Wade; Diana Barnato Walker; Nancy Bird Walton; Claire Walters; Ernest Waldron West; Dr Trevor Weston; Colonel and Mrs Whitbread; Ann White; Anthony Whittome; Lee Whitsell; Hilary Harvey Whittle; Owen Williams; Rita Wilson; Nancy Wise; Brian Wolfe; Ken Wood; Bill Wordsworth; David Wynne-Morgan

Companies, institutions and organisations:

Air BP; Associated Speakers; Beaufort Air-Sea Equipment Ltd; Berrow's Newspaper Group; Bowden House Clinic; Bridgeman Morris; British Aerospace; British Women Pilots' Association; Brompton Hospital; Civil Aviation Authority; CSE; *Daily Mail; Daily Mirror*; Dudley Road Hospital, Birmingham; Elizabeth Arden; Entertainment Inc. Ltd; Equity; Esso Petroleum Co. Ltd; Fédération des Pilotes Européennes; Goddard Space Flight Center; First Cross Ltd; Fleet Air Arm Museum; Freshwater Property Management; Girls Venture Corps; Goodyear Great Britain Ltd; Guild of Air Pilots and Navigators; *Harpers & Queen*; Hodder and Stoughton; Institute of Aviation Medicine; International Aeradio; International Forest of Friendship; International Women's Air and Space Museum; International Wool Secretariat; Lombard North Central PLC; National Portrait Gallery; National Temperance Hospital; Nestlé; Newbury Helpline; Newbury Public Library; Newfoundland Museum; Phillips West Two; Ninety Nines; Poole and Dorset Adventure Centre; Priory Hospital, Roehampton; RAF Museum, Hendon; REME Corps Secretariat; Riverside Health Authority; Royal Naval Air Suadron, Yeovilton; Royal Society of Medicine; Smithsonian Institute; Special Forces Club; Tennant Housing Trust; Thuxton Flight Centre; Tiger Club; V.A.D. (R.N.) Association; Worcester City Council; Whirly Girls; Zonta.

Illustrations: the following have kindly made photographs available:

David Hurlstone and David Morris, Sheila Scott's executors; Mrs P. Gibson (portrait of Sheila's mother); John Turner (photo of Sheila with Peter Korda); Institute of Aviation Medicine, Farnborough (polar clothing); June Mendoza (portrait)

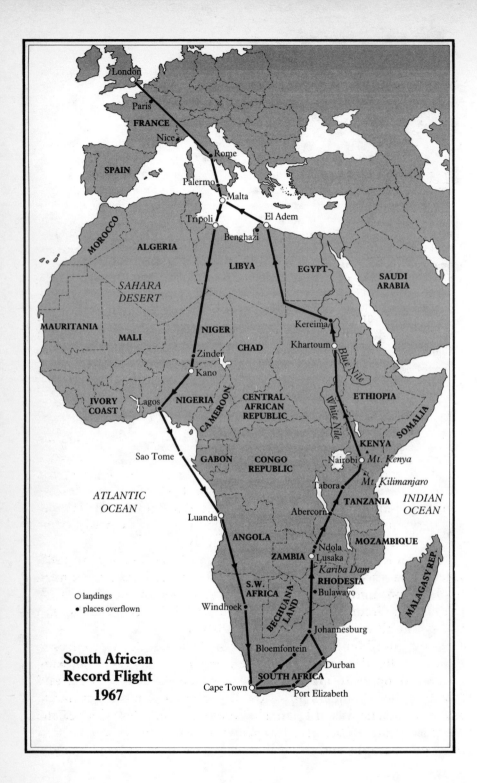

South African Record Flight 1967

London
Paris
FRANCE
Nice
SPAIN
Rome
Palermo
Malta
MOROCCO
Tripoli
Benghazi
El Adem
ALGERIA
LIBYA
EGYPT
SAUDI ARABIA
SAHARA DESERT
MAURITANIA
MALI
NIGER
CHAD
Kereima
Khartoum
Zinder
Kano
Blue Nile
IVORY COAST
Lagos
NIGERIA
CENTRAL AFRICAN REPUBLIC
CAMEROON
ETHIOPIA
White Nile
SOMALIA
KENYA
Sao Tome
GABON
CONGO REPUBLIC
Nairobi
Mt. Kenya
ATLANTIC OCEAN
Tabora
Mt. Kilimanjaro
TANZANIA
INDIAN OCEAN
Abercorn
Luanda
ANGOLA
MOZAMBIQUE
Ndola
ZAMBIA
Lusaka
Kariba Dam
○ landings
● places overflown
S.W. AFRICA
RHODESIA
Bulawayo
MALAGASY REP.
Windhoek
BECHUANA-LAND
Johannesburg
Bloemfontein
Durban
Cape Town
SOUTH AFRICA
Port Elizabeth

Introduction

LITTLE DID I think, as I admired Sheila Scott's elegance and courage from afar during her few brief years of flying glory in the 1960s and early 1970s, that I would ever meet her, let alone know her so well that I would be with her when she died. When I was a young wife and mother, struggling with domesticity, Sheila Scott was my heroine – although I am not normally inclined to hero-worship. I followed her progress from one record-breaking solo flight to another with a mixture of awe and envy – envy that even after many hours in a minute cockpit she could emerge looking as if she had just left an expensive session in a beauty salon, and awe that she dared to undertake her long, lonely ordeals in the first place.

No sooner had she completed one solo flight round the world than she was planning another. Between 1965 and 1972 she broke over a hundred records, many of which still stand. She was, as her publicity handouts claimed, living proof that it was possible to combine femininity and success – and success moreover in aviation, still very much a male-dominated world. Then, as suddenly as she had flown to fame, she was no longer news.

It was a few years before her death that I first met her, in 1985, when I was researching for a book about women pilots. She sounded hesitant, but agreed to let me visit her, although she warned me that, as her circumstances were now considerably reduced, her flat was not at all what she would have wished.

As we talked on that first meeting she made veiled references to things she dared not talk about. She seemed nervous, chain smoking as she sat opposite me in her small basement sitting room and hunching her shoulders forwards. I wondered, but did not like to ask, how old she was; if I had, she would no doubt have lopped the usual six years off her age. Her hair was, as it always had been in press photographs and television interviews, immaculately blonde,

1

held back from her forehead by a hairband, and she had obviously spent some time on her make-up. There was a tautness about her bone structure which suggested tension.

Her flat was not the setting I had imagined for a retired heroine. A steep, narrow, open-runged staircase led down to it from the pavement. The sash window in her front room was so opaque from the constant cigarette fumes that it scarcely needed the concealment of the full-length net curtain. A narrow passage went straight from the front door past the small cluttered sitting room, a bathroom exactly the length of the washbasin and bath and the width of bath and toilet, and an equally small and cramped kitchen. The bedroom was little more than a wider extension of the passage. There was nothing luxurious, nothing elegant: it felt and looked like a place in which to survive, rather than to live.

By the time we had run quickly through Sheila's life story, the 'Darlings' which had dramatically underlined disaster areas – of which her life had clearly been full – had become less frequent. Already I was aware of the great effort which had gone not only into her flying achievements, but also into the public image she had presented during her heyday – quite how much of an effort I did not fully realize until much later.

There are people with whom one feels an immediate rapport even on a first meeting, and so it was between us, although it is difficult to say why – especially as it was apparent that we would differ on many things. It was a tribute to Sheila's generosity that she did not resent my intrusion, since I was writing on a subject for which she had been collecting material for years. Later, after my book had been published and had met with her approval – 'You told it how it was,' she wrote to me – she brought out a case of cuttings and notes: 'I could have saved you a lot of work,' she said, 'if only I'd known you better then.'

It was a chance remark of Sheila's towards the end of our first meeting which led me to my next book, about a German woman test pilot who, although technically a civilian, during the war flew such revolutionary aircraft as a glider the size of a jumbo jet and a manned version of the V1 which was to have been used for suicide attacks on Allied shipping. 'Hanna Reitsch – you must include Hanna Reitsch,' she said. 'Hanna was the greatest: she was never forgiven for her patriotism, you know.' Sheila admired patriotism as much as she admired courage. When I later received a commission for a biography of Hanna Reitsch she was delighted.

'Darling, you must come to Vienna.' It was Sheila on the telephone, a few months later: there was to be an annual get-together of the European Women Pilots' Association, of which Sheila was then president. 'There will be lots of people there who knew Hanna.' As I set out for Vienna with her, I was not sure whether I was her protégée, or her protector against the many plots and disasters which seemed constantly to threaten her. She undoubtedly had problems to contend with that weekend – problems about which she uttered dire warnings on the plane; on this occasion, at least, they were neither of her own making, nor imagined – although perhaps she exaggerated their significance.

The European Federation of Women Pilots – or, to give it its French title, La Fédération des Pilotes Européennes – meant a lot to Sheila. It meant as much to its French founder, who was determined that her language should be used for all Federation business and whose representative in Vienna spoke no English. Almost immediately a wrangle over whether English, as the international language of aviation, or French, as the mother tongue of the organization's place of origin, should be used in committee discussions. Sheila, who was not a good chairman, was in despair. Somehow I found myself appointed interpreter, an uncomfortable position as I was not even a member of the organization.

At last, late in the evening, the committee disbanded. 'Thank God for that,' said Sheila. 'Now let's have a quiet drink.' I had hardly taken the first sip when Sheila clutched my arm, staring fixedly across the hotel bar. 'They're here,' she whispered.

'Who's here?' I asked. She seemed to be looking directly at an inoffensive young couple.

'They – you know who I mean,' she hissed. 'They track me down everywhere. Even here. I'm never safe.' She was convinced that she was being followed by agents of some sinister undercover organization; after that, I was with her on many other occasions and in many other places when 'they' suddenly appeared.

Her fear seemed, briefly, real enough – but could it have any substance other than in her own deluded imagination? Was it a symptom of mental illness, or a hint of some real danger? Either way, she was clearly under such strain that I feared she would be unable to cope with the social functions which had been laid on for us by the Austrian Aero Club. I did not then know her well enough to realize that of course she would rise to the occasion, looking magnificent in a long, high-necked green evening dress for a dinner and ball under a full moon, and flirting elegantly with the men in full-dress uniform.

When I invited her to stay with us for Christmas I kept my fingers crossed that the rest of my family would like her, for all her oddness, as much as I did, and that we would be spared the sudden stare and whisper of paranoia. We discovered yet another Sheila, a Sheila who could sit on the floor talking to a six-year-old without being patronizing and throw herself into games of charades without minding that for once her elegance was dishevelled. This was a Sheila who might have been, a family Sheila with an ability to care about each one of us as much as about herself, a warm, loving person waiting to be released from the cage which she had created around herself.

It was perhaps because we accepted Sheila as she was, and she us, without questioning, without setting limits or conditions and without infringing on individual privacies, that our friendship was never marred by friction. At times we found her exasperating – and vice versa; we often disagreed, but could agree to differ. I felt that she was lonely, although she knew many people, and hope that we made her less lonely for a while.

Sheila often felt – sometimes with cause, but more often without – that she was being used or plotted against not only by nameless agents but also by those closest to her. It was for that reason that I hesitated before suggesting to her that I might write her biography; but eventually, several months after we both knew that she was dying, I did suggest it, tentatively. She welcomed the idea.

I doubt whether it has come out exactly as she would have wanted. Since her death I have found out much that I can understand her wanting to forget; it was all, however painful, part of her. Some people may feel that I should neither have probed into areas of her life which she had kept secret, nor have revealed the negative aspects of her personality. There may still be many things about her which I do not understand; I have certainly had to leave out many details, and many people, because of restrictions of space.

But I hope that, by accepting her weaknesses as well as her strengths, and by attempting to understand her, I have shown her for what she was: a remarkable and an unforgettable person, who overcame many difficulties – some of her own making – and who showed as she approached death the strength and the courage which she had often, but not always, displayed in life. One of her closest friends, Elizabeth Overbury, begged me to 'come up with something that is – Sheila Scott!' It is up to her and others to judge whether I have done so.

1

If Sheila Christine Hopkins had been granted one wish as a child, it would have been to have a mother as well as a father. She could remember neither what her mother looked like, nor the sound of her voice. The shadow of a slim, dark-haired woman who held out her arms at the top of a lawn haunted her dreams. 'Why did she leave me?' she asked herself over and over again. As no one explained, Sheila assumed with the egocentricity of childhood that somehow, although she did not know how or why, she had driven her mother away. Her guilt combined with resentment to isolate her in her own unhappiness. Although she could not at the time have defined her feelings, she felt robbed of her identity.

If it had not been for the misery of having been abandoned by her mother, and the stigma of her parents' divorce, Sheila's background could hardly have been more stolidly stable or solidly middle-class. 'It was,' as one of her cousins told me, 'very *Forsyte Saga*, very Victorian, with very strict old-fashioned values. We always had a living-in maid, with a daily cook and bottle washer' – the pre-war trappings of financial and social comfort and acceptability.

Sheila's father, Harold Reginald Hopkins, was the third child and only son of a baker who had moved to Worcester in 1912. Her grandfather, William Hopkins, had sold his village bakery near Rugby and was planning to emigrate to Canada; but when the *Titanic* sank the long sea voyage suddenly lost its appeal, although by then his brother was already in Ontario. William took his family to Worcester instead, where he established a new bakery business.

Although Harold was too young to join up when war was declared in 1914, he lied about his age, only to be invalided out in 1915 with a steel plate in his skull. Although this made him a war hero in the eyes of his five sisters, it was an unnecessary and silly accident in which he had lost an eye: with his few remaining men, Harold, a

6

non-commissioned officer, was resting behind a clump of rocks, sheltering from Turkish gunfire, when a cigarette card of a film star fell out of his pocket. As he leaned forward to pick it up, he was shot.

His disfigurement, and the recurrent headaches from which he subsequently suffered, made him perhaps more withdrawn and taciturn than he might otherwise have been. Nevertheless the one-eyed war veteran, heir to W. H. Hopkins and Co. – by then a flourishing business with its own shop – was one of Worcester's most eligible young men. In January 1921 Harold Hopkins married Edyth Kenward, daughter of a local tailor and outfitter. Sheila was born fifteen months later, on 27 April 1922.

Those who had darkly predicted disaster for the marriage were all too soon proved right. Edyth Kenward had been considered flighty at school; her reputation as 'a rake', 'a bad lot' and 'a one for the men' was remembered and brought out during gossip over the teacups when she began to associate with, of all people, touring actors, a class of person regarded with the deepest suspicion by the provincial worthies of Worcester. It was for one of these touring actors that she left her husband and daughter.

As no one in the Hopkins family ever spoke openly about her after her defection, it is impossible to apportion blame or to establish why it was that, after only four years of marriage and three of motherhood, Edyth's flightiness apparently reasserted itself. All Sheila was ever told was that her mother had run off with a comedian whom she had met when his company was playing at the Worcester Playhouse. This was, in the eyes of the Hopkins family, disgraceful behaviour, and not to be forgiven. Infidelity might, given a modicum of discretion, have been condoned; but not desertion, nor, worse still, divorce. All photographs of Edyth were destroyed, and the Hopkins family closed ranks over the gap as if she had never existed. But although they behaved as if they had forgotten her, they never forgave her.

It seems inconceivable that Edyth can have vanished totally without trace – indeed she cannot have done so immediately, as there was the matter of the divorce to settle before she was free, and this must inevitably have meant that she and Harold remained in contact at least through their solicitors. But as far as Sheila was concerned, her mother never again showed any sign of affection or even of interest in her. If Edyth wrote letters, Sheila was not told; if she asked how Sheila was, or sent news or photographs of herself, this information was never passed on. Sheila grew up convinced that she had had no more than a passing importance for her mother, and that even during those first few years she had merely been tolerated, but never loved.

In the summer of 1926 Edyth Hopkins remarried, in a registry office in Kensington. The only time her name was ever mentioned afterwards was when Sheila misbehaved. Then she overheard dire mutterings about 'turning out like her mother'. This, it seemed, must be avoided at all costs; but as Sheila had no idea what her mother was like, she could not tell to what extent she took after her. A photograph of Edyth shows dark, brooding eyes, a full mouth, a wistful expression. It is a sad, sensitive face, but bears little obvious resemblance to Sheila, who never saw the picture: it was given to me by one of her school friends, who felt it better to keep it from her.

Until she was ten Sheila lived with her grandparents, where she was equally spoilt by them and by any of her aunts who happened to be around; the two youngest were still at first living at home, and the other three, two of whom were already married, in flats above the Hopkins shops. Apart from her continuing grief and guilt at the loss of her mother Sheila had no reason to be unhappy, and was outwardly a happy, cheerful child, although she was capable of a most determined scowl under her thick, heavy fringe.

She adored her father, of whom she saw little; but every now and then he would attempt to compensate. She looked forward to having him to herself occasionally for a whole day, and treasured the memory of their visits to the zoo, the circus, the fair, the swimming pool and – most exciting of all – to Alan Cobham's Air Circus. This was her sixth birthday treat; the fierce-looking man who glared at her through dark goggles when she objected to being strapped into her seat in the open cockpit of his flimsy canvas-covered aircraft was Cobham himself. Afterwards she had a confused but happy memory of noise and smells and the feeling of the wind in her face as she looked down at houses which had suddenly become no larger than toys beneath her.

When Sheila was ten, her father remarried. His second wife was Aileen Harper, the quietest and shyest of the three daughters of a respectable and respected Worcester brewer. She was generally considered gentle, ladylike, pleasant enough, not unattractive. Sheila thought her elegant and admired her dress sense, and was pleased about the wedding, at which she drank her first champagne: it made her feel sick. But Aileen had little idea of how to approach a prickly, motherless child, and even less sensitivity to the problems of a rebellious, unhappy teenager.

Sheila found Aileen's cold perfectionism and meticulous insistence on cleanliness, godliness and tidiness alarming and impossible to live up to. There was, initially and always, one vital ingredient missing in Aileen's attitude to her stepdaughter: affection. Aileen did her duty to the best of her ability, and was generous enough in her provision of toys and clothes – especially clothes: the one lasting lesson Sheila learnt from her was how to dress well – but she made it all too clear that being a stepmother was a duty rather than a pleasure. It was not long before Sheila was, as she put it, 'frightened to death' of her stepmother – not that Aileen was ever physically violent; but her almost constant disapproval undermined Sheila's precarious self-confidence.

She must have seemed to Aileen precisely the harum-scarum wild child likely, unless some discipline could be instilled, to follow in her mother's disgraced footsteps. But in the cold, clean, sterile atmosphere created by her stepmother, Sheila felt that nothing she could do would ever please her. As she was incorrigibly untidy she was constantly in Aileen's bad books, and was often locked in her room as a punishment. Pathetically, she tried to buy Aileen's favour by giving her little bars of chocolate; but when her own pocket money ran out, she helped herself to that of her friends – which of course brought more trouble down on her head.

From kindergarten to sixth form Sheila attended the Alice Ottley School for Girls, a private establishment at which her great-grandmother had been a founder pupil. Her school friends disliked Aileen almost as much as she did: they all knew that Sheila was no angel, but resented the way Aileen criticized and belittled her even when they were present. 'Aileen was a bit of a dragon, and snobby,' one of Sheila's school friends told me; 'the stricter she was, the more Sheila went the other way – her aunts were more sympathetic, and quite jolly.'

Sheila longed for affection, but even her father never openly or spontaneously showed her any love. He expected to have his dogmatic opinions unquestioningly accepted by three generations of women; and as she grew up Sheila felt that he was more interested in his later activities as an alderman and as chairman of the

Worcester racecourse than he was in her. He showed less enthusi-asm than his father for the business, which he inherited at about the time he remarried; but inevitably this too made considerable demands on his time, and he had little left for his daughter.

Bringing up children was, in Harold's conventional view, woman's work, and so he left it to Aileen. Although he had a fierce temper, Sheila could only remember him ever shouting at her once, when she was sixteen or seventeen. Aileen had bought her her first long dress and high-heeled shoes, for which she was grudgingly grateful, and she was all ready to go to her first ball; Harold forbade her to go. She was staying with an aunt, who attempted to remonstrate. 'You can't treat her like a child, Harold,' the aunt pleaded, but in vain. Quite why Harold was so angry, Sheila was not sure; she suspected that it was because she was to have been escorted by a young cousin of her stepmother's.

Aileen nevertheless allowed Sheila to mix freely with her own cousins; as Kathleen Turner was the only aunt still living in Worcester, she saw more of her and her only son, John, than of any of the others. John, who was several years younger, looked on Sheila as a big sister, a role thrust on her particularly on Sundays, but one which she did not mind: Sundays would have been even more boring and empty without the ritual of fetching John, walking with him to church where they were met by Aileen, and then, after Sunday lunch, taking him for another walk while the adults snoozed or chatted by the fire.

Sunday church, for which Sheila was expected to wear a hat and gloves and carry a handbag, was important to Aileen. The weekly ritual established in Sheila a lifelong mistrust of established religion, based partly on her conviction that Aileen went to church only for show, and partly on her resentment of the fear which seemed to her an essential ingredient of the Christian faith; but she was never able to free herself from a deeply religious instinct.

Later, Sheila often gave an impression of a childhood totally devoid of fun and affection. She spoke so little of her family that many people imagined she had none; and indeed she felt so alienated by her stepmother, and by her rejection by her own mother, that she often felt as unloved and unwanted as if she had been an orphan. But there were happy times with her cousins, who considered her an extrovert, to offset the loneliness. At Christmas the Hopkins family had great convivial family get-togethers in the largest of their premises: twenty-five could sit down to eat Christmas dinner with all the trimmings. Although Sheila looked forward as much as anyone else to these occasions, she felt apart, almost an outcast, over-sensitive to the contrast between her own loneliness and insecurity and the stability and companionship of the other branches of the family.

Sheila was older than all her cousins and to the adults appeared to be the ringleader in any scrapes; she was even blamed when Peter Hurlstone's experiments with her new chemistry set caused an explosion in Aileen's kitchen, although this was no more her fault than his. It was of course Sheila who, to the alarm of three boy cousins, put a match to a firework which had failed to ignite during a Guy Fawkes party in her grandparents' garden. The firework exploded in her face, with a flash which she thought at first had blinded her, and creating an acrid stench of burning hair. Sheila, lucky to escape without serious or lasting injury, was left with badly singed eyebrows and hair.

She was so terrified of what Aileen would say that she hid behind the sofa. Aileen's insistence that she should continue to attend school in spite of her strange singed appearance seemed to her the cruellest punishment her stepmother could have devised: even at that age she was very conscious of her appearance, and hated to appear foolish or inelegant.

Perhaps with an element of snobbery, Sheila resented, and whenever possible avoided contact with, the bakery. Like her cousins, and her aunts before them, she was roped in to help behind the counter on Saturdays or during school holidays – but whereas the others enjoyed doing so, Sheila hated it, and as usual blamed Aileen.

This was, however, not her bitterest memory of her stepmother's strictness. When she was fourteen, Sheila was caught secretly experimenting with Aileen's make-up. Her hair at the time was long and thick – one of her school friends has described it to me as 'Titian – a fantastic rich deep auburn'. Aileen's punishment for illicitly using make-up was subtly spiteful – she made Sheila have her hair cut to a short bob. That, at any rate, was the way Sheila remembered it: she never forgave her, although she could not blame on her stepmother the short-sightedness which was discovered at the same age. Having to wear glasses was even worse than being punished, and she did so as infrequently as possible.

When Sheila was sixteen, and John Turner ten, the two families shared a holiday in a friend's bungalow at Highcliffe near Bournemouth. For the first time Sheila showed impatience with her young cousin, when she was chatted up on the beach by two young men.

'You'd better walk back through the woods,' she said. 'I'll catch you up later.'

'I don't know the way,' John protested.

'You'll find it,' Sheila said, propelling him firmly by the scruff of his neck on to the path. John later discovered that she kept up a correspondence with one of the young men until he was killed during the war.

Her school friends would not have been surprised that Sheila had put a romantic encounter on the beach above her duty to look after her young cousin. She had by then already established a reputation for promiscuity which they secretly envied as much as they deplored. It was a more refined form of rebellion against the stiffness and restrictions of her home life than her earlier deliberate scruffiness and surliness, not to mention her occasional but memorably violent and melodramatic outbursts of temper both at home and at school: when she was angry or upset, which was often the case, she would hurl her satchel ahead of her into the classroom, and could clear the cloakroom pegs of the other girls' coats and bags in two minutes flat.

Sometimes she did not appear at school at all for several days, but spent the time searching in vain for her mother. Her absence would be preceded by a hoarse whisper: 'I think I may have a lead.' Although she undoubtedly made the most of any opportunity for drama, her unassuaged longing to find Edyth was no act. It had become an obsession. The more unspoken criticism of her mother she sensed at home, the more she longed to trace her. To have been deliberately abandoned, and to know nothing about the woman whom she was told she resembled only when she was being criticized, was still as unbearable as it was incomprehensible.

Sheila's friends forgave her for behaviour which they would not have condoned in anyone else because they were sorry for her, and because, however badly she behaved, she was exciting. 'She was great fun, and she was popular with the staff,' one of them told me. 'She was a devil, and there was some jealousy of her spirit; but she was a very good friend – and fantastic-looking.'

Her less adventurous friends were usually ready to join in

escapades organized or thought up by Sheila. 'Do you think your father would let you come to Solihull with me?' Sheila asked a classmate who was hoping to become a nurse. 'We could sneak a look at an operation.' Aileen's sister was matron of a nursing home in Solihull; she never knew that the two girls climbed on to a flat roof overlooking the operating theatre, and peered unseen through a glass dome throughout an appendectomy.

On several occasions Sheila was suspended from school, but on the whole the staff as well as the pupils were more lenient with her than she deserved – because of her obvious unhappiness, and because in spite of her many misdemeanours no one could dislike her or stay angry with her for long. Sheila knew all too well how to batten on to this sympathy, and how to ensure that she was the centre of attention; she was even suspected of staging fainting fits during assemblies so that she would have to be resuscitated by a favourite games teacher.

Her apparent susceptibility to fainting had, however, no ill effect on her prowess at games; she was tall, slim and long-legged, and threw herself into sport with considerably more enthusiasm than she showed for academic work. She excelled in swimming, in which she held life-saving badges, and was good at lacrosse, netball and tennis; but the preliminary to any match for which she was in a school or house team was inevitably a search for some vital piece of her clothing or equipment. Before sports days, she would practise her high jump and long jump during the dinner hour – never content with jumping well, she was determined to jump better than anyone else, and usually succeeded in doing so. For a while she was determined to become an Olympic swimmer or athlete – or at the very least a games teacher on the model of the one whom she admired.

At other times, she dreamed of fame on the stage. In amateur dramatics, as well as in sport, her competitive and self-dramatizing instincts came into their own. She played Queen Elizabeth in one school pageant, and her own great-grandmother, one of the school's eleven founder pupils, in another. But however well she performed, whether in public or in private, her friends did not consider that her stepmother ever gave her enough support – although both Aileen and Harold were punctilious about attending speech days.

Sheila failed her school certificate examination – for no other reason than that her social life and her obsessive searches for her mother had left her neither time nor energy to work for it. For the first time Aileen openly supported her when she was then threatened with expulsion – which probably had something to do with being caught in a coffee bar with a boy from the local grammar school, or may have been connected with the crime of reading *Lady Chatterley's Lover* under the lid of her desk; or it could have been for a combination of misdemeanours.

Instead of being expelled, she was, yet again, suspended; during her suspension, Aileen kept her locked in her room so that she would have no choice but to work. Even when she returned to school Sheila was still under strict surveillance, and therefore for once gave all the necessary attention to her studies. As she had a retentive memory, the result was that on her second attempt she received more than adequate passes in every subject.

During the last few years of her school life Sheila was part of a gang which included several Alice Ottley girls and a number of boys from the local grammar school. Education in those days was still strictly segregated in Worcester, and the Alice Ottley girls were most emphatically not supposed to consort with grammar school boys. There was a double distinction in that Alice Ottley was a private school, as well as an all-girls establishment, so the ban was social as well as sexual. This, of course, made the boys from the grammar school seem all the more attractive.

Sheila's school bag bulged every day, not with school work but with clothes to change into for after-school assignations. She was considered exceptionally attractive, and had no shortage of willing male attention. Those who did not know her, or did not like her, thought her sex-mad; her friends felt that through her many and varied sexual encounters she was desperately seeking the attention and affection which were lacking at home.

She fell in love for the first time with the local dentist's son, John Pimley. It was an innocent enough relationship by the standards of some of her later affairs; but to her envious classmates it seemed little less than a 'purple passion', especially as John's ability to play the drums gave him an extra element of glamour. Although he was three years younger than Sheila, they were soon considered an established couple.

Surprisingly, in view of the puritanical restrictions which her stepmother normally attempted to impose on her behaviour, Aileen did not object to the many hours Sheila spent with John, even when they were alone together in the attic where he practised his drum playing; Sheila's explanation was that John was teaching her to play the drums, and she certainly had enough natural musical ability to pick up some rudimentary knowledge – it was later one of her greatest regrets that she had never imposed enough self-discipline to persevere with any musical instrument, and had given up piano lessons at the earliest opportunity.

As part of the gang, they went together on swimming expeditions and to parties at which they played murder in the dark and sardines. Gradually the gang's activities became more sophisticated, with dancing at the Cadena café and at the Winter Gardens in Droitwich, where John played the drums. There was a feeling of safety in being part of a crowd.

After Sheila's second, and successful, attempt at matriculation, she left school to become a nurse: the war had by then started, and she had vague ideas of being a second Florence Nightingale. She embarked on training in Birmingham, and made a point of turning up at the Cadena looking glamorous in her white uniform; Harold and Aileen were no doubt as relieved that the defiant schoolgirl had chosen a responsible and respectable outlet for her energies as she was to escape from their rigid and restricting home.

The first thing Sheila bought when she left home was a packet of cigarettes. Both Harold and Aileen smoked, although not heavily, and from the age of fourteen onwards Sheila had been puffing surreptitiously – for once uncaught and unpunished – through an open window at cigarettes taken from one of the packets they left lying around the house. Smoking was a symbol both of being an adult, and of defying her stepmother. As she smoked her first few deliberately adult and independent cigarettes, Sheila felt confident that she could handle any new experience which came her way.

2

SHEILA CONTACTED HER maternal grandparents in a last desperate attempt to trace her mother. They told her, as she put it, to 'lay off'. By then Edyth had a third husband, who presumably knew nothing about her eighteen-year-old daughter. Husband number two had apparently committed suicide. Sadly, Sheila resigned herself to never meeting her mother or knowing whether she had any half-brothers or sisters.

Before she had completed her basic nursing training at Birmingham's Dudley Road Hospital, Sheila left to become a VAD – a volunteer nursing auxiliary – at the naval hospital in Gosport. The move took her farther from home, opened the doors to a variety of experiences both professionally and socially, and satisfied her patriotism.

Whether it was made voluntarily is another matter: one of her cousins told me that there was 'some sort of hoo-haa at the time, something to do with a young doctor and Sheila thrown out of somewhere'. He assumed that her crime was sexual; given her reputation at school, and the strict public attitudes of the time, this would not have been surprising. The older generation of the Hopkins family was far too 'close' to talk openly about anything contentious. It is, however, equally likely that her nursing training came to an abrupt end either because of a serious back injury, for which she was given heroin as a painkiller, or because she was caught using heroin less innocently. She was introduced to the drug, either medicinally or socially, during the war by a young doctor, but although she later said that she had first taken it after breaking her back I have found no record of such an injury. The vague memory of veiled rumours and Sheila's move from Birmingham to Gosport may therefore be linked with her introduction to heroin.

The glamour-and-glory image of naval nursing appealed to

16

Sheila, as did the distance from Worcester and the rich new social opportunities it offered. She mixed at parties with officers, doctors, men from old aristocratic families – and of course with other nurses and volunteers, some of whom would not have considered such work during peacetime.

The professional side of nursing was, however, less to her liking: even before she left Dudley Road her sense of vocation was wearing a little thin. The tiring routine of the ward, the essential combination of naval and hospital discipline, and the emotional toll of trying, as she put it, to patch up mangled bodies every day, eroded it even further; and I find it difficult to imagine Sheila cheerfully emptying bedpans. She had always become easily depressed – but as swiftly elated; the constant proximity of death was so disturbing that whenever possible she deliberately escaped into a social whirl to avoid thinking too deeply about the implications of her job or the war.

At parties and dances, fear and depression were temporarily banished and the pleasures of the moment could be enjoyed as fully and as rapidly as possible. When she was posted from Gosport to London, where she lived in a nurses' hostel in Kensington, her social life became even more hectic and she was, according to an older girl from her school who was also in London at the time, 'always going places and ready for adventure'. Her biggest adventure was undoubtedly falling seriously in love with Peter Korda, whom she met in London in 1943. Peter, who was introduced to Sheila and her friend Rita at a party as 'Mr Black', was tall, dark and handsome; he was also, even more impressively, the son of the well-known film director Alexander Korda. After the party, Sheila asked Rita: 'Do you know who he is?' Both girls were awed at having met the son of one of the most glamorous figures of the age.

Although officially Peter appears to have been employed as a wartime ambulance driver, and to have been a conscientious objector, he hinted intriguingly at connections with the Free French and at secret journalistic assignments. His aura of slightly taciturn mystery immediately marked him out and made him exciting, and it was not long before 'Mr Black and Mrs White', as Peter and Sheila called themselves, were considered inseparable. Rita thought Peter delightful, although he struck her as a quiet and very private person. Sheila was less flattering: 'Peter wasn't a very nice person,' she told me, without explaining, 'but I was very much in love with him.'

That both Peter and Sheila had wicked stepmothers – his, whom he loathed, was the film star Merle Oberon – was an instant bond between them.

For a while, Sheila enjoyed having a 'country boyfriend' – John Pimley – and a 'town boyfriend'. She still saw John when she went home to Worcester, although her weekends there were infrequent. When John visited her in London, she made excuses to Peter that she had unexpectedly to do extra weekend nursing duty. When she was telling me about this, I asked her how long she managed to continue two-timing without repercussions. The question surprised her: 'I never really thought of it like that,' she said; but the town and country boyfriend arrangement came to an end when Peter became jealous, perhaps one of the reasons why she did not consider him very 'nice'. He was nevertheless too important for her to risk losing him; although she remained afterwards on friendly terms with John, and later with his wife, she accepted Peter's possessiveness.

Nevertheless the romance ended, after two years, with a row. Sheila either could not, or would not, remember what it was about. If Peter was, as seems likely, the father of the child she had aborted during the war, this could well have been the cause of the row which ended their relationship; so, of course, could any number of smaller disagreements, or an accumulation of aggravations; or the row could have been one of those silly quarrels which start from something insignificant and end with things which can never be unsaid. However much she may have been in love with him, and whether or not she had hoped to become his wife, Sheila resented the limitations he imposed on her. 'I had a much better social life after Peter Korda,' she told me, 'and I can't remember feeling unhappy when the affair ended.'

Pregnancy was, as Sheila admitted, always her great fear, but although she told me about two abortions – one during and one after the war – she was vague about the possible paternity: the first child might have been Peter Korda's, she said, but she was not certain. As for the second . . . it was all so long ago. . . . The operation itself nevertheless made a lasting impression, not least because of the expense of £150 each time, paid in cash to a Harley Street gynaecologist whose activities as a society abortionist were, of course, illegal.

When Sheila told him on her first visit that she was pregnant, he gave her a severe telling-off: she must never say that word. 'You mean you have not had a period,' he told her. Having satisfactorily rephrased her problem, he agreed to give her 'a minor operation to regularize her periods'. She described a steel cage which he had had constructed in his consulting room so that his operations would not be interrupted by air raids. After an injection into the uterus, Sheila was sent home to wait, and bled for two days, It was, she admitted, 'pretty horrific'; but she clearly found the alternative of having the baby unthinkable.

Neither her father, nor her stepmother, nor in all probability either of the two potential fathers, ever knew about Sheila's abortions. In spite of her tendency to dramatize any situation, she was capable of being as secretive as any other member of her family. Whether or not she should give birth was, she considered, her decision, and hers alone; if she ever regretted it, she was not prepared to admit to any regrets, nor to having felt any guilt. Her own experience of being, as she felt she was, an unwanted child, no doubt contributed to her determination not to bring another unwanted child into the world. The social pressures against being an unmarried mother were even greater at the time than the moral condemnation of abortion, since one was inevitably public and the other could be undertaken in secrecy – indeed, as abortion was a criminal offence, secrecy was essential. Sheila would moreover have found it unbearable to admit to an unmarried pregnancy, to her stepmother in particular, and to risk being told that she was no better than her own mother.

Whether it was her pregnancy, or her abortion, or something to do with drugs, or nothing in particular which ended Sheila's affair with Peter Korda, the relationship led to some useful introductions, not least to Alexander Korda, with whom she remained on good terms even after she was no longing speaking to his son. They met over tea at Claridge's, where he had a permanent suite in which from time to time he entertained Peter and his friends. Alexander Korda was impressed – as were most people – by Sheila's looks: 'My dear, have you ever thought of going into films?' he asked. The question reawakened her schoolgirl dreams of the stage.

It was also at Claridge's and therefore probably also through Alexander Korda, that in January 1945 Sheila met the editor of *Good Morning*, a daily paper for the submarine branch of the Navy. With ideas of earning some money by writing about her experiences as a VAD, she covered one side of a sheet of pale blue Claridge's writing

paper with notes about the editor's 'likes' – 'nice, simple straightforward style' – and dislikes: 'common fault – too flowery – writes
better than it reads'. What was emphatically not wanted was
'romancing on life' or anything smacking of an 'official government
brochure', for instance 'Wrens get up at 6 a.m.; brekker 8, etc'.

Later in the year an article entitled 'My First Day' was printed in
Good Morning under the name of Susan Christin RN, VAD. Susan
Christin was presumably no other than Sheila Christine Hopkins,
as the same name appears on a handwritten draft, in Sheila's
writing, for a piece to be called 'Nelson's Town', as well as on
typescripts of a further two articles which I found among her papers
('Night – in a Wrennery', and 'Factory Wrens'). Sheila's later
anecdotes about her naval nursing life are certainly identical to the
experiences described by 'Susan Christin' – her favourite being her
misunderstanding an instruction to do the 'heads', the nautical term
for toilet, and instead attempting to de-bug the scalps of the startled
but amused patients. The articles, however, showed little of the
'personal angle' and 'fresh style with a lot about the Wrens
themselves' requested by the editor, nor could the style be described
as 'snappy'. 'Nelson's Town' tails off after a cliché-ridden beginning
and does not appear to have been finished.

If these efforts were an indication of Sheila's literary ability at the
time, it was just as well that when the war ended it was as an actress,
rather than as a writer, that she decided – with Alexander Korda's
assistance – to seek fame and fortune. She was by then tired of the
discipline of nursing, and of the poor pay, and wanted to do
something as different, and as exciting, as possible.

Because she looked like Deborah Kerr, Korda took Sheila on as
the star's stand-in at Denham. Initially this meant getting up
uncomfortably early, travelling by train to the studio, being made
up so that she was ready to stand in during lighting and technical
rehearsals, then standing round drinking coffee for much of the day;
the hours of waiting to be called left plenty of time to hope and to
dream. The routine became more agreeable when Sheila became
friendly enough with Deborah, who was a year older, to travel to
and from the studios in a chauffeur-driven car provided by
Alexander Korda. Deborah's was a lifestyle to which, in spite of the
hard work which went into her success, Sheila felt that she could
happily become accustomed, and she convinced herself that she too
would soon become a star.

Not long after the end of her affair with Peter Korda, and before she had time to establish herself as an actress, Sheila became engaged to an army officer, Rupert Leahman Bellamy, whom she had met at a party. She knew even before she became Mrs Bellamy that she was making a mistake, but she was too proud, too obstinate, and perhaps too optimistic to back out of the marriage once she had given her word. Quite why she agreed to marry a man she was never in love with remained as much of a mystery to her as to anyone else, although there are several probable partial explanations: one, that she married on the rebound from Peter Korda; another, that Bellamy appeared to offer her security, which she felt that she had always lacked, and which she was sure she would never have found with Peter Korda. Then there was a side of Sheila which always, despite her outward rejection of accepted rules and stereotypes, wanted to conform, especially to social standards; she did not question that marriage was desirable and inevitable, and assumed in a vague, undefined way both that to become a respectable married woman was her ultimate role in life, and that life after marriage was, in spite of her own parents' break-up, bound to be happy.

Rupert Bellamy was the epitome of respectability; an Old Harrovian, he was a major with the Royal Army Ordnance Corps, and had been promoted during the war to acting lieutenant-colonel. No doubt part of his initial attraction for Sheila was that his apparent solidity and reliability was a contrast to the men with whom she had previously associated, and particularly to Peter Korda. Later she liked to give the impression that she had been much younger, little more than a child, when she rushed with her eyes open into a marriage which she knew was a mistake: in fact she was twenty-three, and Rupert fourteen years older.

Bellamy's parents lived 'in considerable style', according to another Old Harrovian and Army contemporary, Michael Scott; his older brother, who was the favourite son, had been killed during the First World War. Rupert had acquired a BSc in engineering at Oxford, where his studies took second place to his interest in wrestling and party-going, and had then done the practical part of his training with Vickers Armstrong at Barrow-in-Furness; his face had been permanently pockmarked by acid burning during a submarine accident. His father subsequently financed a motor business at West Grinstead in Sussex. 'The tuning of sports and racing cars was the main interest,' Michael Scott told me. 'Rupert competed at trials and at Brooklands, but not with any great distinction.'

When the motor business came to an end in 1935 – probably because his father withdrew his financial support – Bellamy was commissioned into the Royal Army Ordnance Corps; he arrived at the depot in Portsmouth in a 4½-litre Bentley, and was the only one of the twenty-five on his Army initiation course with a private income and who could therefore afford to hunt. 'He was not an easy friend,' Michael Scott admitted, 'too much money and always a bit larger than life and inclined to be intolerant of those who couldn't or wouldn't match his style. He was a great party-goer, although unusually among young officers of those days he drank practically nothing. He had a vast circle of girlfriends and could always raise one or two at short notice for any occasion in the offing.'

Another Army contemporary, Jocelyn Tateman, remembered Bellamy as 'a thorough gentleman' – and rich. 'He didn't take the Army very seriously,' he told me. 'He wanted to enjoy himself.' In 1936 Bellamy was serving in Malta; some time after this he was attached to the British Embassy in Turkey, a posting which apparently ended hastily because of an association with the wife of a member of the Embassy staff.

Sheila no doubt hoped that access to Bellamy's money would make her life easier, especially if the dream of dramatic fame failed to materialize. By marrying him she felt that she was taking out an insurance policy against personal failure, and that she would be independent of her family; that this meant being dependent on her husband did not occur to her – and of course nothing could make up for the fact that she found him neither physically attractive nor particularly amusing.

A few weeks before the wedding, Sheila took her fiancé to meet her friends in Worcester. The gang had gathered at the Raven Hotel, where they greeted him with a deathly silence which they realized afterwards must have been both rude and hurtful: he was not at all the man any of them would have expected for Sheila. She was the glamour girl of the gang, the one who was always most vibrant, most attractive, most alive; and they could not imagine her as the wife of this rather ordinary man whom they found, even in his officer's uniform, undistinguished and almost old enough to be her father. Somehow they had expected someone more dashing and romantic –

more like Peter Korda, in fact. Although his companions on his pre-war Army course had found him easy-going and good company, Rupert seemed to the Worcester gang stiff and stilted.

Sheila's father and stepmother, however surprised they may been at her choice of bridegroom, set about planning for a full-scale London society wedding. A week before the wedding, Sheila had flu. She felt so demoralized that she confided on the telephone to her father that she had cold feet about marrying Rupert. Harold advised her to wait until he arrived in London before making a decision; but somehow neither of them broached the subject again when they met.

The day before the wedding, Peter Korda turned up to plead with Sheila not to go through with marrying a man whom he considered to be totally wrong for her. The Korda family was so influential that, at a time when for most people foreign travel was out of the question, Peter told Sheila that his father would get her away to France until all the fuss died down. She refused. It was only six months since the end of their affair, and she was still at least a little in love with him; if he had begged her to marry him instead of Rupert, she might have done so – but otherwise he was the last person she would listen to, or perhaps the last but one, the last being her stepmother.

On the morning of the wedding day, Aileen went into Sheila's room: 'Are you quite sure you want to go through with it?' she asked. 'You don't have to, you know.' Appearances meant a lot to Aileen; wedding gifts had already been accepted and put on display, guests were due to arrive within a few hours for a white wedding at Holy Trinity Church, Brompton and an expensive reception at the Rembrandt Hotel; in the circumstances Aileen's willingness to call the whole thing off implied that she cared more about Sheila's happiness than Sheila was ever prepared to give her credit for.

There was nothing Sheila would have liked better than to cancel becoming Mrs Rupert Bellamy; if anyone other than Peter Korda and Aileen had suggested she could escape, she might have listened. But her pride would not let her back down in front of either of them, and so she went through with the ceremony. As she walked up the aisle, she was trying to swallow back her tears. At the reception, she made it obvious to her bridesmaids – one in pale blue, the other in pink – that she was reluctant to leave and be alone with her husband. For years afterwards, she was convinced that anything which went wrong in her life was a punishment for making vows in church which she knew to be false.

At least Bellamy could give Sheila a comfortable home; but she very much hoped that he would not insist on living in it with her. When he was posted, first from one part of England to another and then to India, she refused to leave their London house in Queens Gate Mews. Her excuse was that she had to be in London to further her acting career: she was still hopeful that sooner or later – and quite possibly sooner – she would be as great a star as Deborah Kerr. In the meantime, as Mrs Bellamy she was able to afford acting lessons which she could never have paid for without her husband's allowance; places at drama school after the war were difficult to obtain, but Sheila was taught privately by Elsie Wagstaff, one of the top teachers at the Central School in London. She also enrolled, again no doubt at her husband's expense, on a Lucie Clayton modelling course.

It was important to Sheila to retain, or perhaps to create, her own identity, even during the brief period – a matter of months at the most – when she thought of herself as Mrs Rupert Bellamy; and so she needed a professional name. Sheila Hopkins sounded too prosaic; Sheila Bellamy sounded better, but not independent enough – and in any case she did not intend to remain Bellamy's wife for a day longer than she had to. There was something compact but yet potentially glamorous about Sheila Scott – Scott being both an old family name, and as good a name as any, with sufficiently adventurous connotations to offer unlimited promises of success. And so Sheila Christine Hopkins chose to be known not by her maiden name, nor by her married one, but as Sheila Scott. 'A titter went round the family,' one of her cousins told me. At about the same time she changed her appearance dramatically by becoming a blonde, and completed her transformation with cosmetic surgery, for which Bellamy's money again presumably paid.

For five years, Sheila was haunted by the old proverb: 'Marry in haste, repent at leisure.' Nevertheless she did not behave as if she was married. She so rarely spoke about her husband that few people realized she had one. Within less than a year of her marriage, Sheila had acquired such a reputation for wild behaviour that the more sedate or puritanical of her acquaintances did not wish their names to be associated with hers. Whatever her acting pretensions, she spent much of her time in bars and clubs, where according to those who disapproved of her lifestyle she was not averse to being picked up by any attractive man. 'She used to sit in the bar looking gorgeous and picking up the chaps who came in,' a friend who was less disapproving put it. 'She was absolutely gorgeous, with a wonderful voice, full of fun and go, with lots of friends. She had an American Army officer boyfriend who was very good-looking.' 'There were so many men,' another woman whom Sheila considered a close friend told me. According to the same friend, Sheila's life at the time – she was talking about 1946 – was 'unhappy, mixed up, sordid'. Although this woman did not wish to talk to me, when I was told that Sheila had been on heroin I rang her and asked whether this was one of the things she did not wish to discuss; she admitted that it was. All she knew was that Sheila had phials of white powder, and that when she asked her: 'Is that what I think it is?' Sheila replied: 'Yes – so what?' 'I used to think: "My God, do you know what you are doing to yourself?"' the friend told me.

The question remained both unasked and unanswered. Sheila may not have cared; her life was physically full, but she felt an increasing spiritual emptiness and loneliness. Professionally, it was also all too often empty, and it was not until 1948 that she gained her Equity card. 'There do seem to have been an awful lot of men, don't there?' Sheila remarked one afternoon when we had been talking back over her life. 'The trouble was, I was always falling in love, always thinking the new man was the only one, but it didn't last – but I only ever had one lover at a time, and I never stole one from a friend.'

For nearly two years, she kept up a pretence for Harold and Aileen's benefit that all was well between her and Rupert. It was her father-in-law's suicide in July 1947 which revealed the deception, and which caused an even greater rift between Sheila and her father and stepmother than already existed. Rupert's father, Frederick Bellamy, for whom Sheila had a greater affection and admiration than she had for his son, was so appalled when he learnt that he had cancer of the liver that he decided to take his own life while he still had the dignity to do so. A month before his death, he made a will in which his groom, chauffeur, secretary, head gardener, his wife's maid Gwendoline Bugg, his godson and various charities were mentioned, as was the Association of Wharferers of which he was a leading member. He left well over a quarter of a million pounds – a sizeable sum in 1947 – an estate in Devon, and a London wharf and dock which bore his name, as well as the family home in Devon; when Sheila later said that her husband, or at least her husband's family, had owned three manor houses and estates, it was only a slight exaggeration.

The first Sheila knew of her father-in-law's death was a phone call from Aileen.

'Why aren't you with Rupert's mother?' Aileen asked.

'Why should I be?' Sheila said.

When Aileen and Harold discovered not only that Sheila and Rupert had separated, but also that Sheila had embarked on an acting career, there was, as she put it, 'a huge row'. In their eyes, separation or divorce and acting were equally dishonourable, and their worst fears about Sheila turning out like her mother had been realized.

It was not as if Sheila could go home and say proudly: 'Look, I'm an actress, and a bloody good actress.' In her heart of hearts, although she was just good enough to be on the books of the top theatrical agencies, she felt that she had failed as Sheila Hopkins, and as Sheila Bellamy, and that she was already failing as Sheila Scott.

Of the five years between her marriage and her divorce, Sheila later wrote that during this time she had met the man whom she should have married, but it 'was too long for him to wait'. She presumably meant the theatre director Richard Bird, with whom she had an affair, and whose birthday she entered in her diary – always a sure sign that the person concerned was important to her at the time. Strangely, although she told me that with Dickie she did considerably more entertaining – at his expense – than with Peter Korda, and although I have spoken to several people who knew him, I found no one who was aware that she had ever been emotionally or sexually involved with him. There could be several reasons for this: their discretion – which hardly ties in with her claim that they entertained together; the fact that he was thirty years older than Sheila, and so seemed to onlookers more of a father figure than a likely lover; and the complication that Dickie Bird was married to the actress Joyce Barbour, although this does not necessarily rule Sheila out as his mistress and a potential second wife.

Interestingly, in view of the determination to divorce him, Rupert's name was also entered a dozen times in her 1949 diary, only slightly less frequently than Dickie's. Both, however, took second place to hospital and doctor's appointments, from which it appears – as these included sessions with a Harley Street consultant psychiatrist and at the National Temperance Hospital, as well as with an organization called Hopeline – that she was making an effort to get to grips either with her drug addiction, or with a drink problem, or perhaps both. In June she made several diary entries of 'Ampoule', as well as entering 'Start B. tablets'. This could fit in with her having been put on an official maintenance drug dosage combined with tablets to combat withdrawal symptoms as the dosage was gradually reduced.

The week before the first 'Ampoule' Sheila left the Garrick Theatre, where she had been understudying Harriet Johns in *Meet Mr Callaghan*. To Jack Allen, who had a lead role, she did not seem star material, although she appeared ambitious and was 'longing to get on': but he felt that she was in the wrong business, was too humble, and was neither glamorous nor tough enough to succeed. Frank Thornton, a fellow walking understudy during the same year on a West End production of a Robertson Hare play, *One Wild Oat*, considered her very pleasant, but a bit wooden as an actress and – directly opposing Jack Allen's opinion – more of 'a glamour girl – the night club type': he had started doing portrait photography, and did some portraits of Sheila.

She was, however, at last employed regularly enough to justify calling herself an actress. As well as the two West End under-studying jobs, the year included a repertory production of *The Chocolate Soldier* in Southsea; 1950 started with her first lead role, at the Palace Theatre in *Rain on the Just*, a new play by Peter Watling.

Despite this new-found employment it was probably through her association with Dickie Bird, rather than as an actress, that Sheila was invited to society cocktail parties and dinners such as one given in the autumn of 1949 at Claridge's in honour of the Greek Hollywood film producer Spyros Skouras. According to Gerald Pawle, who had taken over from Sir Robert Bruce Lockhart as Atticus on *The Times* and was representing his editor, 'it was a lavish affair, the guest list including many household names in politics and industry as well as a decorative contingent of film and stage stars'. Pawle found himself seated at dinner between the British film actress Anne Crawford and 'an extremely pretty blonde girl who announced herself as Sheila Scott'. He found Sheila 'by far the more entertaining', and by the end of the evening he had secured both what he termed 'some arresting quotes from the Hollywood mogul on the likely future of the film industry', and an invitation to see Sheila on stage in Watford.

Looking back on that repertory production on a January evening in Watford, and rereading the brief notes which he jotted down on his programme, Gerald Pawle does not seem to have been unduly impressed either with the play, or with Sheila's performance: he too described her as 'wooden' on stage. 'She wasn't a God-given actress, although she was very attractive,' he told me, 'and she didn't have any great potential, although she was perfectly competent – but I was not surprised that one never heard of her as an actress.'

Nevertheless his trip to Watford was the start of a friendship which lasted for several years, although he was never one of Sheila's great loves. They went out to dinner in Chelsea together, or to the theatre; she was always good company, and was certainly good to be seen with because of her glamorous looks, but he found her lonely, reserved, 'difficult to enthuse about anything'. 'She did not let herself go,' he told me. 'One never quite knew what was on her mind.' During their first dinners together, in 1950, it could well have been her impending divorce.

It was not until nearly five years after their separation that Bellamy agreed to a divorce, and then only after he had beaten her up. It was the only time he ever became violent with her, although the provocation, particularly her drug addiction, must have been severe. She felt that it was partly out of guilt over this one incident that he gave in about officially ending the marriage. He insisted on divorcing her for desertion, rather than allowing her to divorce him – it was, after all, not his choice that they had lived apart, so there was no reason why it should be his rather than her reputation which suffered; but he agreed to make her a settlement.

The decree nisi was granted in June 1950, followed a month later by the decree absolute, on the grounds of Sheila's desertion without due cause for at least three years. After the divorce, to Sheila's indignation, Rupert went back on his word and stopped her allowance; as she had made her determination to be independent of him eminently clear, and as there was nothing to prevent her from earning her own living other than the precarious way she had chosen to do so, there seems no reason why he should have continued to support her.

Rupert Bellamy retired from the Army on a major's pension in

1951, and married again a few years later. According to the sister of his second wife, he had 'done his back in' while he was in the Army, and subsequently 'led the life of a gentleman'. Sheila saw him twice in 1951, but not after that; she did not meet his second wife, nor did she know that they had children. He died in 1973, leaving approximately a quarter of the amount left by his father. Sheila rarely mentioned him, even to her closest friends, and resolved never to marry again unless she was 'so head over heels in love' that she 'could not see straight'.

3

THROUGH THEATRICAL AND modelling agencies, Sheila was able to obtain enough work after her divorce to support herself; but there was little to spend on luxuries, and often little enough for even the essentials – which included make-up and hair. She became expert at looking as if she had spent more on her appearance than she had, and at making new clothes from old. But she was aware of a gnawing sense of failure; her career all too often took a poor second place to anything else which might crop up – be it a new man, or a trip to the South of France – and she was often depressed. She felt that she was nothing, and that her life was futile and empty.

A new love affair could fill the emptiness for a while, but Sheila was instinctively puritanical and often felt guilty. She continued to hope that each experience might be meaningful and permanent, and to seize the pleasure of the moment – parties, night clubs, restaurants and other people's first nights; occasionally over a period of some weeks there were fewer social engagements and more rehearsals, leading to a short run in a provincial theatre, a small part in a London production, a couple of equally insignificant film parts, or more understudying for a successful West End play.

Often there were such long periods without work that people who met her then were unaware of her professional involvement with the theatre. 'I'm sure she was not acting when I knew her,' Johnny Wodehouse, later Lord Kimberley and one of her self-confessed lovers, told me. 'She didn't know how to act, either in a play or in a film or in everyday life; and she wasn't modelling, as far as I knew; but I rather think she may have been on the fringe of Buddhism or something.' Buddhism intrigued her, but although she was attracted by its principles the practice required more self-discipline than she was willing or able to give it; when she was propositioned by her guru, she gave up her Buddhist studies in disgust.

'Sheila was the love of my life,' Lord Kimberley told me. 'We met in the Battery Bar in Dover Street – our eyes met across the room: it was electric – the earth trembled.' Whether or not it also trembled for Sheila, they became, briefly, lovers. He did not, however, think of marrying her, or even living with her – 'I think one of my wives must have been around at the time,' he explained, 'but I was certainly in love with Sheila.' He was between the second and third of his six wives.

Johnny Wodehouse, ex-Eton, Cambridge and the Grenadier Guards, was two years younger than Sheila, although he always thought he was several years her senior. By his own account, he was then tall, lean, fair, athletic – 'The girls seemed to like me,' he told me – and a member of the British bobsleigh team. As far as he knew, he was Sheila's only lover; he rarely gave her any warning of an impending visit, and never saw a sign that any other man had been either in the Chelsea bedsit she was at first living in or at the flat to which she moved in November 1953.

While he was still between wives, he and Sheila went to France together. 'Let's go to Le Touquet,' he suggested on the spur of the moment one weekend.

'What a lovely idea,' Sheila said. It was just the sort of impromptu adventure which appealed to her, and which stood in the way of any serious progress with her acting career.

The weather in Le Touquet was so bad that they decided to carry on to Nice, and spent an unplanned fortnight in the South of France. As they had taken no luggage with them, this meant buying a complete new set of clothes each – for which Johnny paid.

Many people have, like Lord Kimberley, described Sheila to me as 'strikingly beautiful', but few have seemed so moved by the memory of her 'lovely smile'. 'She was intelligent, fun, and wonderful to love,' he told me; but on their last few meetings he found her so 'weird' that he expected her to have a nervous breakdown: 'She needed a psychiatrist – she was slightly potty.'

Although her flat was on the seventh floor, Sheila was convinced that she was being watched, sometimes through the window of the bedroom – a physical impossibility, in Johnny's opinion – and sometimes through a non-existent hole in the ceiling.

'It is really rather frightening to be lying in bed when you've just made love to a beautiful woman, and she tells you that someone is boring a hole in the ceiling to watch you,' Lord Kimberley told me.

For several hours at a time, he went on, Sheila could appear perfectly normal; then her eyes would take on a glazed, staring look, and she would say: 'Tell him to go away.'

'But darling, there's no one there,' Johnny reassured her. She did not believe him.

It was not only in bed that she thought she was being watched; she was equally convinced that she was being followed in the street. He would not, he admitted, have been surprised to hear or to read that she had committed suicide; but his concern about her 'peculiar behaviour' did not inspire him to seek for her the psychiatric help which she obviously needed.

In October 1952 Sheila went to see a gynaecologist called Edward Sugden; he was well known in theatrical circles as a discreet and sympathetic abortionist, and had featured as co-respondent in a divorce case between a minor actress called Barbara, Lady Beaumont, and the husband through whom she had acquired her title. As Sheila obviously knew Lady Beaumont, whose name appeared occasionally in her diaries, it is possible that it was through her that she had met Sugden.

Whatever the reason for Sheila's first appointment with Sugden, it was not for an abortion; and their relationship soon became considerably closer than that of doctor and patient. Within a few weeks his name was featuring regularly in her diaries; he had become Teddy or T.S., and his date of birth had been added; Johnny's had been dropped. Sheila fell in love with him more thoroughly, and for longer, than with anyone else, and hoped to become Mrs Sugden. For a while they lived together, and Sheila was 'completely happy'. She shared Teddy's interest in living things, in particular lizards and birds; they lived what she called a bohemian life, and she discovered undefined 'new concepts' through music and books. It was, however, not long before she became possessive, and Teddy, who considered clothes and mealtimes unimportant, resented being hassled when he was late for a meal or looked rumpled and scruffy.

Various people who knew him slightly have described Sugden to me as having an air of distinction, and of looking either like 'a little toad' or like a teddy bear. Although one side of his face was partially paralysed, the result of a childhood ear infection – he hated being photographed – women apparently found him attractive. Sheila told me that he was 'a loyal and wonderful and very brave man' whose courage had been demonstrated in a dramatic wartime rescue during the Blitz, and was further in evidence in his professional expertise.

Although when she met Sugden Sheila's attempts to establish herself as an actress were showing some reward, they were always half-hearted, and soon tailed off almost completely. Once their relationship was established on what she hoped would be a permanent basis she was supported by Sugden; her social life nevertheless flourished during their affair. She saw a mixture of people from the theatre and from middle- to high-ranking social circles at venues such as Maxim's, the Orchid Room, Les Ambassadeurs, the Jacaranda, Romano's and Le Drap d'Or, and she listed addresses in Switzerland and in Antibes, Juan les Pins and Cannes in the South of France. Sheila continued to visit various theatrical agencies in search of work – and to make, and presumably keep, appointments with several doctors and hospitals. One of the doctors she saw told me that, although she gave him Sugden's name as her GP, he never answered any letters about her.

Most of Sheila's diary entries were made in her almost illegible handwriting, and usually in pencil. Only four were made in capital letters, three of these in 1952. On 4 March Sheila wrote 'PAY COURT', sandwiched between Cardiff on 3 March and Blackpool on the 9th. The place names refer to a provincial theatre tour, which started at the King's Theatre in Southsea towards the end of February and continued via Streatham and Golders Green to Hammersmith: it was both her longest and her last professional theatre tour, although she made spasmodic later appearances on various stages. In May she again wrote 'COURT' in capitals, and in August 'TREATMENT STARTS'.

What 'court', and what treatment? I have been unable to trace the 'court', and think it unlikely that it refers to someone of that name, or to Cranmer Court, where she lived both with and without Sugden for several years; in any case, no other name was ever considered significant enough to warrant capital letters. The only conclusion I can draw is that, shortly before she met Teddy Sugden, Sheila was in some sort of serious trouble, probably financial.

As for treatment, this was almost certainly connected with her drug abuse and psychiatric problems; one of the doctors mentioned was a consultant psychiatrist. It is, however, possible that it could refer to a course of beauty treatment – hair and beauty appointments figured frequently in her diaries, and must have cost her a considerable amount over the years; but they were normally entered simply as 'hair', or with the name of the person who was to give her treatment, and even the 'great bleach disaster' – when she made a mistake with the proportions in her blonde dye – was not entered in capital letters.

In Febuary 1954 Sheila again entered 'COURT' in the mysterious capital letters, as before without explanation. By then, Teddy Sugden had become such a fixture in her life that she had included his measurements at the end of her previous diary: he had surprisingly small feet – shoe size 8½ – for a man not otherwise daintily built, with a 40½-inch chest, 36½-inch waist, 43-inch hips and 16½ collar size.

Sheila had by then no regular source of income, and was being supported entirely by Teddy. A Mrs O'Donnell, whom Sheila described to me as 'a wonderful home help', was paid by Sugden: her role appears to have included keeping an eye on and looking after Sheila for him, as her behaviour was again – or still – peculiar enough to cause concern. Mrs O'Donnell was, according to a woman friend, 'very protective of Sheila', who was 'very nervous at that time and always saw Reds under the bed', as well as being convinced that she was receiving threatening telephone calls. Sheila herself later wrote that there were many 'coincidences' which she was sure did not happen by chance, but that she was afraid to face up to what this meant in case others thought that she had taken leave of her senses; she felt that she was living in two worlds, 'as though in a mirror'.

But to her cousin John Turner, who visited her with his fiancée and two other friends at about this time, Sheila appeared perfectly rational. They telephoned her when they were in London with a few hours to spare before going to an ice hockey match at Wembley: 'Come over,' she said immediately. 'Sheila must be doing all right,' they commented to each other while she was in the kitchen making tea. To their horror, she then told them she had been recording their conversation on a new tape recorder; it was a considerable relief to John when she found that she had not switched it on properly.

At the end of her 1956 diary, Sheila made a sad and enigmatic three-line entry: 'People are hatched, matched & dispatched: No waiting; Beware of the cat.' She had made references to marriage in the preceding entries: 'Elizabeth London's wedding', 'John P[imley] pre marriage', 'J.H. marriage S. France etc'. The cat was Teddy Sugden, against whose name Sheila drew a cat and, to whom she referred on several entries in her diary as 'Pusscat', once even writing 'Love & kisses Pussycat'.

In spite of Sheila's hopes, the relationship had become increasingly one-sided. Although he was still fond of her, and felt responsible for her, Teddy Sugden had decided that he could not live with her. As a doctor he was well aware of her considerable psychological problems, and of the fact that they were compounded by her drug taking. She made several efforts to come off heroin, but each time turned to vodka, sometimes drinking as much as a bottle at a time. This merely exacerbated her paranoid symptoms, while at the same time threatening to create a new addiction.

It was clear that Sheila desperately needed some meaning to her life. She was finding the social round, enjoyable though it may have been in itself, increasingly futile; lovers, and a husband, had come and gone, but even if she still hoped for a permanent relationship with Sugden this in itself would not have been enough – she had to find a new and independent outlet for her energy and ability, which were considerable but lacked direction. She realized that she had failed as an actress, and practically cut herself off from her family – indeed she did not feel that she had, or had ever had, a family; nor, more seriously, did she feel that she had found, or created, her own identity. She knew neither who she was, nor who she wanted to be. Heroin and alcohol provided no more than brief and illusory relief from her depression.

There must, she thought, be more to life than this – this being, at the time, her affair with Sugden, bars and clubs and parties, and occasional modelling, interspersed with trips to the South of France in the summer and skiing, at which she never excelled, in the winter. In an attempt to earn her own living, although so long as she was being supported by Sugden this was not an urgent necessity, she had tried designing and making après-ski wear: she made occasional lists of measurements and some rough sketches, and obtained a few commissions, but she had too little business sense or indeed commitment to make it a paying proposition, and soon grew bored with it. Living for the moment and trying anything which was going had lost its appeal: she felt that she had tried most things, including Buddhism, and found nothing. She had even visited fortune tellers, in the hope of seeing fame and success, and perhaps marriage to

Sugden, in the crystal ball or the tarot cards; and I suspect, although I have been unable trace her, that a Mrs Ouis whom she saw several times was a spiritualist.

A new name, Duke, had started to appear so regularly in Sheila's diary that at first I assumed he must have replaced Teddy Sugden in her affections, although at the beginning of the diary she gave her name optimistically as Sheila Scott-Sugden. It was not until I traced Duke that I both ruled this out, and discovered about her heroin addiction. Duke's full name was Hilary Duke Woolley: this solved another mystery, as the name Hilary appeared separately in the diaries on several occasions.

Many things which I had not previously understood made sense after I had heard Duke's story. I had already realized that Sheila had made a deliberate break with her previous life: this had made it difficult to fill in the twenty years from the beginning of the war to the time when she started flying, as she had cut herself off from all her old friends and activities. Now I knew why, and why she had later written of 'sampling the vices and virtues and discarding some of both'.

By 1957 Teddy Sugden was trying both to ease out of his relationship with Sheila, and to help her to stand on her own feet without drugs, and without him. He had a new, and much younger, much more straightforward, girlfriend, although at first neither she nor Sheila knew about the other. But, perhaps for the first time in her life, Sheila felt emotionally dependent on and possessive of someone. It was, however, no use her breaking the drugs habit merely to please him, although this in itself would have been a strong incentive – enough perhaps in the short term, but not a long-term answer. She had, somehow or other, sooner or later, to be psychologically independent.

Although Sheila found it difficult to admit that she was in the wrong, she at last admitted both to herself and to Sugden that she had to come off drugs once and for all, and that she needed help. Once she had set her mind on something, she was – as she had proved by her insistence on going through with her marriage, and with then embarking on an acting career – determined not to go back on her word. At the age of thirty-five, she wanted at last to start her life again. Having once made this decision, she accepted Teddy's advice and followed his instructions to the best of her ability. During 1957 she spent some time, at his expense, in a luxurious private psychiatric nursing home in Roehampton in south London, where she was diagnosed as paranoid schizophrenic.

To combat the inevitable withdrawal symptoms, after she left the nursing home Sugden prescribed a course of injections; but this on its own would not be enough, nor would any further hospital treatment – he knew that Sheila must find something to absorb her interests and to challenge her abilities. At the same time, she needed companionship: it was largely through loneliness that her life was in such a mess.

This was where Duke came on the scene. He had met Sheila several times socially, and liked her. One of his closest friends was Paul Romney, to whom Sugden confided Sheila's condition. Although Paul, who was a bachelor and who found Sheila attractive, would gladly have taken her on, Sheila could not stand him – perhaps because she knew that he was attracted to her: the last thing she wanted to cope with was another complicated emotional entanglement. She was in any case not yet ready to admit that her relationship with Teddy Sugden had no long-term prospects.

Paul outlined the problem in confidence to Hilary Duke Woolley. Duke, a qualified architect and trained artist who had returned to what he called his 'ancestral farming roots', was on a small farm near Lymington in Hampshire with his wife and daughter. 'The last thing I needed at the time was any extra responsibility,' he told me. 'I was mainly wondering how to keep afloat financially.' But he liked Sheila enough to want to help her. 'It was,' he said, 'a strange relationship – basically a rescue operation.' So Duke was not Sheila's next lover, as I had first thought, but, in conjunction with Teddy Sugden, her saviour.

Although Duke knew that Sheila had been on heroin, and was told that she had been introduced to it by a young doctor when she was nursing during the war, he was not given, nor did he ask for, any detail. With the support of his wife, an ex-SRN who found the case interesting, he took up the challenge that Sheila presented. Whenever he was in London, he stayed at her flat, where he rented her spare room. He took her out to dinner and the theatre, and at weekends drove her to his home in Lymington, where she got on well with his wife and daughter. When he had to go away, he was worried about leaving her alone. 'Wouldn't you like someone to stay with you?' he asked her. 'You might be lonely.' He did not feel that he could say what he really meant, which was: 'Look you're odd. You're not fit to be on your own.' Sheila, who after all was used to living alone, no doubt welcomed the respite: he considered her obtuse because she did not seem able to grasp what he was getting at.

People to whom he introduced Sheila socially during his rescue operation always remarked afterwards: 'There's something odd about that woman.' He gave no explanation for her oddness, but privately agreed; it did not surprise him when Sheila told him that she had once been in a padded cell at St Stephen's Hospital in London. Like Johnny Wodehouse, only less intimately, he found her paranoia disconcerting: she was still convinced that people were looking through the windows of the top-floor flat or boring holes in the ceiling to spy on her, and that the loft was bugged. When Duke assured her that there was no one there, and that the loft could not possibly be bugged, she said darkly: 'Ah, but you don't know.' Sometimes she would suddenly strip all her clothes off and sit looking at the television screen stark naked, without taking anything in. There was, however, Duke assured me, 'nothing sexual about this – it was rather as if she was trying to be free'.

Sheila often thought she was being followed in the street, both on foot and by car. On journeys down to Lymington, she was constantly looking behind them. As soon as she saw another car for more than a few minutes, she insisted that Duke slow down until it overtook them – only to be replaced by another.

In public, in restaurants or theatres, he was not able to relax: although she never did more than raise her voice and become loudly argumentative, he was always afraid that she would do something drastically embarrassing, like stripping off and dancing on the table. She was, however, perfectly rational in public, and for much of the time in private, until one of the frequent occasions when she became suddenly and severely depressed; then he would seize hold of her until the worst had passed – but he always wondered what might happen when he was not there and she was in one of her down moods.

When she was behaving rationally, Duke enjoyed Sheila's company; he found her always good value socially, tautly beautiful, and often both interesting and amusing. 'She was very brave and rather glamorous, dressed well and appropriately, knew how to

behave in company of all sorts and was generally kind and gentle,'
he told me.

There were occasional moments of light relief – like the episode of
the lizards, the beret and the Harrods monkey house. Teddy Sugden
had given Sheila some miniature lizards, sleepy little creatures
called axolotls which made no attempt to crawl out of the bowl she
kept them in; she told Duke in great excitement one day that he had
promised to give her a new one: 'Will you come to Harrods to help
choose it?' she asked him.

One lizard looked much like another to Duke, but he accompanied her willingly enough. Sheila was wearing a woollen beret
with a diamanté clasp which an occupant of the Harrods monkey
house clearly found exciting: it stretched out a paw, whipped the
beret off Sheila's head through the bars and started to play football
round the cage with it.

The beret, or the diamanté clasp, immediately became Sheila's
most treasured possession, and she demanded it back. The assistant
was reluctant to retrieve it, and pointed out that before opening the
cage he would have to seal off the entire floor. 'I don't care – I must
have it back,' Sheila insisted, 'it has great sentimental value.'
Although the assistant was less familiar with Sheila's hysterical
tendencies than Duke, he knew it was wise to give in: the floor was
sealed off, and Sheila's beret, still complete with clasp, was returned
to her. Duke was both embarrassed and amused by the incident,
and relieved that it had been resolved without a public scene.

After a few dinners and theatres in London, and what he termed
'occupational therapy' in the country, he felt that Sheila's mental
state was improving. As well as weekends in Lymington with his
wife and daughter, the country therapy included staying occasionally at a carnation farm near Fordingbridge which was run by Bunty
Stockwell, a friend of Duke's wife – they had been in the British
Ladies' Ski Team at the Winter Olympics in 1947. There Sheila
could be on her own as much as she liked, or could help Bunty pack
carnations into boxes while they talked. But although her time in the
country was undoubtedly therapeutic, Sheila was not at heart a
country girl. She refused adamantly to take up horse riding, which
was suggested as a suitably extrovert and absorbing new interest.

Sheila spent Christmas 1957 at Duke's farm, reaching it, by taxi
from London, at 4.45 a.m. on Christmas Day. Apart from the
unexpected time of her arrival, she fitted in happily with the family

celebrations. In the New Year she went to the Earl's Court Boat Show; but sailing, or anything else nautical, did not provide any more than horse riding the absorbing interest that Teddy Sugden felt she needed. Nor did driving, for which she showed as little enthusiasm as natural ability.

The early part of 1958 dragged on, with fewer social engagements than Sheila had ever had. Duke did not feel that she had many real friends, nor did she make any new ones at the time; and if she was determined to break away from her old lifestyle, then the break had to be equally with people who had been part of it. Her diary until September had few entries other than numerous dentist's appointments, and several with two different doctors, one of whom was again a consultant psychiatrist. Duke noticed that she was becoming increasingly fascinated by the aircraft she could see on the Heathrow approach: 'She used to rush to the window to watch them, and seemed as excited as a small child,' he told me.

Then, very faintly, as if she almost dared not write it, Sheila made an entry in her diary in September: 'First flying lesson, Elstree'. She had found her new interest, which soon became an obsession, almost a drug. Through flying, she was able to stay off heroin and to recreate her identity.

That so few people knew that Sheila had ever had a drug problem is a tribute to the discretion of those who did; and it explains her choice of words when she told me that Teddy Sugden was 'loyal'. If he, or Duke and the small group of others who helped Sheila to overcome her addiction, had ever betrayed her confidence in them, it would have destroyed the new life and the new image which she was at last able to build for herself. She started with the odds so very heavily stacked against her – even if she had stacked them herself – and won the biggest battle of her life.

4

SHEILA'S INSTRUCTOR AT Elstree, David Ogilvie, did not find her an easy pupil; she was nervous, with what he termed 'an instability element'. He told me that he would have been reluctant to take her on if he had been aware of her previous psychiatric history.

Her tuition was paid for by Teddy Sugden, who had warned Duke that Sheila would probably turn against those who had helped her. Although she did not do so, she was so absorbed in her flying, and in the new friendships she was making through flying, that she gradually saw less and less of Duke and his wife. In November, she wrote in her diary: 'N.B.! I rang Duke!' She wanted to tell him that on the next day she was to take her first flying exam, for her private licence.

Optimistically, she wrote on the day of the test: 'The Last Day Facing the Past!' It was not, however, as easy as she had hoped to put the past behind her, and the next day's entry was disconsolate: 'Lost the flying exam'. In the New Year she made a fresh start, at Thruxton in Wiltshire: the instructors at Elstree, who were beginning to despair of ever getting her successfully through her PPL – her Private Pilots' Licence – breathed a sigh of relief that someone else was taking over the responsibility.

Suddenly the idea of learning to drive began to seem attractive, as a way of travelling each weekend to Thruxton; and so, in April 1959, Sheila embarked on a course of driving lessons: after a dozen lessons she failed her test. By the autumn she had, at Teddy Sugden's expense, failed it four times. She found learning to fly almost as difficult, but far more enjoyable.

It was not until she had had numerous flying lessons at Thruxton that her instructor, John Heaton, at last considered her ready for a solo flight, nine months after her first lesson at Elstree. By this time, however, nothing was going to make her give up, although she was

41

prepared to admit that she was not 'a natural pilot' – an opinion shared by many who admired her persistence more than her initial aptitude. After the triumph and excitement of her first solo at Thruxton, Sheila entered even more fully than usual into the spirit of a flying club party in the evening.

For the previous two years she had abstained almost totally from alcohol, on Teddy Sugden's advice. I cannot judge whether she was, as some have maintained, 'pissed out of her brain' when she fell while she was clearing up after the party, or whether, as she herself maintained, she merely slipped on a crisp. Sober or drunk, she broke one arm and had a suspected fracture of the other.

Less than a week later, with one arm still in plaster, Sheila pronounced herself fit to resume flying. This was reluctantly allowed, but only so long as she had a qualified pilot with her. When at last, after two months, the plaster was removed, she was at first reluctant to fly solo again: her initial nervousness had returned, and it was only after John Heaton had sent her up again and again, for several days running, that she regained her self-confidence. She had been beginning to doubt whether she would ever learn to fly, but could not bear to admit failure. When she at last received her PPL it was the proudest moment of her life. She had by then made a further break with her past, by moving into a flat in Park West, off the Edgware Road.

In the autumn Sheila became the proud owner of her first aircraft, a Tiger Moth converted with a covered rather than an open cockpit into a four-seater Thruxton Jackaroo. With some initial assistance from Teddy Sugden, she bought it on hire purchase. The day before it was delivered, she met her stepmother for tea – the only time Aileen's name was ever mentioned in any of her diaries; it was perhaps an indication that at last Sheila felt she had an acceptable identity of her own.

As she wanted her aircraft to be 'feminine' she insisted on having it painted pale blue and silver, with white upholstery. She felt that a mere call sign – in her Jackaroo's case G-APAM – was impersonal, and christened it *Myth*, the Greek word for a female moth. Thruxton was the home of the Jackaroo, for which its creators were keen to gain publicity; and as the first woman owner of a Jackaroo and certainly the most elegant and attractive, there was no one better than Sheila to publicize it – which she did on television early in November.

One of the aspects of flying which appealed to Sheila was undoubtedly the social life, the easy-going camaraderie of the flying field and soon of the aerial racecourse. Having felt lonely and isolated for so much of her life, she found for the first time companionship among people with whom she felt she had something in common, although few were quite as obsessive. She joined as many flying clubs as possible: Thruxton and Elstree, the Royal Aero Club, the Tiger Club and the British Women Pilots' Association. Beverley Snook, who for many years was an official of the Royal Aero Club and who met her when she was learning to fly at Thruxton, told me that Sheila was considered 'a very beautiful girl', and that 'everyone fancied her'. Among those who did was one of the instructors, who chased her round the airfield. Sheila even claimed that he had had the curtains in the room she slept in at Thruxton shortened so that he could look through the window at her; this sounds reminiscent of her earlier paranoia, but was said jokingly, and bore no relation to her earlier conviction that she was being followed and watched. She had apparently made such a complete recovery that, although many people who knew her during her early flying years told me that she was always tense, and smoked heavily, there was no suggestion of any mental illness, and certainly no suspicion that she might ever have been on drugs.

On the whole, she was made more welcome by the men than by the women, to some of whom she seemed 'an alien animal' and 'fairly bad news' – 'beautiful, thin, determined, a glamorous thing swanning around with men swooning at her feet and doing things for her'. Since she was indeed beautiful, thin and determined, and since the men were intrigued enough by her looks and her determination to be willing to do whatever they could to help her, it was perhaps an inevitable image. It did not at first occur to Sheila that she was putting the other women's backs up – although she was aware of some resentment – nor did she intend to do so; nevertheless some of them thought that she was 'a tart' because she appeared to have no income, but plenty of time and enough money to fill it with such an expensive hobby as flying. Simon Ames, a fellow racing pilot and an official of the RAeC, put it less bluntly: 'She may have had an income from a circuit of people for the time they spent with her.'

Even Sheila's closest friend, Elizabeth Overbury, was unable to tell me how Sheila financed her flying: 'I did not ask, and she did not tell,' she explained. 'This was part of our friendship. We each respected the other's space.' She knew only that Teddy Sugden paid the rent – which several other people told me was paid by Alan Cobham.

It was Catherine Sugden, who after living with Teddy for several years married him when they were on holiday in Cyprus in 1963, who supplied the answer to Sheila's financial position. 'Of course Teddy paid for her flying,' she told me. It seemed perfectly natural and acceptable to her that, although Teddy and Sheila had never been married, he had given her the support he would have given to an ex-wife. Although at some point he transferred the lease of her flat to her name, to avoid complications should anything happen to him, he continued to pay the rent. Catherine did not know the details of Teddy's financial support, but confirmed that he paid for all Sheila's initial tuition, and assumed that he continued either to make her an allowance or to give her money when she needed it.

'Teddy was very fond of Sheila,' she said, with no tinge of jealousy, 'he just couldn't live with her – but he was very proud of her flying.' Through flying, Sheila had become emotionally independent of Teddy, and was aiming at becoming financially independent. It was his name, and the address and telephone number of his consulting rooms in Half Moon Street, that she continued to give for emergencies in her diaries; and it was at Half Moon Street that she carried on seeing him, but as a friend – 'a loyal friend', as she put it – rather than as a lover. His pride in her flying was as much an incentive as her own ambition, and she was not yet ready to replace him with any other man, although to some extent *Myth* took his place in her affections. She felt that she and *Myth* were a partnership in a way which she had never found possible with any lover.

Sheila was already beginning to compare herself with Amy Johnson, who was her example and her heroine. There were indeed certain noticeable similarities – both women had started flying on the rebound; both had to contend with psychological difficulties and even mental illness, and both failed in their attempts at marriage and at pre-flying careers; neither found flying easy, nor was a natural pilot, but both persevered with a dogged determination which, once they had decided what they wanted to do, allowed nothing to stand in their way.

What Sheila wanted to do to start with was quite simply to fly as

often and for as long and as far as she could with her little Jackaroo –
and as fast as she could make it go. Encouraged by the engineers
who had converted it and by fellow club members, she decided to
enter the 1960 National Air Races, little expecting to do well. She
had six months to learn the techniques of flying at speed over a set
course and to absorb the complexities of aerial racing regulations.
Although she had no radio, she made several flights to the Channel
Islands – crossing the English Channel seemed to her a great
achievement for such a small aircraft without navigational aids, and
was indeed a longer sea crossing than Amy Johnson had made when
she set out for Australia. It was at a rally in Jersey that she won her
first trophy, a small award presented to her by Lady Brabazon:
although it was to her that it was awarded, Sheila felt that it had
really been won by *Myth*.

If flying to the Channel Islands seemed daring, it was nothing
compared with another aerial expedition the same year, to Spain
and Tangier, with two male pilots as passengers. The range and
speed of the Jackaroo meant that they had to land and refuel every
two hours. But 'the thrill of being in North Africa', the excitement of
the Seville Easter Fair and of bullfights, and the beauty of the Costa
Brava and the Pyrenees from the air, as well as the sense of
achievement at having actually flown safely there and back, more
than made up for such minor inconveniences.

Although Sheila's diaries usually contained little more than
scribbled reminders about future appointments, with only an
occasional comment, during 1960 she made several longer entries in
an otherwise empty five-year diary. When she had delivered *Myth* to
White Waltham, ready for the first of the national air races – from
London to Cardiff – she wrote that she 'felt very proud of her, and
didn't like leaving her picketed there, although she had so many
other precious planes for company'.

On the morning of the race she woke up 'feeling grim', and
convinced that she would not be able to fly 'for toffee'. 'I didn't think
we had a hope of qualifying after seeing all those experienced boys,'
she admitted. But, with considerable back-seat encouragement
from her instructor John Heaton, who was acting as co-pilot and
was one of the most experienced men in air racing, she did more
than well enough to do so. She relived her excitement in enthusiastic
but sometimes illegible detail:

We overtook a few turbulents . . . Geoffrey overtook us and then an Auster streaked ahead. Vis. was not good. Round the West Pylon – nearly there. Over the sea I can see the coastline but not the aerodrome until the last minute. There seemed to be a gaggle of us together. The last two minutes were an hour of suspense. I . . . begged *Myth* on. – Geoff's off course, perhaps I can pip him – keep straight *Myth* nose down – to hell with the trees. A yellow Tiger flashes between us, & we're over the finish one second later. Wow – we're fifth in the overall results in the London–Cardiff. Geoffrey is third, which is wonderful for Jackaroos. I am delighted. . . . We bedded *Myth* down for the night. Usual Shell & Dunlop tents for drinks. Glamorgan Club for a meal, Park Hotel & another meal. No drinking, & bed at midnight. Feeling very mixed up and grinning.

Next day, she was 'a bundle of nerves' until it was time for her start, and afterwards filled several pages with her excited description of the triumph she shared with *Myth* and John Heaton:

. . . Myth was holding her own. Sweat was rolling down my face, & my head was practically through the windscreen. John was shouting encouragement. Heavens – I nearly missed the right spot to turn on the horizon – an awful swerve – hope I haven't lost too much speed. We've got round two laps, & I haven't seen anyone, & they haven't caught us. My heart is bursting with excitement – my left foot is asleep – I can't feel it, & the right feels cut in two by the rudder bar – my hands are clenched on the throttle, & the stick, & I try to relax – past the 1st and 2nd pylons – two more laps to finish – I feel glorious, & beg & cajole *Myth* to do her utmost – she does, wonderful beautiful girl – John says that they are on our neck – keep straight – turn steeply – steeply vertically, & pull out on the next spot – Lord it takes every ounce of strength – we are on the straight – I see the hangars first, then the yellow pylon – nose down – luckily most of the trees are to the side – just skimmed a broken down me – we're at the pylon – we're at the finishing line – nose down & still more. Dear, precious wonderful *Myth* – she's done it again – how I love her – John is shouting, grinning – we are both incoherent, & look back at the others streaming behind us – this time we've won – wow.

At the prizegiving, Sheila was presented with a model of the de Havilland National Air Racing trophy, and discovered that at that stage the number of points she had gained made her air racing champion of her class so far for the year. 'This is a great joke, and such fun!' she wrote, although it meant that she and *Myth* would be heavily handicapped for the King's Cup Air Race, for which they had just qualified. A few days later, she made another entry: 'I still can't believe we're in it [the King's Cup] – I'm really terribly thrilled, & am very grateful for my luck this year, & particularly some dear people's encouragement, & backing.' The 'dear people' whose encouragement she valued included two acknowledged patriarchs of British aviation, Lord Brabazon and Sir Alan Cobham.

On the day before the King's Cup, in which she acquitted herself adequately but not outstandingly, Sheila made one further entry in her five-year diary:

I do so want to do well this year – partly though fear lest there isn't another time – . . . I'm scared because I've started to live again, & enjoy life, & I'm afraid lest it's all taken away again. I can't imagine life without flying now. It's been the most wonderful thing in my life, & in spite of all the scheming, & bitcheries from certain directions – I've found more sheer beauty, mystical qualities, & sheer overwhelming happiness, & a sense of belonging, & minor accomplishment, than I could ever have imagined. It's incredible when I remember the other things – that I've been given a chance to see it all afresh, in spite of starting still in the nightmare, & sometimes even to this day it comes back – but the sky soothes it away, & I try to believe the others were right, & I imagined it all. Sometimes I believe I can soar right over it to sheer freedom.

When Bev Snook said to me: 'Sheila Scott burst into flying out of the blue', he was speaking more accurately than he realized. The next few years were the happiest of her life. Spurred on by her success in her first air race, she entered everything she could; and in between races she flew to as many rallies as possible; when she was neither racing nor rally flying, she concentrated on learning, both practically and theoretically, about aviation. She practised aerobatics, as a new member of the Tiger Club; threw herself into instrument and night flying; struggled with wireless telegraphy – she was given a six-channel radio for *Myth* as a birthday present, and collected crystals so that she would eventually have enough channels for any foreign flying which might crop up.

Although the moods of despair which had always alternated with those of elation were still inclined to engulf her from time to time, alone in *Myth* she found it impossible to remain depressed or unhappy, and could relax in a way which she had never found possible on the ground, or with other people. She discovered 'a new dimension', both physically and philosophically: 'a certain purity of thought' which she could never recapture on the ground, and a freedom, a sense of beauty, of magnificence and even of grandeur which was almost religious in its intensity. Something, or someone, seemed to be looking after her when she flew: she considered her *Myth* symbol to be a lucky charm and was aware of 'some yet unexplained energy in the higher levels of the atmosphere'.

In spite of her professed devotion to *Myth*, as early as January 1961 Sheila was dreaming of becoming the owner of a Piper Comanche, a larger, faster, more streamlined and considerably more expensive aircraft than her Jackaroo. She went as far as asking British Executive Air Services Ltd at Oxford Airport about maintenance costs; the reply, giving an estimated annual outlay of £835, pointed out that it would be 'a pretty expensive airplane to own'.

During the summer of 1961 Sheila earned her first money from flying, as drop pilot with *Myth* for a parachute club. In the following winter, she concentrated on the theory needed for her commercial licence: she did not find it easy, but managed to prove herself adequately conversant with aviation law, flight planning and the mathematics essential for aviation. Her flying training followed in the spring, in a Chipmunk at CSE Aviation, Oxford, although she still looked longingly at the Comanche 250, with its cruising speed of 160 m.p.h. and its four-seater comfort.

Then, armed with all the necessary examination and flying test results, she met her first serious setback since she had started flying: she was refused her commercial licence on the grounds of short-sightedness. Her explanation was that her test coincided with what she thought to be flu, but which turned out to be infective hepatitis, and that this must have affected her sight. For a few weeks she was grounded, and had to drop out of an instructor's course on which she had just embarked at Thruxton. Her short sight, and her refusal to wear glasses in public, earned her an undeserved reputation for being stand-offish: 'I've seen someone come towards Sheila smiling, and she hasn't even seen them,' Elizabeth Overbury told me. 'If I was with her, I'd marshal her back.'

Although she had been refused a commercial licence, Sheila's morale was boosted and her achievements with her Jackaroo the previous year were rewarded by the BWPA's Jean Lennox Bird Trophy. Even better, in practical terms, was her involvement with Cessna Aircraft, an American firm which wanted to boost sales in Britain – and enlisted Sheila's help in doing so by offering her 'various beautiful Cessna aeroplanes' to show off in air races, and by paying her as a demonstrator. She still owned – and adored – *Myth*, but in 1962 raced both a Cessna 175 and a chocolate brown Cessna 150. With the latter, she was second in an Open Handicap Race and won a Ladies' Race at Thruxton – during which, according to the commentator, John Blake, she lost count of the laps and flew an extra one: 'Everyone else did an extra lap too, just in case Sheila was right – which made the whole race take a lot longer.'

In 1962, Sheila flew John Blake in the Comanche to Hungary for the World Aerobatic Championships, at which he was the British team manager and RAeC representative. After landing at Budapest to clear customs, they were given a local interpreter – more, John felt, to keep an eye on them than to help them with language difficulties. On their approach to the smaller grass airfield where the competition was to be held, one of the three green lights indicating that the undercarriage was down failed to come on. Not daring to risk landing on a grass strip with no emergency facilities, they turned back for the main airfield. Sheila was keen to land as soon as possible.

'There it is – there's the airfield,' she suddenly exclaimed. 'I'll go straight in and land!'

'No, Sheila, it's not the right one,' John said, while the interpreter behind them became very excited and said 'No – no – no!'

On the airfield which Sheila had wrongly assumed to be the one they had just left they could see rows of fighter planes which had certainly not been there before. Had Sheila landed it would undoubtedly have caused a serious incident, but fortunately she was made aware of her mistake in time to divert and carry on to the correct airfield. There they could still only get two greens, and the full emergency service was alerted: but their only problem was, as they had suspected, a faulty bulb, and the undercarriage was functioning correctly.

Nevertheless the aircraft was wheeled into a hangar so that this could be checked. Security was tight, with armed guards on duty; but Sheila kept forgetting this and wandering into the hangar – only to be marched out each time by one of the guards.

Photography from the air was strictly forbidden, because of the nearby secret fighter base on which she had nearly landed; but John and Sheila photographed everything possible, both on the ground and in the air. 'It was a creepy feeling, being on the wrong side of the Iron Curtain,' John admitted, 'so as soon as the competition was over we were anxious to get back – everyone was a bit nervous.' They were waiting for clearance to take off when, to their alarm, a huge official car with a motorcycle escort roared up behind them.

'Help!' they thought anxiously.

The occupant of the car was the airport commandant: he merely wanted to say goodbye to Sheila – and to give her her camera, which she had left behind.

There was more drama as they approached Vienna. Visibility was good; they had been cleared to land and were already letting down. John was looking down to one side at the ground, and Sheila was fiddling with the radio controls, when suddenly the cockpit went dark: an Austrian Airlines Viscount was letting down immediately above them. Shaken but unharmed, they landed behind it. Nothing was said about the incident, and they could only assume that the Viscount pilot had been oblivious to their presence.

It was the final excitement of what John termed 'an hysterical journey'; but he considered Sheila a safe and competent pilot whose only problem was lack of experience. 'She was not a natural,' he told me, 'nor did she have the experience of a commercial pilot – but she was never dangerous, although she could be forgetful.'

'Not a natural' was an expression many people used of Sheila as a pilot; but those who had flown with her or raced against her always qualified it by adding that she 'worked hard and took a lot of trouble'. 'She found it difficult,' Simon Ames – for several years an official of the Royal Aero Club – told me, 'but she had lots of adrenaline, and the more she did, the better she got.'

Sheila made her first visit to America for a Cessna Sales Week in Wichita, Kansas. She found American aviation more relaxed, even more friendly and considerably cheaper than in Britain, and was impressed by the luxurious week of sophisticated ground and air entertainment and sales training laid on by Cessna. Even better was the opportunity to fly, albeit as a passenger, from Wichita to New York – 'as far as flying over four European countries, but without the fuss and bother of international boundaries and customs formalities', as she put it, adding that Americans did not realize how simple flying was for them in comparison with the British: it was even possible, to her amazement, to fly small private aircraft over New York, which at night was 'something magical'.

Determined to make the most of any aviation opportunities which might present themselves while she was in the United States, Sheila took a medical test for an American commercial licence in New York, where her eyesight was considered perfectly acceptable. When it was suggested that she should take her commercial licence in America she needed little persuasion, especially when she was offered the hospitality of Bill and Lee Whitsell, the owners of the Flying 'W' Ranch in New Jersey, while she worked towards commercial and instrument ratings.

The Flying 'W' Ranch was, as Sheila said, probably the most unusual airport in the world, 'a pilot's paradise', with two tarmac runways and Wild West decor both inside a luxury restaurant and bar, and disguising the outside of the modern classrooms, hangars, a Link trainer building (housing an aircraft simulator for instruction) and maintenance buildings. The staff were dressed as cowboys, and dinner guests arrived in private aircraft for an evening at the Ponderosa, a motel on the far side of the airfield. There could not have been a greater contrast to the Nissen huts and club bar at Thruxton. Sheila plunged with enthusiasm both into the air and ground work for her ratings, and into the accompanying social life. Her confidence grew as she gradually disentangled such differences in terminology as tracks instead of courses, and courses instead of headings, and coped with landing and taking off at Washington DC between monsters like 707s and Gulfstreams.

While she was at the Flying 'W' Ranch Sheila was included in the family life of the Whitsells, who had four children – the youngest a baby a few months old, the oldest eight. She shared Bill and Lee's fear as the Cuban crisis presented what seemed at the time an imminent threat to the eastern coast of America. When, at the height of the crisis, Bill had to leave the ranch on business, he made sure that his aircraft was ready for Sheila to fly his wife and children to safety if the worst came to the worst. Lee and Sheila stocked up with food ready for a siege and turned the cellar into a bolthole. Night after night they sat together wondering whether that would be the night, and whether they would have time to fly out or would have to sit for days in the cellar. Although they were less frightened, according to the accounts of both women, than they would have expected, the thought that an H-bomb might fall on them at any moment gave them, as Sheila put it, 'an odd blank feeling'. She and Lee felt very close to each other; then, of course, 'fortunately the Cuban crisis blew over and we returned to normality'.

Normality for Sheila towards the end of her time in America included being made a Member at Large of the 99s, an inimitably American association of women pilots whose founder president, in 1929, was Amelia Earhart, America's flying heroine. In 1929 there were 117 women scattered across America who had pilot's licences; when they were invited to form an association, 99 of them turned up for the first meeting – hence the whimsical name of the association. Its intentions were, however, serious: to promote air-mindedness, to ensure equal rights in aviation for women, to fight for various aspects of safety and progress in aviation, and to act in many ways as a women's institute with wings. Men were not banned; but depending on whether they were themselves pilots, or were the husbands and boyfriends of pilots, or merely had an interest in supporting women in aviation, they were allowed to become only 66ers, 45½ers or 33ers. An American all-women's air derby, flown coast to coast across the United States and lasting a week, was also held for the first time in 1929 – shortly before the setting-up of the association – and gained an equally whimsical name: the Powder Puff Derby. But the 99s and the Powder Puff did much to prove that women pilots were as competent as men, to force the men to take them seriously, and to persuade the American public that flying was safe.

Sheila did not object to the whimsy, and approved of the association's aims and activities. 'This is no dreary women-only club,' she said, '. . . the Ninety-Nines are also of great service to general aviation.' She was agreeably overwhelmed by the hospitality of the New York section, which invited her to the inauguration of their new governor, a far more lavish occasion than any social event put on by the British Women Pilots' Association. Sheila was neither the first, nor the only, British Member at Large; Freydis Sharland, who had flown during the war with the Air Transport Auxiliary and whom she had met in 1960 when they had acted as joint hosts to a group of 99s, had been similarly honoured, but had been quite content to remain 'at large'. It was Sheila's enthusiasm and initiative which launched a British section of the 99s later in the year, and which listed the support of Sir Alan Cobham.

She returned from America with an American commercial pilot's licence and instrument rating. But she was still unable to fly commercially in Britain, although she had been made a freeman of the Guild of Air Pilots and Navigators.

In April 1963, Sheila came to the regretful but inevitable decision to part with *Myth*. She advertised in the Mutual Aid column of the *Tiger Rag*, the Tiger Club's monthly magazine: 'For Sale: Happy and well cared for Jackaroo seeks kindly home where she'll be given the sort of treatment to which she's supposed to be accustomed.' Benjie Benjamin, who later wrote a privately published book about the Tiger Club and who considered himself 'a dear friend' of Sheila's, flew to Thruxton to try *Myth* out with her – she hoped he might be able to find the right person to be the next owner of her beloved first aircraft. Although he realized that Sheila did not then have 'a lot of hours to her credit', he was not prepared for her nervousness on take-off: she was so cautious that he became frustrated at her slowness. This made her even more nervous, although John Heaton in the control tower was chatting reassuringly to her over the radio and gave the all-clear for take-off. Still Sheila hesitated, until Benjie became so impatient in the passenger seat that he urged her: 'For Christ's sake, Sheila – go!'

'I can't,' she wailed, 'it isn't clear.' She pointed at some jets en route for Farnborough some distance away and a good three thousand feet up.

John Heaton, who as her instructor was aware of how nervous Sheila was when she had a passenger, said patiently: 'It's OK, Sheila. You can go.'

Smiling anxiously at Benjie, Sheila asked: 'Are you sure?'

'Yes, Sheila,' he replied, looking round the empty circuit, 'Go.' At last she plucked up the confidence to take off.

It was not until a year later that the sale of *Myth*, to British Skydiving Ltd for the sum of £975 – paid in two widely spaced instalments – was completed. Although Sheila was delighted, as this meant that the Jackaroo would stay at Thruxton and would be both well cared for and put to good use for training in parachute drops, she was so upset at parting with *Myth* that she could not face doing the handover herself. By then she was flying a borrowed Piper Comanche based at Kidlington, although she flew a Jodel in the 1963 King's Cup and a Cessna the following year – but was not placed on either occasion.

For three years running, Sheila and her co-pilot Beryl Saunders beat all other women entrants and many of the men in the Comanche 250 at an air race meeting in Sicily which was unofficially considered the world racing championship. Their hat-trick won them a challenge trophy and enough money for a holiday in Capri before they returned; they celebrated with champagne, and Sheila embarked on a brief but idyllic love affair with a wealthy Italian jet pilot: she called him 'a real man', but did not divulge his name.

After another prolonged European tour in the autumn, to Germany and then across the Alps and the Mediterranean to Morocco, where she was joined by Beryl Saunders for a North African rally, Sheila returned to America. She was there for only a few weeks, into which she managed to cram enough helicopter training to gain her licence and multi-engine helicopter rating, her seaplane rating, and to take a high-altitude course for civilians. Her helicopter instructor was Dottie Young, a tiny but determined woman who had just become the first female helicopter examiner in America and had already done much to make helicopter training available to civilians. Among Dottie's two hundred or so pupils some were, according to her own description, 'just curious', while 'some couldn't afford a rating and some couldn't hack it'. Sheila 'hacked it', at half the cost of helicopter instruction in Britain, although at first she could hardly be said to enjoy it: it was so different from flying a fixed wing aircraft, and seemed, initially at least, considerably less dignified.

Almost as if it had done so on purpose, the elderly helicopter in which she was to have taken her test had an engine failure shortly after take-off. Sheila Scott, the British racing pilot who had chosen to fly in America, was by then so well known on that side of the Atlantic that the Brantly helicopter factory came to her rescue with a brand-new – and therefore alarming – helicopter so that she could after all take the test. In spite of her nervousness and inexperience,

Sheila was considered by Dottie Young competent enough to gain her helicopter rating, and became Whirly Girl number 79. A Whirly Girl is a female helicopter pilot; the association of Whirly Girls was started in 1955 by Jean Ross Howard, who made herself Whirly Girl no. 13 – she was the thirteenth woman in the world to fly a helicopter. Whirly Girl no. 1 was the German pilot Hanna Reitsch, who flew the world's first viable helicopter before the war both outside and in a vast covered stadium in Berlin.

Dottie Young and her newest successful helicopter pilot were both pupils on the next stage of Sheila's self-inflicted training for all aviation eventualities. This was the first civilian high-altitude course at the FAA Academy in Oklahoma. According to the published account of American journalist Tony Page, the only other woman on the course, they 'decided to kinda huddle together in the chamber and look at each other in great horror if one committed a social error'. Although Sheila was by far the heaviest smoker, Tony Page admitted that she 'won the stay' at a simulated 29,000 feet without oxygen. 'Strangely enough, my writing remained the same throughout,' Sheila commented, 'maybe because it was illegible anyway.' After sixteen hours of training over two days, various practical tests and a written paper, the three women and seven men on the course each received a blue high-altitude card to attach to his or her flying licence.

Sheila's enthusiasm for the American way of doing things had gained sufficient momentum for a British chapter of the 99s to be formed, with an inaugural Thanksgiving party soon after she returned again from America. Freydis and Tim Sharland – who became a 45½er – dressed up in Red Indian costume for the swearing-in ceremony, which was given official recognition by the presence of John Stonehouse, Parliamentary Secretary to the Minister of Aviation, an ex-RAF pilot and a personal friend of Sheila's. The new association did not go down too well with some of the BWPA members, who considered its glamorous image to be unnecessary and even counter-productive. There was rivalry and unstated jealousy between the two organizations from the start, partly because potential finance no longer had a single focus, and partly because of the publicity received by the 99s – although the establishment of the British chapter was acknowledged in the BWPA winter newsletter.

The small group of women who belonged to the British 99s took no notice of the implied criticism of the older organization, and formed close, mutually supportive bonds of friendship. When Beryl Saunders, who was a pilot with Dan Air and whose hobby was aerobatics, was severely injured in a crash while practising, Sheila galvanized the other members into contributing towards private hospital fees and insisted that Beryl should not be treated as a vegetable. Although Beryl could not speak, Sheila was so convinced that her brain was still alert that she bought her a typewriter. 'Where did you learn to fly?' she asked her. Beryl typed 'Massachusetts' without faltering, which proved Sheila's point.

The *Tiger Rag*, which called the 99s an 'illustrious organization', also felt it worth mentioning that Sheila had been awarded the Amelia Earhart trophy – given annually in America – 'for her extraordinary achievement whilst in the USA in obtaining, within the period of three weeks, her commercial seaplane and helicopter ratings plus her multi-engine instrument rating. To cap these awards Sheila also found time to take a High-Altitude Course in a pressure chamber and also to qualify for jet flying. A magnificent record.'

In March 1965 the BWPA magazine got round to reporting Sheila's achievements during the previous year, although it made no mention of the Amelia Earhart Award, and the nearest it came to praise was the comment: 'Busy girl.'

5

AMY JOHNSON FLEW a Tiger Moth to Australia after only seventy-five hours of solo flying – which was just what Sheila would have liked to have done with her Jackaroo; but common sense and lack of money prevailed, although she continued to dream. In the meantime she was looking for some record to break, to test herself and to prove something – although quite what, she was not sure.

She investigated the possibility of using a Mosquito which could be converted and overhauled in Australia. Having abandoned that idea because of the cost, she considered a borrowed Mustang in America. But there was little enthusiasm for record attempts from the British end, where it was generally felt that the pioneering days were over and flying was assumed to be either a commercial career, or for fun.

Sheila was, however, determined to set herself a goal. Still thinking in terms of the Mustang, she went through lists of unbroken records and found her answer: in 1953, a British pilot called Fred Dunkerley had set up several records between London and other European capitals in a twin-engined Miles Gemini. It was, she decided, high time his records were broken – but rather than challenge them one at a time over several weeks, as he had done, she decided to try for them all at once, as a record-breaking endurance test spread over thirty-six hours. 'It was only 2300 miles in a day and a half, and, one would think, simple enough,' she said optimistically. Secretly – although not very secretly – she hoped that this would be a 'dress rehearsal for something bigger'.

Once she had set her mind on the attempt, she refused to be deterred by setbacks imposed by bureaucracy, apathy or incredulity from those who could not see why she wanted to break records, or even by lack of money. The preparation took six months, from December 1964 until May 1965. Simon Ames and John Blake, who headed the Aviation Centre of the Royal Aero Club, gave the venture their and the club's blessing, although it inevitably involved them in many hours of extra work. Sheila had set her heart on a Piper Comanche 400, a powerful single-engined sporting executive aircraft not yet available in Britain but which she had flown a few times in America. The president of Piper Aircraft International at Geneva, Ian Forbes, himself a keen racing pilot, agreed to lease one on unusually favourable terms. The first hurdles had been overcome: she had official recognition and the promise of an aircraft.

There were still innumerable time-consuming details to be sorted out – route planning and permissions, official registration of the various records to be attempted, and publicity; the private satisfaction of record breaking could not be enough. Without publicity, there would be nothing to offer as a lure to sponsors – and sponsorship was vital; Teddy Sugden's allowance would by no means cover the costs. The *Sun* offered Sheila £750 for an exclusive story on the preparations. Even with an extra £250 from BBC2 for filming rights, this was far from enough to finance the attempt – but it helped, and it ensured excellent exposure. Firestone tyres, Champion spark plugs and BP petrol all promised support, although most manufacturers of products which Sheila would – or could – be using merely wished her luck, pointing out that their advertising budgets for the year had already been agreed.

In April, Marjorie Proops included a photo of Sheila in a *Daily Mail* column attacking male attitudes to women's success. The main targets of her page were jointly the Jockey Club's intransigent ban on women members, and male chauvinism in aviation. 'Men regard the air as primarily their province and they suspect a woman who is actually qualified to fly in THEIR sky,' she wrote. ' . . . I guess they think that when a woman moves into what they regard as an entirely male field, she must be a peculiar kind of woman: tough and unfeeling. Which, when you meet a flyer like Sheila Scott, is obvious nonsense.' She described Sheila as 'an attractive, feminine woman who is crazy about flying . . . a competitive racing pilot [who] has about forty trophies to prove she can handle a plane in tough contests against men'. Sheila's approaching record attempts could not be mentioned because of her exclusive contract with the *Sun*.

The dates for the attempt – two days in May – were fixed before Sheila had ever seen the aircraft she was to fly. A reporter from the *Sun*, Margaret Jones, was with her when she went to inspect it in

Geneva, only a fortnight before the take-off date to which she had committed herself. 'It was like the first meeting between a top jockey and a highly bred racehorse,' Margaret Jones wrote; 'even an outsider could sense the feeling of sensual pleasure, admiration and respect that airwoman Sheila Scott felt for *15 Papa*.'

In recognition of the newspaper's sponsorship, *15 Papa* was temporarily renamed *Sunpip*; Sheila insisted on preceding this with *Myth* for luck, and so the Piper Comanche 400 became for a while *Myth Sunpip*.

Among the pre-flight press coverage was an article entitled 'Fashion when a woman is flying solo'. It featured a photograph of Sheila in 'her No. 1 flying suit' of peacock blue stretch silk, her legs long and slim in tapered pants, her feet in matching gaberdine boots, her hands thrust into the pockets of a semi-fitted double-breasted jacket with a mandarin collar – or it could have been her second flying suit, of fine navy blue mohair, again with matching gaberdine boots. With her, the article revealed, she would have a hat box containing a blonde wig styled by René – whose hair-dressing establishment she visited regularly – and an emergency overnight bag she called RON (Remaining Over Night) in which she carried mini make-up supplied by Elizabeth Arden, another name which featured regularly in her appointment diary.

The arrival of the Comanche at Kidlington, where CSE, a company set up by Lord Waterpark and Lord Kildare, had the UK franchise for Piper Aircraft, provided an opportunity for instructor Frank Thomas as well as Sheila to try it out. They made several short flights together and one dummy run, turning just short of the Dutch coast, a few days before the record attempt. Although she was 'anxious and edgy', Frank had confidence in her as a pilot: 'She was an extraordinary person. She never seemed very brave or very clever, and was very nervous and unsure of herself. But once she'd decided to do something, she did it. I never doubted she would, although it often seemed unbelievable.' The engineering staff at CSE shared his feelings, and on this and other occasions willingly put in long hours of extra time on Sheila's behalf.

The last two days were, as Sheila put it, 'grim'. She retreated from the telephone and from her own rising panic to a hotel near Northolt. The weather was too bad for any practice flights, and she was beginning to wonder if she would have to postpone her attempt. One of *Myth Sunpip*'s radios went out of action, and there was a long hassle about getting a replacement through customs. It seemed almost miraculous – or perhaps it was *Myth*'s luck – that the weather report for the first day of the attempt was favourable, and that everything went without a hitch. Firestone provided a Rolls-Royce to take Sheila to the airfield at Northolt, which she had been given permission to use by the RAF. By the time she arrived, Bill Trollope, who was acting as her chief engineer, had run up the engine and checked the aircraft over: as a young man he had helped Amy Johnson with *Jason*, the Tiger Moth with which she flew to Australia. Airline pilot Captain Peter Macdonald, whom she had roped in as ground assistant, was waiting with her maps and flight plans, and Philip Mayne, the RAeC time keeper, was in position. To her surprise and gratification, all her sponsors had gathered to see her off, and waited to welcome her back.

Feeling tense but confident, she took off on time from Northolt to The Hague. It was only at Northolt that she was to land. The first leg brought the hoped-for three records – London–The Hague, The Hague–London, and London–The Hague–London. Then it was London to Brussels and return, non-stop – another three records. The first day, 19 May, finished with the third set of records, with Brussels as the turning point. As usual, once she was in the air the tension – sometimes verging on hysteria – which Sheila had displayed under the pressure of the last few hectic days of preparation was replaced by a feeling of peace and a total concentration on the complexities of flying and navigating at speed. The only problem was caused by a ten degree deviation in the compass, which Ian Forbes confirmed and attempted to rectify in the evening.

Simon Ames sat at Leavesden throughout both days following Sheila's progress: it was his task to log her records officially, in those days a slow and laborious task involving a book of logarithm tables – *Norie's Nautical Tables* – and an old-fashioned calculator looking more like a typewriter with a wind-up handle. He felt that the Comanche 400 was 'a bit more than Sheila could cope with' – she had gone, with very little experience, from an aircraft capable of 100 m.p.h. to one which could do 250 m.p.h., and had to get used to the problem of navigating while flying at speed; it was, Ames said, to her credit that she not only managed this, but did exactly what she had set out to do, and 'was well organized, well prepared and reasonably calm' – although as usual she chain smoked nervously throughout the ground preparations, and continued to smoke in the air.

Next day, again without landing except at Northolt, Sheila repeated the process, with longer return flights, one to Belfast, one to Dublin. She had broken all fifteen records in thirty-six hours, of which ten and a quarter had been spent in the air. By the time she climbed out of the aircraft, in front of television cameras, she was more tired and colder than she ever remembered. Her average speed on the various legs had varied from just under 187 m.p.h. on the way to Dublin to just over 210 m.p.h. on the return flight, when she had the wind with her. Firestone took out a full-page congratulatory advertisement in the June issue of *Flight* magazine, with a photo of Sheila and *Myth Sunpip*.

Afterwards, her pride in her achievement was tempered by a feeling of let-down; but she had successfully tested both herself and the aircraft, and had proved that record breaking was still possible in spite of the restrictions imposed on aviation by modern technology and bureaucracy. With dreams of more records never far from her mind, before *Myth Sunpip* was returned to Geneva Sheila clocked up the fastest speed – 207 m.p.h. – at the Manx Air Derby; but she was by then so heavily handicapped that she finished in sixth place. For the first time, Elizabeth Overbury was her co-pilot; although they had often competed against each other, until their half-dozen practice flights before the race they had never flown together. Elizabeth found Sheila as competent as she would have expected.

As president of the British 99s Sheila had ardently campaigned for greater recognition of women in air racing, and she was rewarded by the inclusion of a Ladies' Race for the first time as part of the 1965 National Air Races. There were nine entries, all but two from members of the British 99s – which was a more exclusive club than the BWPA, and accepted only women who were professional pilots or were exceptionally highly qualified. Heavily handicapped in a borrowed Comanche 250, Sheila soon overhauled the majority of the slower aircraft and just before the finish passed the leader, Christine Hughes, who was flying the BWPA's Condor and was one of the two entrants who did not belong to the 99s. It was a fitting tribute to her efforts in setting up the 99s in Britain that Sheila became the first recipient of the Air Challenge Trophy provided by Champion spark plugs. Lady Pamela Huntly, a successful – and wealthy – racing pilot, was also in a Comanche 250 and was even more heavily handicapped than Sheila, but retired from the race.

Pam Huntly, who had met Sheila in 1962, admired her as a pilot and as an organizer – 'She organized it all very well,' she told me, referring to the 99s and to the women's race which they initiated. Although she considered her 'very nervous and jittery' on the ground, their friendship was never marred by any disagreement, and on the one occasion when Sheila piloted her Pam found her 'very different in the air – very calm, relaxed; she couldn't have done it if she'd been jittery'. Nor would Pam have trusted her to fly her own Comanche – as she once did when she found herself after a rally in France with both a car and an aircraft to bring back to England – if she had not had faith in Sheila as a pilot.

In August, in America, Sheila was asked what she planned to do next. Without thinking, and to her surprise, she heard herself say that she intended to make an attempt on the solo round-the-world record. Having said it, she felt immediately committed. It was time to follow the lead of her heroine, Amy Johnson – and to do so, Sheila persuaded herself, not for personal satisfaction and fame (although she hoped for both) but for Britain. She would do better than Amy: she would fly first to Australia and then back to England, making the flight the first solo circumnavigation by any British pilot, and the longest solo flight ever undertaken. Although she had no money, she did not let this deter her: she was confident that this time sponsorship would flow in – if not for her, then for the greater glory of her country.

The preparations for such a flight could – indeed should – have taken anything up to two years. Sheila had eight months, starting with a trip to Geneva to discuss the possibility of again using *Myth Sunpip*. For a deposit of only £100 she became the nominal owner of the aircraft – quite how she would pay the remaining £16,900 she would work out later. Sir Alan Cobham was perhaps the one person who might have talked her out of carrying on; his appearance at race meetings long after he had ceased to participate actively was thought by many to be because of his admiration for Sheila. She had an even greater admiration for him – as indeed did everyone in aviation – especially as he had, in a sense, introduced her to flying as the pilot of the aircraft in which she had had her first unforgettable birthday joy-ride. But when he asked her to marry him, she turned him down; she looked on him not as a lover or a potential husband, but as a father figure.

In aviation circles Alan Cobham had long been regarded as one of the great pioneers. In 1935 *The Complete Book of Aviation* had paid tribute to his achievements: 'Sir Alan Cobham has done, by his survey flights and air publicity campaigns, more than most men to increase interest in the air.' In Sheila, he recognized the determination and pioneering spirit which had taken him on long-distance flights in the 1920s. Although he was already over seventy his interest in aviation was unabated, and he supported her ambitions wholeheartedly – egging her on, rather than holding her back. She had also enlisted his support for the 99s, and in November 1965 was the first recipient of their Sir Alan Cobham Achievement Award 'for her contribution to the furtherance of active aviation'.

What Sheila needed more than awards, and even more than money, was a manager, a financial adviser, someone who could handle the multitudinous paperwork which soon engulfed her. Letters, telephone calls and personal encounters optimistically aiming at sponsorship were all too often fruitless. She was never easily able to accept the disappointment of being made a half-promise over a dinner table, only to find that nothing further came of it, and felt repeatedly let down. There were, however, promises which were kept, and which gave considerable practical help. Champion spark plugs, for instance, confirmed in writing in November 1965 that the company would provide Sheila with a supply of spark plugs sufficient for her trip, technical assistance in the USA and whenever possible overseas, photographs and PR coverage at her various stops, and 'upon completion the sum of $1000 US for the accomplishment'. In return, they intended to make full use of the firm's support for her record attempt in their advertising.

Gradually other sponsors came forward, usually with offers of free equipment rather than of cash. All this of course helped, but as time went by and 27 April, Sheila's birthday and the date set for the start of the round-the-world flight, approached, she became increasingly frustrated and agitated. She knew that she had taken on more than she could cope with, but she was not prepared to admit defeat. On occasions she made her irritation all too clear; some potential sponsors took this in their stride, but others were antagonized. When Nestlé's supplied her with several tubes of condensed milk (which she greatly appreciated – it was a quick, easy and tasty way of gaining energy and nourishment during flight) she was genuinely grateful; but this did not prevent her from saying to a friend, 'Six bloody tubes of milk! – and they call that sponsorship!' 'We had no difficulty in dealing with Miss Scott, and got good cooperation in return for our sponsorship,' I was told by a representative of the company, which also supplied Sheila's coffee powder.

'On the few occasions I met Sheila I found her to be intelligent and attractive,' another sponsor in kind commented. 'When certain things got delayed or went wrong prior to the flight she tended to get somewhat agitated, but possibly this was to be expected.'

From other sponsors Sheila was given tyres, a life raft and a life preserver, airway manuals and charts, fuel and a promise from the major aviation fuel companies of worldwide assistance, navigational equipment, clothing and make-up. 'My memory of Sheila is that she was full of nervous energy with an enthusiasm and persistence of a high order for the project she was engaged upon,' said Ted Hawkes of BP. 'She evidently had great problems in securing adequate finance for her flights and, I think, hated having to go around seeking funds or aid in kind. This was reflected in the apparent hostility she sometimes showed in negotiations with her sponsors but, notwithstanding the occasional difficult encounter, she was greatly admired for her courage and persistence. There were some, though, that took offence at the brusque manner she could adopt.'

The preparations left virtually no time either for flying or for social life. Sheila had become, briefly, a ballooning enthusiast after a six-page letter inviting her to 'an unknown destination' in Holland had led her to a fantasy world. Rechristened Champagne, she had made various strange vows and had been treated to the sublime peace and majesty of floating over the flat Dutch countryside in a basket suspended from the belly of a balloon called *Utrecht*. This, she claimed, had been what she had been striving to find ever since she had discovered the 'joys and frequent heartbreaks of flying'. Whatever it was that she felt dimly she had experienced 'up there' in *Myth* was 'experienced more vividly'.

'Why do we have to go to Holland for this?' she asked Anthony Smith, who was at the time the only balloonist in Britain. Anthony, who had been quite happy ballooning in the cloud-cuckoo-land of Dutch castles, or across Africa for television programmes, took note of the question. 'Sheila acted as a catalyst,' he told me. Spurred and badgered and even bullied by her, he wrote to everyone who had contacted him after seeing his ballooning films; the result was the inaugural meeting of the British Balloon and Airships Club, of which he became founder president. Sheila was able to take a few hours off to attend the meeting and give the club she had been largely responsible for initiating her full verbal support, but was too deeply involved in her powered-flight record-breaking projects to indulge in the more peaceful pastime of ballooning.

While she pestered potential sponsors, and pored over maps on the floor and the bed of her flat, *Myth Sunpip* was undergoing conversion in Geneva ready for their joint ordeal. It was on one of her visits to Geneva that she met Donald Campbell, whom she turned to for advice even though he was deeply embroiled in his own record-making plans with his speedboat *Bluebird*. She admired his patriotism, his 'complete individuality' and 'heights of courage', and considered him 'a truly great sportsman'. Campbell in turn sensed an equally adventurous spirit, although he could not see how Sheila could possibly keep to her intended take-off date. They discussed the possibility of death in their various undertakings, and considered Sheila the less likely to survive. Nevertheless Campbell organized a press conference and luncheon for Sheila in London to try to attract sponsorship for her flight.

Among the many people she had written to was Norman Lonsdale of the World Record Club. 'She thought this was a good tie-in – her world record attempt, and my world record club,' Norman Lonsdale explained. It was at the lunch given by Donald Campbell that he and Sheila met. 'Campbell was very gung-ho, very this-is-good-for-Britain,' Norman told me. 'I talked to Sheila and told her I thought I might be able to do something.' It was the start of a long and supportive friendship, although the support was always somewhat one-sided. Norman Lonsdale came closer than anyone else, at least for a while, to filling the emotional gap in Sheila's otherwise full life.

'What a sweet person, what an endearing person, what an utterly charming person, what a beautiful person, what a refreshing person, what a dedicated person,' he eulogized more than twenty years later. He might have added, 'what a naïve and totally disorganized person', since this is what he also considered her. His help included a small financial contribution – smaller than Sheila might have hoped, but he made up for this by providing the luxury of a music system and tapes for her aircraft and, most important of all, assistance with the organizational side of the project, as well as constant patient caring moral support. Although he thought that Sheila should abandon the whole idea, because she quite simply could not afford it, he realized that she would not do so: and so he set about making as much of it easier for her as he could.

In many ways, he was just what she needed: had he not been married, and with no intention of leaving his wife and children, Sheila would certainly have considered him a potential husband. 'What a fool I was not to marry Norman and settle down with him when I had the chance,' she once said to me; but her memory was providing a chance of marriage where none had existed. Nevertheless they were considered by her friends a handsome couple, and although Sheila was never possessive – she had learnt that lesson with Teddy – she was as much in love with him as she had time to be: flying and her aircraft still came first. She described Norman to me, before I met him, as 'tall – thin – kind and charming – with an impish sense of humour'. He also had some business sense, which Sheila, in her impetuous search for a way of proving herself and becoming famous, had had neither time nor inclination to acquire.

'I always think of Sheila in her living room in Park West surrounded by fourteen thousand sheets of paper, with the phone ringing constantly, coffee mugs everywhere, one or two temporary secretaries not knowing what the hell was going on,' Norman told me. 'There was this rather crazy woman talking to them about the North Pole and the Zambesi, giving no introductions, straight off giving them notes on compass courses, telling them to call Champion's about spark plugs, saying that the propeller was being polished, saying just get on to Leavesden. . . .' Her secretaries came and went, few staying for long; coping with Sheila, and being paid very little for doing so, but being expected to understand what she wanted and to devote themselves wholeheartedly to ensuring that she had her own way, was not something for which temps were trained. Nor was being on the receiving end of one of her hysterical outbursts, which were becoming more frequent under the pressure to which she had subjected herself.

Norman took the brunt of much of her rising panic and increasing feeling that she was being persecuted. Her mental balance, so carefully maintained during the years since flying had restored it, was again insecure. Although he knew nothing of her previous history of instability, Norman felt that because of her lack of understanding of the legal, financial and diplomatic problems of what she had undertaken she blamed people and events: she was sure everyone was letting her down, and developed a persecution complex. 'In the months before her world attempt she got a glimmer of what she'd let herself in for, but it was too late to back out,' he told me. 'She was also financially into it, tied into it in a business way so that she had reached the point of no return – but underneath she realized that she was in a pickle, which started the sense of insecurity.'

'The correct course,' according to Norman and many others whose advice Sheila did not want, 'would have been to abandon the whole project because of lack of funds – but Sheila went ahead, proving that where there's a will, there's a way.' He was by no means the only person to be dragged into her determination to find a way. Bob Pooley, for instance, whose firm Air Tours provided her with some of her navigational equipment, remembered the run-up to her world attempt as 'very fraught', with telephone calls which, although she always started by saying that she had no time, might last for half an hour or more. After one forty-five-minute telephone conversation, Sheila sounded so desperate – 'Darling, I'm not getting any help at all!' – that he dropped everything and rushed from Elstree to her flat. 'When I arrived, there were already about a dozen people there flapping around her,' he told me. 'It was a bit of a wild goose chase; but Sheila was always under such pressure because of lack of time.'

Among the many tasks that needed time was working out exactly which records Sheila was going to attempt on the way. Each one had to be agreed in advance. Sheila had frequent meetings with Simon Ames, who found what he termed the interaction of being involved with her over the paperwork exhausting. He often had to listen to tales of woe; Sheila was secretly and unkindly referred to at the RAeC as 'Look what they've done to me now!' No one was ever quite sure who 'they' were, but conversations with Sheila became increasingly a conspiracy in which whoever she was with was included in 'we' and almost anyone else was 'they'. On the few occasions when Norman Lonsdale attempted to put this into perspective, he had to admit defeat. 'Who are "they"?' he asked her, 'and who are "we"?' She was unable to give any rational answer, and became upset if he persisted with the question. He tried to tease and laugh her out of her increasing paranoia: 'What are today's disasters?' he would ask – and all too often Sheila would tell him.

Nevertheless somehow, gradually and chaotically, the details began to fall in place. There were radio, television and press interviews. Throughout it all Elizabeth Overbury, who was one of Sheila's many occasional volunteer helpers as she struggled with the organization, considered her 'bloody marvellous'. So, in spite of her demands, her occasional hysteria and their exhaustion, did everyone else involved. Then, with only a few weeks to go, she was told that the Piper Comanche 400, *Myth Sunpip*, with which she felt she already had a strong relationship, was unsuitable; instead she should use a Piper Comanche 260, which with its lower horsepower could carry more fuel in proportion to fuel consumption. With the faster, greedier Comanche 400, it was pointed out, there was no margin for error over the long Pacific crossing and she ran the risk of ditching.

Sheila was in despair. She knew that she had a clear choice: to cancel the attempt, or to accept the opinion of the experts. Cancellation was unthinkable; she was too involved, both financially – she had sold jewellery, cashed in her savings and insurance policy, and committed herself to too many people whom she would be letting down if she pulled out – and psychologically. If it had been only up to her, with no considerations such as the reputation of the Piper Aircraft Corporation to think of, she would have chosen to take the risk. She spent a miserable Easter trying to find a way of obtaining a Piper Comanche 260 at a reasonable price – there was one at CSE, but, as it was brand-new and subject to full customs duty, the price put it out of the question unless she could find a major sponsor almost overnight. She felt 'a great roaring emptiness' as she faced the thought that she had failed even before she had taken off.

It was Sir Alan Cobham who came to her rescue, by lending her £10,000 as a deposit on an aircraft and guaranteeing a loan from Lombank. He told Norman Lonsdale: 'By God, I always admired Sheila as a woman – then she told me about this crazy idea. I never thought she'd do it. Then I saw her with all her maps and equipment, and I thought, "My God, an aviatrix!"' When Sheila thanked him for coming to her rescue, he brushed aside her gratitude as a waste of time which should be spent getting on with the job: 'I know you can do it,' he said. There could have been no higher praise, and no greater incentive.

Although Sheila could now go ahead with her plans, there was no way that the new aircraft could be prepared in time for take-off at the end of April. Delaying the departure date meant rearranging international permissions and schedules, and once again contacting everyone with whom various complex arrangements had been made on her route. As the Comanche 260 was considerably slower than *Myth Sunpip*, it was not a question of simply postponing everything by a few weeks; every flight plan had to be reworked and retimed to take account of the slower speed. Even with the unfailingly cheerful unpaid assistance of Bill Hewitt, one of BOAC's top navigators, this took valuable time.

Without Bill Hewitt, Sheila admitted that the planning would have taken her many extra months, and that she would often have reached 'screaming hysteria' through sheer exhaustion; however tense and hysterical she became, he took it in his stride and could make her laugh, and this did as much as anything to keep her going. She had lost twenty pounds which she could ill afford to lose – but there was no truth in the headline which announced 'Woman pilot slims for world record attempt', a garbled report of a press conference at which the need to keep weight down on the aircraft had been mentioned. Although it was essential for the publicity she needed to keep on good terms with the press, Sheila felt so pressurized that she became irritable with reporters, who often seemed to her to be wasting time which she needed for more important tasks.

It seemed as if the paperwork would never end. To add to the frustrations was the greater likelihood now of bad weather beyond India – and, worst of all, Sheila's emotional reaction to changing aircraft. She felt as if she was letting *Myth Sunpip* down even before she had seen the replacement, which she had been told was gold and white; at least, she thought, this sounded feminine enough. When she saw her new acquisition, in a hangar in Geneva, she burst into tears of exhaustion and sheer misery; the gold looked a dirty yellow, the upholstery was a dull black, and 'she was ugly'. 'I don't like her – she's not even feminine – she's a man's aeroplane!' she felt like wailing. Masculine and ugly the aircraft may have seemed; but Piper engineers were already working on the conversion, taking out carpets, seats and soundproofing to save weight and installing extra fuel tanks as well as everything which Sheila had expected to use in *Myth Sunpip*.

The anonymity of the aircraft, rather than anything particular about it, was what Sheila found upsetting. It needed a name, an identity, and somehow this had as usual to be connected with *Myth*. Although the original *Myth* was the only aircraft which had actually belonged to Sheila, borrowed ones had used up so many numbers that the simplest solution, of name and number, was discarded. Eventually she decided on something almost as simple, a punnish play on the repetition of the name and the fact that this was the second aircraft she had owned: the Piper Comanche 260, call sign G-ATOY – which was inevitably the excuse for jokes about playing games – became *Myth Too*. *Myth*'s symbol was painted on its side – or rather on hers: Sheila was beginning to think in her usual feminine terms, a sign that sooner or later she and *Myth Too* would achieve a satisfactory working relationship.

With an American ferry pilot she flew *Myth Too* to Gatwick and then on to Leavesden, which was to be her home base for the final preparations. Both Peter Masefield, managing director of Beagle Aircraft – which Sheila had reluctantly discarded as being un-suitable – and the engineers who were to work on the plane seemed to approve. Sheila began to hope that her ugly duckling might after all turn into a swan. The apparent confusion of final preparations gradually made order out of chaos – the engineers worked overtime, the telephone rang constantly with demands for interviews and information, or with messages of good luck; exhausted friends ran round in circles fixing last-minute details of permissions and foreign currencies and clothing; equipment was fetched or delivered, installed and tested. Reluctantly Sheila gave in to doctor's orders that she must take a couple of days off and do nothing but rest – but found it impossible to relax. Her mood swung rapidly from elation to despair; one moment she felt 'delirious happiness and the sheer excitement of the unknown adventure to come' – the next she was beset by doubt and lack of confidence.

Throughout all the turmoil which surrounded her, and which was of her own creation, she remained somehow immaculate. As Rodney Burbeck put it in a long article entitled 'Why a woman wants to fly alone around the world', she looked 'like a Kensington party hostess, eminently at home with canapés and clever chat.

Slim, ash-blonde hair perfectly placed, delicate hands fluttering'. 'If all goes well,' Burbeck had written not long before the change of aircraft postponed her take-off, '. . . she will return at the end of May after completing the longest solo flight ever made in a single-engined light aircraft. And she will be the first British pilot to fly solo round the world. If all does *not* go well, Miss Scott will not take off at all, and it will be due to lack of money – money that should have come from British backers.' Sporting sponsorship had not yet caught on in Britain, and breaking records seemed to many more of an ego trip than an effort of patriotic pride.

Amy Johnson was often in Sheila's thoughts as she planned to follow her route to Australia as closely as possible. Simon Ames felt that she was beginning to identify with her heroine, who had, as he put it, also often been rude and ungrateful. Sheila would have put it differently: she believed in some unexplained form of extra-sensory communication, which she felt accounted for various 'strange co-incidences'. She was, for instance, searching for an airfield in India on a map one day when the telephone rang: a woman called Elizabeth Gray told her that she was writing Amy's biography, asked for some technical information, and then mentioned the very same place in India. A few days before her scheduled departure, Sheila received an unexpected parcel: it contained Amy Johnson's jewellery box, and a letter from Amy's sister. It was, however, not Amy's record but that of Gerry Mock, one of two American women to have flown round the world, which Sheila was intending to break. When Gerry sent her a telegram wishing her 'God Speed and Good Fortune' she felt that this was yet another lucky omen.

Finally, by 17 May, only three weeks late in spite of everything that had had to be fitted into those weeks, it looked as if all had after all gone well, at least as far as starting. Sheila had staked everything on the flight. According to Rodney Burbeck, if it succeeded she could expect to get it back several times over 'by selling her story and "selling" her name to sponsor products'; in spite of the considerable sponsorship she had been given in kind, and several financial contributions – Donald Campbell was reputed to have put up several thousand pounds – she had, to Norman Lonsdale's alarm, run up a £20,000 overdraft. The cost of the operation even before the change of aircraft had been estimated at £30,000 – approximately a pound a mile. As for selling her story, she had somehow found time to dictate the first few chapters of her autobiography, and intended to bring it up to date on the way.

The question asked again and again by reporters was not how the flight was to be financed, but why Sheila was undertaking it in the first place. None of her answers seemed to give an adequate explanation. She loved flying, she said, because of the sense of freedom, and because in the air there was never time to be bored; and a flight round the world was 'one of the few great flights left to do – so why not do it?' As Rodney Burbeck put it, 'several very good reasons come to mind . . . most of them concerned with the danger involved in flying thirty thousand miles in a light aircraft'. Sheila was well aware of the dangers – far more aware of them, and with considerably more experience as a pilot, than Amy Johnson had been when she had set out with 'the confidence of ignorance'. She faced the possibility of danger, and even of death, with what Donald Campbell called 'cold courage', and dismissed the suggestion that people who, like herself and Campbell, voluntarily placed themselves in danger had a suppressed death wish. 'If I fail,' she told Rodney Burbeck, 'someone must try again. If I am to be killed I would like it to happen while I am doing something I love.'

6

ON THE MORNING of her departure, 18 May, Sheila at first showed more panic than cool courage. Everything seemed to be going wrong – the cloud base was low, there were people rushing round asking questions and thrusting sandwiches and coffee flasks at her, and she longed to be alone. She had her wish briefly under the hairdryer: whatever was going to happen, she was determined to set out looking her best. Norman Lonsdale was waiting to escort her to Heathrow Airport; while they waited, he recorded an encouraging tape for her to listen to on her way. It told her not to worry, and not to be too proud to give up if necessary; it told her that there were friends waiting to help her; it told her that she was wonderful and that Norman admired her enormously – in fact it told her almost everything that she might have wanted to hear, except for one thing: it did not mention love.

In the car, Sheila seemed in no fit state for flying: 'She'd had no sleep, smoked non-stop, was rampaging until the last minute,' Norman told me. 'And then she opened the door, all tranquillity, and was ready to fly off.' First, however, there were numerous formalities to be endured – weight checks to conform with the procedure for registering record attempts; customs to be cleared; the flight plan for the first leg to be filed; and a farewell reception.

'Smile, Sheila' – 'Look this way' – 'Turn towards us' – She was not wearing her glasses, and so the sea of faces was a confused and confusing blur; she knew Norman was there, and Sir Alan Cobham, and Teddy Sugden; the British 99s had turned out en masse, led by Elizabeth Overbury and Pam Huntly, to whom Sheila had said: 'Why don't you fly alongside me as far as India?' John Blake, with his unmistakable moustaches which climbed halfway up his face, was the RAeC official starter. Among the well-meaning crowd, Sheila felt overwhelmed and alone.

At last, after speeches and presentations – a scroll from the Guild of Air Pilots and Navigators, orchids from the Tiger Club, cash from the 99s towards hotel expenses en route – Sheila thought she was about to escape into the freedom and solitude of her cramped cockpit, certain that no ordeal in the air could be more nerve-racking or exhausting than a heroine's farewell when as yet she felt that she had done nothing to deserve it. *Myth Too* was standing waiting under the statue of Alcock and Brown, whose flight across the Atlantic in 1919 had earned them a place among the early pioneers of aviation. Sheila paused beneath the statue and touched it for luck, looking up into the stone faces and wondering if they too had felt as bewildered and intoxicated as she did. The symbolism of the moment and of Sheila's gesture was not lost on the television cameramen and press photographers; this was the picture which should have dominated reports on the departure of Britain's most glamorous post-war long-distance solo pilot.

Bill Hewitt walked with Sheila to *Myth Too*, and at the last minute pushed a floppy rabbit with protruding teeth into her hands. Sheila immediately christened her new mascot Buck Tooth, and sat him on top of the fuel tank which dominated the interior of the cockpit. She started to taxi towards the runway, then, to the astonishment of the friends who were waiting to see her take off, turned round and taxied back. Her main radio was not working. Through exhaustion, frustration and embarrassment she was near to tears, and hid her eyes behind dark glasses as she stepped out of the cockpit. This of course was the photograph carried by several newspapers the next day. It was more than she could do to keep smiling and answer questions cheerfully. 'I'm terribly disappointed,' she said, her voice trembling, 'but these things happen.'

It was early evening – a glorious sunlit spring evening – before the radio was ready. By then Sheila felt 'quite blank, and not at all capable'; but VIP treatment from the Heathrow control tower, and almost non-stop messages of good luck and best wishes over the radio from other aircraft, soon boosted her flagging morale. It was not, however, long before she was encountering a series of failures, first with one of her radio compasses, then with the radio which had already caused trouble, as well as with the pitch control of her automatic pilot. On a relatively short leg, the autopilot was a luxury rather than a basic necessity; as she had a back-up radio compass and radio, these should not have caused any serious problems –

except that, since they were unlit, as soon as it was dark she had to use the main cabin light to see them; this meant that she could not see out of the cockpit. There was the added irritation that in turbulence over the Alps she spilt coffee down her smart new flying suit.

Because of the delay in her departure, she had to make a night landing at her first scheduled stop, Rome. Although it was midnight when she arrived, the glare of television cameras met her as she taxied to the control tower, and she had to endure the bewildering nocturnal publicity until she was rescued by 'Mac' McDonald of BEA. Instead of sleeping, she spent most of the night waking people in London with telephone calls about her faulty equipment. It was not until Ian Forbes had assured her from Geneva that his top man, Phil Peterson, would arrive in Rome first thing in the morning to sort out her problems that she finally went to bed – only to be woken by the telephone three hours later: she had deliberately become news, and like it or not this meant constant attention from the press.

All time spent on the ground seemed to Sheila like time wasted as it jeopardized her chances of setting new records. She had, however, no choice but to wait in Rome for the new equipment promised over the telephone. Phil Peterson arrived on the first possible plane and immediately started work, flight testing the aircraft, recalibrating the autopilot, making adjustments and rigging up a dim light over the instrument panel. He showed Sheila how to install a new radio which was to arrive from London during the early hours of the morning, then flew back to Geneva. By six the following day Sheila had, with the help of 'Mac' McDonald, switched radios and was ready to leave for Damascus, via a short stop in Athens; she wanted to leave early to avoid the thunderstorms which were likely later in the day, and to land in daylight in Damascus.

But there was another two-hour delay because, according to Sheila's account, the customs officer did not like any of her papers and wanted a new sort. This was followed by an eerie and turbulent flight through a thunderstorm which coincided with an eclipse: day seemed to have turned into night. Time kaleidoscoped into a sequence of take-offs from, landings at and flights over unfamiliar territory, messages from passing aircraft, hospitality, flowers, paperwork, refuelling, jumbled enticing glimpses of exotic places, instant friendships and all too little sleep. The heat was often intense, both in the cockpit and on the ground, and over the desert sand and dust stung her eyes and nose. Buck Tooth was grinning reassuringly whenever Sheila glanced back at him. But whatever the discomforts, and in spite of recurring problems with equipment and the time irritatingly consumed by formalities on the ground, Sheila was happier than she had ever been. She listened to Rachmaninov's third piano concerto on Norman Lonsdale's music system while she flew.

She telephoned Norman from every stopping point, expressing elation at arriving, saying how kind people were, and then almost always launching into some disaster story. She was often frightened, especially when monsoon weather and equipment failure coincided; then she felt lost and isolated in the cockpit as she was buffeted alarmingly by the turbulence. Her first experience of the violence of tropical weather was in a monsoon thunderstorm between Karachi and Delhi, when she was again having problems with her radio: she decided to divert to Jaipur.

Three days later, on the way from Calcutta to Bangkok, she made another unplanned landing – again because of bad weather and with radio problems – in Rangoon. An engineer attempted to sort out *Myth Too*'s wiring problems: 'It's all quite mad inside,' he commented. At least while he was trying to solve the problem Sheila was able to sleep for five hours – the longest unbroken rest she had had since leaving London.

By the time she had taken off from Rangoon in the dark, found that none of the instruments she needed for blind flying were working, had landed there again and had sat up all night and through the morning with the engineers while they tried to trace the fault, she felt more than tired. In spite of the tablets from her emergency medical kit, she was suffering from dysentery; her many mosquito bites were itching unbearably, but at least she had taken her malaria tablets regularly; and the steamy heat of the monsoon was making her feet and legs swell even more than they would have done anyway after sitting for hours in the cockpit. The extra-large shoes which experts in aviation medicine at Farnborough had insisted she would need had seemed a joke when she had bought them – but without them her discomfort would have been even greater.

The weather she had avoided by landing at Rangoon was nothing compared with that on her way to Singapore. Monsoon rain beat against the aircraft, which was tossed about by the turbulence. This was caused by thunderstorms which she could not avoid because she could not see through the rain. On the approach to Singapore, lightning flashed along the wings and as she twisted and turned in the turbulence she began to wonder if she would ever regain control. Her one comfort was that she had been promised a complete overhaul in Singapore.

There was another plaintive telephone call to Norman – 'Darling, you'll never guess what they've done to me now!' – when she discovered that no one knew anything about the promised overhaul. With the imperiousness of total dedication, Sheila assumed that it was the duty of any engineer to work all night if necessary to ensure that she could take off with minimum delay. Engineers from Anrite Aviation and from the Royal Air Force eventually agreed to do so in Singapore.

Ten days of alternately flying alone and struggling with publicity, bureaucracy and equipment failure, without a single night's uninterrupted sleep, had taken their toll. Sheila woke next morning feeling unsteady, sick, giddy and feverish. She had again had only five hours' sleep. Had she realized that the airport at Bali, her next stop and at least eight hours away, closed at sunset – and that sunset was at 4 p.m. – she would have stayed in bed. By the time she had been taken for a Chinese meal, and had found a hairdresser where she had a shampoo and massage, she felt considerably better. The comfort and hospitality of the Singapore Flying Club added to her recovery.

The long flight to Bali passed quickly; Sheila had by then become used to not being able to rely on her radio. On the last leg before Australia, over the islands of Indonesia and the Timor Sea, her thoughts wandered from the danger of the 'shark-infested waters' which looked so serene beneath her – her tape-recorded accounts of this and other flights mentioned sharks so often that it seems she was obsessively afraid of them – to Amy Johnson's excitement when she first saw Darwin. Australia was at last not only in reach, but in sight: 'This was one of the most satisfying moments of my life,' Sheila recorded.

In Darwin there were press interviews which she could not refuse, and offers of hospitality and invitations which, because of the time they would have taken, she could not accept. An encouraging telex from Bill Hewitt told her that the round-the-world record was still well within her reach: on her present schedule she would make it in twenty-nine days, with nearly five days in hand. 'Keep going Sheila if needed carry the damned aeroplane,' he finished.

'Already carrying aircraft as camel objected,' Sheila replied, '. . . Contemplating departing on BOAC as they take good care of you worldwide. Love to you and them all.' BOAC had indeed taken good care of her whenever possible throughout the outward flight to Australia, although as hers was a private venture they were under no obligation to do so.

The only time Sheila's high-frequency radio had worked satisfactorily had been between Bali and Darwin, but in the morning she found that the aerial was missing – she blamed 'some enthusiastic souvenir hunter' for this 'absolutely heartbreaking' damage. A makeshift aerial was provided, but for six hours over bleak, scrubby Australian desert which seemed unending and unchanging beneath drifting wisps of white cloud she was again out of radio contact. It was nevertheless the most relaxed flight so far, with time to enjoy the luxury of caviar and smoked salmon sandwiches and to put her hair in rollers. As the weather started to deteriorate, and the ground became rugged and rocky, making the idea of a forced landing distinctly alarming, Sheila kept fear at bay by talking to *Myth* and listening to Rachmaninov. She was so tired that she was beginning to make simple mistakes, like attempting to land on the wrong side of the airfield at Mount Isa.

In Brisbane the next day Sheila was greeted by a group of women pilots with orchids and a toy koala bear, and felt honoured to be allowed to sit in the cockpit of the pioneer aviator Kingsford Smith's famous aircraft, the *Southern Cross*. Her first sight of Sydney was at night. When she landed in the dark at Mascot it was to a ripple of applause and a warm reception from the Australian 99s, Peter Masefield's son Charles, and John Day from the World Record Club: 'It is a little like my acting days, but I am so much tireder,' she recorded. There were telegrams of congratulations, and gifts from people who did not even know her; Sheila began to feel that her efforts had been appreciated. *Myth Too* and her equipment were thoroughly overhauled by a team of engineers and radio experts who worked for two days and two nights. It was a well-earned and much-needed respite for Sheila, who found Australia intriguing, hospitable and quite different from the way she had imagined it. She had time to see the harbour, the bridge and the opera house, to visit the Cross – Sydney's Soho – and, since she was not flying, to drink

Beaujolais from a tin, which struck her as very strange. 'This is great fun,' she commented happily.

By the time she set out from Sydney to start the return to London across the Pacific, America and the Atlantic, everything on the aircraft was at last in perfect working order. The source of the problems had been simple enough – some crossed wiring which had caused short circuiting, and vibration. Sheila's problems had not after all, as some had suspected, been imagined, nor had they been caused by incompetence. Given more time for test flights, the faulty wiring would have shown up and been sorted out, and the parts likely to be loosened by vibration would have been identified.

Sheila hoped that the second half of her record attempt would go more smoothly than the first. At last she had confidence in *Myth*: 'I began to love her and told her so.' For the first time she was able to talk into her tape recorder in the air, as she had been given a throat microphone – the one she had been using on the ground picked up too much engine noise to use during flight. This would make the task of finishing her autobiography considerably easier.

Good luck telegrams were read out to her from the Sydney control tower – she kept her tape recorder running, but most of what was recorded from her radio conversations was inaudible – and as she approached Auckland she was given an escort of honour of fifty aircraft. She felt like a 'pioneer airwoman' when she was greeted on the ground by reporters and cameramen, and once again surrendered herself to the care of BOAC. Her only regret was that the fresh fruit she was given was as usual taken away before she took off next day: carrying fruit across national borders was forbidden – most frustratingly as it was often just what she craved most.

In Auckland she was given a parcel wrapped in newspaper by John Batten, whom she described as 'a most attractive man who had once been a Hollywood movie star'; he was, more significantly, the brother of Jean Batten, the New Zealand record-breaking pilot of the 1930s. In 1937 Jean had been awarded the Harmon Trophy after she became the first person to fly from England to New Zealand – the very flight just completed by Sheila. Since then, no British pilot had received the American award, which was given annually for the most outstanding achievement in international aviation. When Sheila unwrapped the newspaper, she found inside it Jean Batten's Harmon Trophy, which she was to carry to England

and which John Batten assured her would get her home safely. 'I don't know whether you are superstitious,' he said.

She felt that she needed a little extra luck as she left New Zealand. She had not expected cold enough conditions to need it, so had not switched on her cabin heater; when she found herself in dense, turbulent cloud with ice forming on the wings, for a few minutes none of her instruments functioned correctly; it was both frightening and annoying, since she knew she should have thought ahead to the possibility of icing.

On the way to Fiji she attempted, with coffee, evaporated milk sucked from the tube and chocolate, to build up her energy sufficiently to stay awake, and at Nandi made a bad landing in rough weather with a strong cross wind. For once there were no crowds or television cameras. Instead, she was greeted by bare-footed Fijian chiefs in long draped skirts and loose shirts; they gave her shell necklaces and she recorded their welcoming music, and decided that this was one place she must some day find time to visit properly. She had to unload as much luggage as possible and send it on ahead to reduce weight, because when she arrived at her next stop she would for the first time take on a full load of fuel.

Sheila felt that she had passed the stage of noticing the aches and pains of cramp and tiredness, and had entered a dream world which was above discomfort. Her confined cabin had become her home, and she felt secure and confident in it, especially while the sun was shining – but the fear of meeting yet more rough weather still lurked at the back of her mind.

At Canton, a minute island nowhere more than fifteen feet above sea level, the entire population of fifty-one 'supermen' who worked for America's NASA space programme turned out to meet her. It was an eerie place from which to take off at dawn with a greater weight of fuel than *Myth* had ever before carried. Everything possible had to be brought forward to balance the aircraft, with extra ballast to bring the centre of gravity forward. Spare clothing was crammed into every corner in the overcrowded cabin. Sheila approached the runway with what she termed 'some trepidation': it was her first maximum weight take-off, and the longest flight she had ever made lay ahead of her, across several thousand miles of empty ocean. It was on just such a flight that after missing Howland, a low, flat island only half a mile across, Amelia Earhart had disappeared on her attempt to fly round the world. At least

Sheila's destination, Honolulu, fourteen flying hours away, should be easier to find.

Myth climbed slowly, heavily but safely to 7500 feet, although Sheila's hands on the controls were sticky with tension. Again, her high-frequency radio refused to function. For hours she flew on and on and on, isolated in the solitary confinement of her cockpit. As her compasses gave different headings and her direction indicator veered by up to fifteen degrees every ten minutes, she was never quite sure of her position. The constant mental effort of calculating her course prevented her concentration from wandering. The fuel tanks made strange banging and echoing sounds which she found alarming until she realized that they were caused by the changes in pressure as the fuel was used up. Buck Tooth carried on grinning, unperturbed by the noises from the tanks beneath him.

After twelve hours a voice called: 'Sheila!' An American Coast-guard Search pilot told her over her VHF radio that he had thought she might be lonely – which indeed she was – and offered to transmit messages for her. When he had to return to base he sent a friend out in a Lockheed Hercules, which flew beside her like a mother hen sheltering its chick under its wing. It was just as well that he did, for by talking to the two pilots Sheila discovered that her compasses were indeed both very much out. *Myth* and the Hercules landed together on parallel runways at Honolulu International Airport, where the FAA – the American ministry of aviation – now took her under its comforting wing.

Honolulu was another place which Sheila put on her leisurely visiting list. She was greeted with twenty-nine garlands of flowers which almost suffocated her with their perfume; traditional kisses accompanied the presentation of each one. The record-breaking pilot Max Conrad, who had just delivered an aircraft from San Francisco, was among the welcoming party; so were the British consul and the women of the Hawaiian chapter of Zonta, an international association of professional women of which Sheila was a member. One of Zonta's rules was that no profession could have more than two representatives in any chapter, and Sheila was proud that she had been chosen to represent British aviation. Even more surprising and gratifying than the garlands and the greetings was a message from Piper International, who had telephoned Pacific Flight Services with instructions that her latest set of problems with the Piper Comanche were to be put in order at their expense.

Sheila's anticipated day of rest in Honolulu was spent on such mundane tasks as getting her washing done and talking to officials about bananas – she had hoped to take some with her, but was eventually allowed only to take a whole pineapple: not the easiest fruit to eat while flying single-handed. She was about to take off on an even longer flight than the fourteen-hour leg between Canton and Honolulu, and this of course again meant a full load of fuel and a maximum weight take-off, with nothing except an empty 2400 miles of Pacific Ocean ahead of her again for eighteen hours.

She took off from Honolulu in style, escorted for half an hour by a Pacific Air Services aircraft piloted by Fred Spencer, who had done the work requested by Piper International. Not long after he had waggled his wings in farewell, Sheila smelt petrol. For once, she was not smoking. She checked her fuel gauges but could find no reason for the fumes, which were soon making her throat ache. When she looked back, a stabbing pain of physical fear almost paralysed her: fuel was leaking from the top of the starboard tank. Buck Tooth grinned idiotically.

'This is a full-scale emergency,' she told herself. She was in a flying bomb – impossible to land with tanks which were, in spite of the leak, still all but full. 'Don't smoke. Open the storm window – let some air in, let some fumes out. Thank heavens I'm not on oxygen' – a few hours later she would have been, and the aircraft would probably have exploded. 'Don't want to die. Want a cigarette – mustn't smoke. Where is the fuel coming from?'

She did the only thing she could do, and switched to the leaking tank in the hope that soon the fuel level would be below the leak. Then she just carried on flying, a little higher than before to remain above the patchy cloud. The noise from the open window was better than the suffocating stench of petrol fumes. After a couple of hours, during which she sat it out, waiting tensely to know if she would live or die, the leak had dried. It was almost certainly, she thought, the overflow vent which had broken; the movement of the aircraft had then allowed fuel to splash out.

The rest of the flight passed quickly and enjoyably, in spite of the lingering smell of petrol in the cockpit. 'This is fun, now that everything is working properly,' Sheila recorded, 'and *Myth Too* is really the most perfect aircraft in the world.' The vapour trail from jets heading for San Francisco was comforting proof that she was heading in the right direction, although when she picked up the beacon on the ocean station *November*, twelve hundred miles from land, she realized that she was south of her intended course.

'Is that a woman up there?' a voice from the weather ship asked. 'Are you alone?'

'Do you mind carrying on talking?' the ocean controller asked next. 'I haven't seen a woman for weeks, and I shan't see one for another two weeks.'

Sheila did not mind at all, and they flirted over the air waves in the middle of the Pacific. The fear of a few hours ago was forgotten, and she was enjoying herself. The mid-ocean flirtation was a morale booster. So was the calm evening with a brilliant, glowing orange sunset, and time to clean up and apply some make-up. Sheila was ready to face anyone and anything.

As she approached San Francisco, she felt as if she could carry on flying for ever, although she had been in the air for nearly eighteen hours. Then the strobe lights which were turned on to guide her in dazzled her, and she was so overcome by fatigue that she had to repeat her pre-landing checks three times before she was sure she had them right.

At five in the morning, with the 99s who had turned out even at such an unearthly hour to greet her, Sheila had a bacon and eggs party in her hotel room, and thought of Thruxton and the 'cook-ups' which had been part of her early flying. Seven years had passed since she had flown her Jackaroo there – seven years which had been fuller and more satisfying than she had ever imagined possible. She felt so exhilarated that she could not think of sleep, much though she undoubtedly needed it.

'Wake up! Wake up! I've done it, I've done it,' she told a sleepy and bemused Lee Whitsell at the Flying 'W' Ranch over the phone. 'And wake Bill up too – tell him I've done it!'

'Done what?' Lee asked.

At last Sheila fell briefly into bed. But she was to have little rest, nor indeed to want it, during the next few days as she flew from San Francisco to Phoenix and on to El Paso, then to Oklahoma, and finally via Louisville to New York. She flew during daylight only, and in the evenings – and sometimes at stops during the day – was, as she put it, 'feted all the way at every landing' by fellow members of the 99s and of Zonta. At El Paso she was given honorary citizenship, rechristened Shining Squaw and presented with an Indian squaw's headband. Then she was escorted by police cars with their sirens blaring to the house of a friend who had erected banners saying 'Sheila Scott – Solo Round the World Flight' – 'a most exciting way of travelling,' Sheila called it. Oklahoma made her an Admiral of Space, a distinction shared only by Bob Hope. In New York, she made an unfortunately public bouncy landing. Tearful exhaustion had caught up with her by the next morning, but was banished by an official luncheon at the Wings Club, at which she was awarded the Amelia Earhart Medal of the Month.

The non-stop congratulations in New York seemed to Sheila premature, and she tried superstitiously but in vain to turn them aside. She still had to fly to Gander, and then across the Atlantic via the Azores to Portugal and on to London, before she could claim success. On the final leg, from Lisbon, she met such strong head winds that her confidence wavered, and she was sure that she could not achieve her aim.

She was laughing and crying at the same time as she touched down at Heathrow on 20 June, thirty-three days and three minutes after she had left, and felt 'a tremendous uncontrollable excitement'. Everything that she had set out to do had been achieved. 'The beauty-conscious air-ace stopped for a moment on the tarmac to powder her nose before being greeted by Sir Alan Cobham and the customs men,' one newspaper reported under a photograph captioned: 'Mobbed by cameramen, round-the-world girl Sheila Scott waves as she arrives back at London Airport yesterday.' 'Round-the-world girl Sheila Scott flew home yesterday – in tears, and £6000 in debt,' the report started. 'She wept from happiness and relief,' another newspaper reported. 'Later, in the airport's Aerial Hotel, she collapsed twice from excitement and tiredness.' Sheila remembered it differently:

> . . . a kaleidoscope of colour, of flowers, of masses of faces and a customs officer opening the door, congratulating me and asking me if I had anything to declare, all in the same breath. As I climbed out on to the wing, there were cheers and masses of photographers all shouting 'Look this way!' 'Look that way!' until I was dizzy and nearly fell off. As I staggered off the wing I was surrounded by friends and officials with arms of flowers, Sir Alan Cobham himself being the first to reach the aircraft. He held my hand tightly as he saw how bewildered I was and said, 'See it through – keep smiling!'

She did her best, until, before she had even left the aircraft, an engineer whispered: 'Excuse me – we must taxi the aircraft away to take the wings off.' Sheila, by her own account, 'turned on him like a wildcat'. She was unaware that in their efforts to help her financially, Norman Lonsdale and a public relations friend, David Wynne-Morgan – whom she called her 'manager' – had arranged a £1500 contract for her story with the *Daily Mirror*, and that as part of the deal *Myth Too* was to be suspended above the newspaper's offices. Norman would have liked a chance to explain this to her in private, but it was too late. 'It was handled very tactlessly,' he admitted.

The tactlessness turned the welcoming reception, which should have been the happiest and most triumphant occasion of Sheila's life, into 'a ghastly nightmare': she felt that removing *Myth*'s wings was a violation of her own and her aircraft's identities. When photographers burst in on her while she was changing, she lost her temper and swore at them. 'The change from the greatest excitement and exhilaration to the sudden hurt of my aircraft being taken away from me was too sudden and I was too shocked to be able to govern my emotions any longer,' she explained afterwards.

'I did not collapse at all,' she told me. 'I was just so angry that I was blazing away at everyone – I was far too angry to collapse.'

Her father sent a telegram from Worcester: 'Well done. Get in touch when rested.'

How to find the money to pay her debts, to keep *Myth* and to carry on flying obsessed her to such an extent that Sheila talked about it even on the evening of her landing at Heathrow. Pam Huntly, who was among those there to meet her, begged her: 'Please, please don't start talking about money now.' 'If Sheila had said nothing that day, more might have been done to help her,' she told me. As a journalist herself, she was only too well aware that apparent carping was bad publicity, and that Sheila 'could be a bit impatient with people' – including reporters.

Simon Ames, whose job with the RAeC was to a large extent a public relations exercise, put it more strongly: 'Sheila barked at people and was very demanding when she wanted things. She wasn't good at "interpersonal skills" – she was so single-minded that she would wind herself into an unpleasant tizzy, which was very embarrassing and put people off. There was always some drama. In a sense, my first real PR job was to rescue Sheila from reporters, although the ones she knew personally were always "darling".'

In spite of her protests, *Myth Too* was flown from Heathrow to Luton, where the Aviation Division of Sir Robert McAlpine & Sons stripped her down before loading her on to a lorry and taking her to the towering *Mirror* building at Holborn Circus. There she was, suspended high above the pavement; 'Great Scott, look what's landed at the *Mirror*', a vast banner headline read. Sheila felt that *Myth* looked 'like a wounded human being, hanging up there in slings'; even the publicity did not mollify her, although later she comforted herself that thousands of people had grown 'to love her too when they saw how tiny and frail and covered in mud she was.'

The aircraft was covered in more than mud: there was hardly any space left on the fuselage between the many signatures and messages from well-wishers round the world. The advertising slogans of the companies which had supplied her equipment were prominent. Although the easiest way of attracting public support for Sheila's financial position would have been to display collecting boxes under her aircraft, this suggestion was turned down by the *Mirror*'s management.

Sheila felt strangely disorientated back home in London as an instant heroine, at the mercy of the publicity this brought – and to which she had looked forward with eager anticipation. The sense of well-being – despite the physical discomfort and occasional fear – that she had experienced on her long solo flight was dissipated by the constant need to react to other people. Instead of the euphoria she had expected there was a general sense of anti-climax. During her flight she had been alone in the air, and had often felt alone on the ground; but somehow she had never felt lonely. In the crowds and the congratulations and the jubilation which now surrounded her she felt isolated and insecure. It was as if she had discovered her own identity, and had then had it taken away.

As a sudden celebrity, she was in constant demand; she had to have additional secretarial help to cope with letters and telephone calls and official functions. At the same time, she was worried about how to pay the debts she had run up, and the bills which continued to pour in. She felt almost as if she was being forced to become a split personality – one side of her was living the glamorous film star existence of fame, and took pride in having 'done something fairly well'; the other side was in debt, worried, and made to feel almost like a criminal for having made the flight.

Although her need for a business manager was greater than ever,

Sheila had unwittingly destroyed any possibility of a continuing professional relationship with David Wynne-Morgan. She lost few opportunities of complaining about the way she considered that she had been let down by her 'unscrupulous' manager; while Wynne-Morgan's initial admiration for her 'tremendous amount of drive, considerable personality and absolutely unlimited courage . . . which was the most attractive thing about her' had been replaced by frustration at her unprofessional approach:

> The reason that it all came to an end was that she was incredibly demanding, demanded an awful lot of my time for which she was not able to pay, and was really unprofessional both in the way that she conceived sponsorship and in terms of honouring the obligations that this entailed.
>
> The only thing that mattered to her was to make the new record attempt. In order to do that, she had to have the money. She was prepared to say anything and do anything to get the money and never considered for one moment the obligations that she had to the people who put up the money. It was that total lack of integrity that in the end made the relationship impossible. It was doing me a great deal of damage, both with newspaper contacts and with other clients. . . .
>
> She had absolutely no business acumen of any kind, but she did have a sort of street-wise ability to lay her fingers on instant money, particularly from slightly gullible men. I do not think she was in any way free with sex, and I do not think she slept around in order to get money. She did, however, make every possible use of her feminine charms to arouse the protective instincts, particularly in men, and initially was very successful at doing it.

Sheila would indeed, as Wynne-Morgan admitted, 'have been extremely hurt to have been told this'; without ever making it clear exactly what she meant, she implied that her manager was in some way to blame for her financial difficulties. She was too tired to think clearly. 'Mentally she was clearly extremely unbalanced,' David Wynne-Morgan told me. 'Sometimes it was much worse than others.' What she needed more than anything else was to rest; but this was impossible.

It took her some time to resume a normal sleep pattern; in spite of her constant tension, she had rarely had any problem in sleeping, but now her sleep was restless and interrupted. Night after night, she dreamt that she was still flying; the familiar vibration and engine noise were so vivid, as was the feeling that *Myth* was responding to the controls, that when she woke she had no idea where she was. She felt that she would never again sleep properly; and when she did sleep, she woke up with her debts still hanging over her.

7

By the time the *Daily Mirror* gave a celebrity luncheon for Sheila, she had almost forgiven the newspaper for the removal of *Myth*'s wings. Among the other well-known guests was Sir Francis Chichester, who understood better than most the way she was feeling: 'The end of a record is not triumph, but sadness because it is all over.'

The Guild of Air Pilots and Navigators presented her with a Silver Award of Merit, the first time this had been given to a woman or for a single achievement, and BWPA gave her a large globe on which her route had been marked out in white tape. But Sheila's new status as a flying heroine left her little opportunity to fly, although she managed to fit in the rest of the season's air races. A week after her return, she competed unsuccessfully in an aircraft provided by the *Daily Mirror* in the first round of the annual National Air Races. When *Myth* was returned to her, they proved an invincible combination in the remaining races: Sheila attributed her successes to *Myth*, always speaking of her aircraft as a person.

The days when she was able to race with *Myth* were luxuries stolen from a calendar otherwise full of engagements on the ground. She found herself the centre of attention in a non-stop social round which was as exhausting as it was gratifying. Five weeks after her return, she had a day off – 'FREE!' she wrote in exultant capitals in her diary; but she did not dare to turn down invitations which might be useful public relations exercises or bring in money. There were, of course, many she would not have wanted to turn down – like luncheon with the Queen and the Duke of Edinburgh at Buckingham Palace, or dinner with King Hussein of Jordan.

She enjoyed being treated as a VIP, which brought her a few unexpected free trips and honorary life membership of Zonta and the Munster Aero Club in Cork. On behalf of the States of Jersey

Tourism Committee, she received an invitation to Jersey from Valerie Bartlett, who worked for a public relations company. On a more personal note, Valerie wrote: 'I've seen your plane down at the *Mirror* and it was about a quarter the size of anything I'd even attempt a flight to Manchester in! HOW did you manage to remain as glam throughout everything – you really did keep the side up.'

Sheila was guest of honour at banquets and parties given by aviation societies and other sporting organizations, and by the Variety Club of Great Britain. As a passenger, she flew to Mantua to receive one of twelve Isabella d'Este awards given to outstanding women; back in England she opened rallies, made speeches, was interviewed for magazine articles, judged a Miss Britain beauty contest, and was invited to appear on chat shows and to participate in panel games. She was even Roy Plomley's guest on *Desert Island Discs*, a sure sign of fame.

In November, six months after her return, a £20,000 Sheila Scott World Flight Appreciation Fund was launched. Its aims were to enable her to keep the aircraft in which she had made her record-breaking world flight, 'to assist in the payment of expenses attributable thereto', and to make it possible for her to make further record-breaking attempts.

The British Women Pilots' Association added its support, with an admission that it was belated: 'An early contributor to the fund was that redoubtable Australian pilot, Mrs Nancy Bird Walton, who appealed to all pilots as she toured round the world this summer to help Sheila raise funds. We should cover our shame in letting an Australian start the campaign by giving generously ourselves.' Nancy Bird Walton, who in the 1930s had pioneered a flying medical service to the Australian outback, had been in England to receive the OBE. Although she had given up flying when the war started, she had continued to campaign indefatigably whenever she saw a worthy cause in aviation. Sheila was, in her opinion, such a cause. One contribution recommended to the British women pilots was to give the equivalent of one hour's flying time: 'If all pilots were to do this we should have the relief of knowing that our star pilot was completely freed from worry.'

There was some response to the appeal; but it had been launched too late, and the heat of publicity for the world flight and for Sheila's allied financial problems had been taken off by the delay. She eventually received £1100 – enough to pay the hire purchase instalments on *Myth* for three months – which had come in in dribs and drabs from individuals, including schoolchildren and a group of London bus drivers.

In the meantime Sheila had been looking for other ways of filling her gaping financial hole, keeping her aircraft and carrying on with her ambitious plans. These included another round-the-world flight, over both the Poles; but throughout the winter she was grounded through impecunity, and *Myth* languished in a hangar. Sheila registered with several lecturing agencies, and rushed from lecture to lecture, earning little enough and exhausting herself even further.

Although the Piper Aircraft Corporation of America arranged a month's promotion tour in the United States, this boosted her morale more than her income; but the company's gift of $4000 helped to pay customs duty on her aircraft – which she greatly resented having to pay: such restrictions were, she said, relaxed for other sportsmen representing their country, which was what she considered herself to be doing.

To add to her problems, Sir Alan Cobham, whose loan had enabled her to buy *Myth*, was pressurizing her to sell the aircraft. By the new year of 1967 she was beginning to think that she would have to give in; then, out of the blue, she received a letter with a cheque for £1000, and an offer of further financial support. It came from a woman called Kaye Maclean, whose husband Archie had flown with the Royal Flying Corps in the First World War and whose son-in-law by a previous marriage had been a Schneider Trophy winner.

Sheila wrote in the first of many letters to Kaye Maclean:

Thank you for your wonderful (and comforting!) letter. To receive such a letter and incredibly kind and generous gesture from someone who had never even met me, must be the nicest thing that has ever happened to me.

Alas the money I owe is almost as large as the National Debt! As fast as I earn anything it goes out to feed what seems an ever-increasing avalanche of bills. I know they are too great for any one person to help me (unless it was a company who used me for advertising or something!) and I simply do not know how to reply to your wonderful offer of help – I am so deeply touched. . . .

In any case whatever happens, I do so hope I shall have an opportunity of meeting you – because your understanding letter is something I could never forget. Perhaps all the more so because although surrounded by wonderful people, I am going through the most intense loneliness and heartbreak since I landed at London Airport, and rarely get the chance to fly in this last attempt to save my aircraft.

I find it difficult to express my feelings as I feel near to tears when I remember your letter, and I can only say 'Thank you' for giving me back some much needed morale.

Norman Lonsdale outlined Sheila's financial situation to Kaye Maclean: although she had already paid 'a great deal for the engineering, equipment and expenses incurred on the flight', she still owed £5500 to Sir Alan Cobham, and £5000 to Lombank at £285 a month. 'If Sheila is unable to complete these payments, she will of course be unable to retain the aircraft, thereby her living as a racing and record breaking pilot,' Norman wrote. He went on:

Usually achievements of this kind receive their due rewards, but in Sheila's case it appears to be the opposite. A group of her friends have therefore got together to start an appreciation fund which has to date collected something under £500. Much of the problem appears to be that people gain the impression that feats of this nature automatically bring huge financial rewards; it is of course certainly not the case.

Sheila wrote to Kaye again a few days later, in response to another letter:

You will be surprised by the above address undoubtedly! Am back in New York for C.B.S. television again. It is quite crazy – people spend hundreds on travelling expenses just for me to appear, but few realize that I am rarely able to even see my own aircraft! However the airlines always look after me well and let me sit in the cockpit – so at least I can pretend to be a pilot still!'

In March, Sheila reached such a state of exhaustion and depression that she was forced to take two weeks off. She returned to find an invitation from Kaye Maclean, with another donation, which happened to coincide with her birthday at the end of April. 'I think you must have become a very special talisman,' Sheila wrote, 'as just at my worst moments, a wonderful letter always comes from you!'

'Alan is trying to force me into selling the aircraft literally within a few days,' she complained later in the letter.

He does not seem to realize that without the aircraft there is no future, and I could never assemble all the equipment, and build up an aircraft like this again, as everything I possess is already invested in it, or the past flight. I have worked solidly now since August 1965 (except for the past two weeks convalescence as I came to a complete standstill physically) for the World Record costs. However, I am hoping my solicitors can persuade him to reconsider the situation for a short while. I had set my heart on breaking another in June, from London to Canada to tie in with the 'Canadian Expo' as well as the numerous races and competitions (& other records) which start at the beginning of May. However may not be able to do the Canadian one. I am seeing far more clearly now after the two weeks rest, but look with some horror at the dreadful mess I was led into after my return.

Five days later she wrote again to Kaye, who had insisted on anonymity as she and Archie did not feel that their families would appreciate the way they chose to spend their money:

Just a note to say that I hear the *Daily Mail* printed something about the aircraft being saved this week and mentioned an 'anonymous man' has saved it!!! I am afraid our secret has leaked out a little bit in my effort to put off Alan Cobham. However, this is just to assure you that no-one knows your name or who you are apart from Norman Lonsdale, my solicitors and myself. I do hope you will forgive the misnomer of 'anonymous man' and also the news which must seem to you premature to say the least. . . . It will be a great thrill to actually meet you in person after all these weeks.

The letter was followed by another, a few days before Sheila was to visit the Macleans in Somerset: 'You know it occurs to me that you do not know anything about me, and that I could be AWFUL! I do not know what to tell you about myself, as my life seems to have been very ordinary. Anyway I enclose one of those PR blurbs to make you smile, and then at least you know my flying history! You both must be very wonderful people to try and help such a complete stranger!'

But the meeting between Sheila and her benefactors went well, and she returned with a 'MOST generous' donation to her fund. Although she still wrote to Kaye as 'Mrs Maclean', she had insisted that she be called Sheila rather than Miss Scott, and looked on her almost as a replacement for her mother, or at least as an extra aunt; her own aunts were proud of her flying achievements, but neither they nor her father showed much understanding of or interest in what was involved, nor were they in a position to help her financially.

Kaye's help had enabled Sheila at least to keep *Myth*; but it was not until she met Mr Ken Wood that she could plan positively for another record attempt. He was about to open a new Kenwood electrical appliance factory in South Africa; she was looking for a sponsor. Amy Johnson's second record was to South Africa – so, not averse to identifying herself with 'Wonderful Amy' once again, it seemed obvious that Sheila should attempt to break this one too. Ken Wood was quick to seize the opportunity to share her publicity by financing her flight: he put up £3000, with the stipulation that no other backers would be allowed.

Sheila immediately told Kaye Maclean, with a mixture of excitement and apprehension: 'Of course I was thrilled and said yes! Nevertheless I had not even thought of the route (full of political problems, and now I find it is the worst time of year for violent unfriendly weather!) or how I keep Alan at bay. However, I am going to do my utmost to try & get the aircraft reset up for the flight, and do three months preparation in one month!'

To Ken Wood, she wrote: 'Bless you for being interested, and for trying to help in a realistic way' – and asking whether he wished his name as sponsor to be released at once, or whether he would prefer to wait until all the possibilities of publicity for Kenwood products had been explored. 'Incidentally, the aircraft herself still draws crowds wherever she goes,' she added. 'Is there such a thing as a tiny Kenwood drinks blender which could operate by battery and I could carry normally in the aircraft now? It would be a great attention-getter.'

With Norman Lonsdale's help, Sheila was trying to establish a company for which Kaye Maclean had offered to put up some initial capital. Although she was eager to accept, she did not wish to seem ungrateful or grasping, and felt that she should offer Kaye a chance to back out, writing:

Although she [*Myth Too*] means everything to me, I would still like to say your support has meant a very great deal to me in spirit (quite apart from your wonderful gift of help already) and that if you feel you should not help me quite so completely, I do understand. You see, although it means so terribly much to save my aircraft, I am worried lest you might be worse off in future because you might have helped me so much. This sounds very muddled. But I hope you understand my thoughts, and know what I mean. I could not bear anyone who has been so completely unselfish and generous as yourself to perhaps have to do without certain luxuries to help me out of trouble, even though it means everything to me.

Kaye did not, however, wish to back down, and negotiations for the formation of the company proceeded while Sheila carried on with her plans for the South African flight. Four days before she took off, Sheila told Kaye that 'it is so different this year – everyone is helping me in the most unbelievably generous way and giving up much of their spare time to help with the flight'. There were, however – or so she believed – a few exceptions: 'the same old ones, who do so much damage and undo so very many people's good work'. Sir Alan Cobham appears to have been one of these: 'Alan is now in the picture vaguely although I have not spoken to him and he took a great of persuading,' Sheila wrote. As she claimed to have taken on 'every single thing to do with the aircraft' herself for some time, she complained that she could not understand his attitude, especially as so much had been done for him on his pioneering flights in the twenties and thirties. 'However I have much to be grateful to him for originally,' she admitted grudgingly.

Once again, she had had to negotiate for complicated international permissions to fly over and into several countries, many of which were in a state of conflict verging on outright war. She had engaged another secretary – a luxury she had gone without for several months – and had, as she put it, 'recaptured Bill Hewitt' to do her flight planning. Doug Bianchi, one of the best-known and most respected figures in aviation, had taken charge of preparing

Myth at Wycombe Air Park. His wife Edna remembered his association with Sheila as being exhausting and often traumatic.

'You know they're trying to kill me at Oxford?' Sheila asked Doug.

She had somehow convinced herself that the technical problems she had encountered on her round-the-world flight had been a deliberate attempt against her life – her old paranoia was re-asserting itself under pressure, although it was usually only to Norman that she made such wild and unfounded accusations. Doug ignored them.

'Are you going to take her on?' he was asked by people who felt that Sheila could be difficult to work either with, or for.

'I'll help anyone in aviation,' Doug replied.

He was as good as his word, and did all *Myth*'s maintenance at cost, putting in many extra unpaid hours. There were long hysterical telephone calls from Sheila late in the evening, when he was too tired to listen. Edna laughed when she told me that once she found Doug fast asleep beside the telephone while Sheila was still recounting some tale of woe.

During the last fortnight before the flight, Sheila appeared seven times on radio and television; on each occasion, she managed to slip in a reference to her sponsor. When she was asked what lessons she had learnt from her last trip, she replied: 'Dozens of things. One is that I need a strong man behind me to organize things. . . . Although I can't see any difference between a man and a woman in the air, I've certainly realized that a woman needs a man on the ground . . . I've been lucky, I've found a sponsor, Ken Wood, on this.'

To a question about what was the point of it all, she countered: 'Why did Francis [Chichester] sail round the world, or why do people climb mountains? We seem to have lost all sense of adventure . . . and this was the very spirit that made Britain great.'

'One often wonders where the record-breaking personal en-deavour ends and the publicity begins, on a thing like this,' the interviewer mused.

'I think you've got it back to front,' Sheila retorted. 'I started off for the fun of it . . . and then I got interested in the sort of goodwill export thing for Great Britain and this has been my main interest this year.'

On the last evening, Sheila was in a panic and told Doug Bianchi that she was sure there would be no fuel at some of her stopping points. His daughter Angie, who in the previous few weeks had got to know her as well as had her parents, pushed her firmly into a chair: 'Shut up, Sheila!' she said.

Doug was already on the phone to establish that there would be fuel wherever it was needed. He then telephoned Norman Lonsdale: 'She's not fit to fly,' he said.

Norman said calmly, 'Oh, let her go.' He knew that, once she was in the air, she would as usual be in control both of herself and of the aircraft. In spite of her outbreaks of paranoia, he considered her a 'very brave woman' and was aware that she only felt comfortable in the air. 'It was the only time she felt safe from "them" and from reality,' he told me. 'She felt one with the clouds – but she was quite aware of the dangers.'

By the morning, Sheila was once again able to put across the public image of the brave lone aviatrix, smiling, cheerful, a little apprehensive but optimistic, and above all immaculately feminine and elegant. 'Everything is good, good, good,' she told reporters just before taking off from Heathrow on 29 June. 'I'm feeling on top – I think I can do it.' She had been called 'Amy Johnson II' in one newspaper headline, over an article which pointed out that Amy had created her South African record in a Percival Gull, a much faster aircraft than Sheila's Piper Comanche.

She was escorted across the English Channel by Ken Wood, who was flown by his company pilot in the Kenwood Beechcraft Queen Air. They found her in cloud, flew with her for a while, then with a last wave and waggle of wings and a message of good luck over the radio she was on her own. Twelve hours later, in the dark, she was in Benghazi in Libya, surrounded by locals who offered her food, transport, a hotel and a choice of three brands of fuel; as a British Army helicopter was waiting to fly her to the British barracks for the night, she turned down their offers of hospitality.

The flight which had begun so well had to be aborted the next day, when it proved impossible to confirm her permission to overfly or land in Chad. After a day of battling with the French authorities, Sheila backtracked instead to Malta, feeling depressed and a failure because she had let Ken Wood down. In Malta, she was immediately accosted by reporters who wanted to know what had gone wrong. 'There was merely a breakdown in one line of communi-

cations,' she replied tartly, before taking off again and returning to
London.

She decided that Fate had come to her rescue when she
discovered that someone had painted a Star of David on the side of
her aircraft – 'I would undoubtedly have had my throat cut at the
next stop, in the desert,' she claimed dramatically.

'Never mind – try again!' Ken Wood told her.

Sheila's second departure was a week after her first, with a new
and longer route to avoid the previous trouble spot. She landed first
at Tripoli, and then had to contend with intense heat over the
Sahara. There was the anticipated violent weather as she attempted
to skirt the inter-tropical front, and a strong head wind which she
feared would put the record out of reach as she flew, after three
hours' sleep, from Luanda towards the border of South Africa.
While she was still flying she was invited to a large air show at
Durban the next day, but did not dare accept until she knew her
commitments to Kenwood.

Her tumultuous reception in Cape Town, complete with an escort
of aerial photographers and a live broadcast of her first words on the
ground, was 'the heady stuff the pioneers had thrived on'; 'and
believe you me,' she added ecstatically, 'I am thriving on it too!' She
had achieved her ambition of breaking the record; it was a mere
7800-mile hop compared with her round-the-world marathon, but
had been a tiring flight nevertheless and, because of the change in
route after the fiasco of her false start, was a thousand miles longer
than Amy Johnson's. Even with the extra distance she had cut four
hours off Amy's time, in just over three days and nights, with very
little sleep.

That evening, to her delight, Table Mountain was lit up in her
honour. She sent a greetings telegram to Ken Wood: 'Darling
sponsor thank you for making it all possible', and then another when
she reached her hotel room to thank him for the flowers which had
been delivered on his behalf.

A series of letters from various Kenwood employees kept Ken
Wood in touch with the mutually beneficial publicity which had
been arranged. There was fulsome praise of Sheila, who, in spite of
official restrictions on advertising on South African television and
radio, managed to make public references to her sponsor in all of her
many interviews. Advertising space in local papers congratulated
Sheila on breaking the record and emphasized the role played by

Kenwood. Last-minute arrangements for her to accept the invitation to Durban included more publicity. She flew there the day after her arrival, and was given 'a rapturous and spectacular' welcome when she touched down at the air show at dusk, escorted by members of the Durban Wings Club in Piper aircraft.

'What an arrival it was,' Ann White, a South African pharmacist and amateur pilot, told me. 'As a member of the 99s, I was there to greet her briefly. That evening, Kenwood arranged a dinner at the Durban Country Club for her to meet some of the South African 99s. An extremely tired Sheila arrived to have dinner with us.' Speeches were made by Sheila – who managed 'a clever and humorous reference to Kenwood food mixers' – and by the British consul-general, who remarked that 'this flight was an achievement that Britain could well be proud of'.

From Durban Sheila proceeded to Johannesburg, where numerous photos were taken of her during various tours and receptions laid on by Kenwood. 'I believe we have made maximum use of Sheila's earnest and sincere attempt to link up every public appearance or press and radio interview with her sponsor,' Ken Wood was informed in London.

Leaving *Myth Too* in South Africa, Sheila returned briefly to England where she competed – unsuccessfully – in the National Air Races in a Piper Cherokee. She was still after the King's Cup – one of the few trophies which had persistently eluded her – and had, as she put it, 'stormed the all-male barricade of the Royal Aero Club Committee' as a member of the Air Racing and Competitions Committee. As soon as the first round of the National Air Races, in Roborough, was over she returned to South Africa to capture the return record from Cape Town to London.

South Africa again gave her the heroine's acclaim to which she was becoming accustomed. She was even saluted by a Boeing 707 which dipped its wings 'straight as a die' over the balcony of her hotel room. The Hellenic football team presented her with enough bananas to live on for a year – she did not record whether she was allowed to take them out of the country with her when she left. Best of all, *Myth* had been completely overhauled by two South African engineers who, she said, 'turned out to be just like Doug Bianchi and his team at home' – high praise indeed, as Doug was still in her good books.

She left Cape Town with a letter for the Lord Mayor of London and flowers for the Queen from the Mayor, feeling a true messenger of good will. The moon obligingly came out from behind the clouds as she took off at midnight, and Table Mountain was again lit up in her honour. 'What a country and what enthusiasm and taste for adventure,' she eulogized.

'I feel honoured that I was fortunate enough to meet and get to know the great Sheila Scott,' Ann White, with whom letters continued the friendship started at Durban, told me. 'She was a very unassuming, kind and gentle person' – a description which might have surprised some of those back home who found her determination abrasive.

Wars and weather had conspired to make the western route back from South Africa inadvisable, so Sheila took an eastern route, although along this too there were political disturbances. It was, she felt, one of the most awesome flights she could ever make; but the support of the Piper Aircraft Corporation eased the difficulties. They fed her on trout and steak in Kenya when she was so tired that she could hardly stand, and left several surprise parcels in the cockpit for her to open when she got bored. There was, however, little time for boredom – although she opened them to boost her morale when she again found herself flying without radio and was hot, sticky, thirsty and so sleepy that she could hardly keep awake. The first two packages contained thirst-quenching sweets and a bottle of what she termed 'Dutch Courage'. The third, which she remembered later on the same leg, when a vivid sunset had turned suddenly to a starlit night with not a light in sight on the ground, was an assortment of perfumes. She tried one, and 'suddenly felt a woman again, instead of a sort of neuter object suspended in a vacuum'.

There were inevitably problems en route, in spite of the efficiency of the back-up on the ground. She had resorted to sending a telegram to the Prime Minister of Sudan to cut through the red tape which was threatening to stop her flight: she had been unable to obtain advance permission to go through either the Sudan or Chad, which was the only alternative. The ruse worked and the Sudanese let her in without paperwork, giving her coffee and fuel. Thinking she had only a nine-hour flight ahead of her, to Benghazi, she did not fill her cabin tanks to the top – a decision which she later regretted when her navigation went awry. This was caused by a combination of pilot error and equipment failure; she miscalculated the strength and direction of the wind, and had problems with both her compass and her radio.

It was dark, and her fuel gauge showed that her last tank was almost empty, when she realized that she was lost. In desperation she turned due north, so that if the worst came to the worst she could ditch in the sea rather than crash on the unseen hazards of the ground. Although she felt calm, she knew that she would be afraid when the engine stopped, which she was sure it would do at any moment. She had already put her life jacket on – and then suddenly, miraculously it seemed, her radio compass picked up the beacon of El Adem, on the coast of Libya but way to the east of where she should have been. Then an English voice asked if she intended to land there. She most certainly did.

The RAF at El Adem greeted their unexpected nocturnal guest as if it was the most natural thing in the world for a lone pilot on a record-breaking trip to get lost and drop in on them. Next day the RAF was expecting her in Malta, and enabled her to make her quickest get-away ever – after a turn-round time of twenty minutes, she was on her way again and over familiar territory.

She was already in contact with the Paris control tower, and felt she was almost home, when she was caught in an unexpected thunderstorm. It was briefly even more violent and alarming than the tropical storms she had flown through on her round-the-world flight. Lightning played along *Myth*'s wings as Sheila struggled to keep control and at the same time to reach for her sunglasses. Hail rattled against the windscreen. At one point the aircraft was thrown over on to its back; Sheila's heavy flight bag fell from its hook on to the controls, spilling its contents.

At last the storm eased. Sheila felt exhausted and dishevelled as she landed at London Airport, where Beverley Snook was first to greet her, just beating Ken Wood who was flourishing a bottle of champagne. Bev opened the door of the cockpit and just managed to pull his hand back in time as it was slammed violently shut: Sheila was not ready to be seen.

Three minutes later she emerged looking immaculate, and did not need too much persuasion to drink Ken Wood's champagne, nor to enjoy the celebration party which followed. She had not only achieved the Cape Town–London record, in well under three days; she had, in spite of a longer route back, cut seven hours off her own time, and had broken or established four major records and several minor ones between cities.

The following day, Sheila delivered the Mayor of Cape Town's letter to the Lord Mayor of London, Sir Ralph Perring. As chairman of the British Committee for Exports to Canada, Perring had spent three years planning and setting up a British Week in Toronto to coincide with Expo 67 in Montreal. During their conversation over dinner at the Mansion House, and afterwards when Sir Ralph and Lady Perring took Sheila back to their flat, her next record attempt took shape. Sheila said that she was vaguely thinking of a transatlantic flight to America; Sir Ralph suggested tying it in with British Week, and flying instead to Toronto. She needed no further persuasion.

8

THE SATISFACTION OF having yet another record to plan for pre-empted the feeling of emptiness and isolation which would otherwise have engulfed Sheila after her return from South Africa. She stayed – to some extent at least – on a high during the intervening weeks; and there were again only weeks for the preparations.

As usual, money was a problem, in spite of Kaye Maclean's offer of £10,000. Early in August Sheila's solicitor wrote to Kaye suggesting that the £5822 still owing to Alan Cobham should be paid directly out of this, as should a proportion of the £2000 outstanding to Piper on HP instalments, and that 'the Company' should be started with £3750. An additional £1000 'from another source' – Norman Lonsdale – would provide initial working capital. Kaye Maclean replied that although the proposals seemed 'to promise an immediate answer to Miss Scott's immediate problems and give her a reasonable chance to make more records in the future', the procedure suggested would make it almost impossible for her to remain anonymous and she was 'most anxious to avoid a leak to the press'.

Although Sheila was suitably grateful, as she could not publicize the name of her anonymous benefactress she did not consider her transatlantic flight to have a sponsor. But many of the British firms which would be exhibiting in Toronto contributed either in kind or towards her costs, in the hope that her publicity would rub off on them. Everything she eventually took with her, from food to survival kit, was British-made. The only thing which was not British was the Piper Comanche; that she made her record attempts in an American aircraft was only because there was no suitable British equivalent. Aquascutum made her flying outfits; her other clothes, for private and public wear in Canada, were provided by half a dozen well-known British manufacturers and couturiers.

In the meantime, Sheila plunged as usual into the British air racing season. Although she was placed in everything she entered, she was so heavily handicapped that she won nothing; the coveted King's Cup continued to elude her. This was more than made up for when she was told that she was to receive the even more coveted Harmon Trophy, an international award for outstanding achievements in aviation.

Her relationship with the Royal Aero Club had, however, deteriorated. She queried the times and distances officially recorded for her South Africa records, and complained about the time wasted by the paperwork accompanying record claims. In September, Simon Ames felt it necessary to write her a three-page letter justifying his calculations in considerable trigonometrical and personal detail – although he did not forget to start by congratulating her on winning the Harmon Trophy: 'This must be one of the most satisfying achievements for you and we congratulate you on it.' He then pointed out the amount of work she had created for him, and others at the RAeC, enclosing copies of every complex calculation made over her South African records on her behalf.

'I am glad to send you these because they will show you precisely the considerable volume of work which has to go into the Royal Aero Club's end of your record attempts,' he wrote tartly. 'A great deal of work by a large number of people has gone into these series and, if anything is to be turned down now, then a lot of our time has been wasted as well as yours!'

Sheila was not disliked, but many people found her single-mindedness trying; and there was a certain amount of jealousy of her success and of the publicity this brought her. 'Many people were nice to her face, and criticized behind her back,' Beverley Snook admitted. He and Simon Ames both found her a good person to have around at Royal Aero Club parties, where she was 'always happy and good fun' and where she was admired, but sometimes grudgingly. As Simon Ames put it, she had started with a clean sheet, and had put her act together. 'There was courage there, and skill for the greater part, and resourcefulness,' he told me. But she was nevertheless at times a thorn in the RAeC's flesh. 'Sheila lived for excitement,' Simon said. 'Compounded with the process of organization, this was a cross to bear for everyone, especially her.'

There were certainly times when Doug Bianchi would have agreed during the many hours he again spent on her behalf before she set out for Canada, especially when she accused him of being 'after her publicity'. The last straw was to be told: 'You're sending me across the Atlantic with an aeroplane which is unserviceable.'

'Go away, Sheila, and don't come back!' Doug retorted, although he did not intend her to take him literally.

As Bill Hewitt had died of a heart attack, Sheila enlisted another BOAC navigator, Bill Robinson – Robbie – to do her flight planning. 'She'd got enough to do to fly the ruddy aeroplane and worry about fuel,' he told me, 'although she was quite capable of doing all the flight planning herself – she knew all the answers, and the questions.' He considered her 'a bit bloody stupid sometimes', and 'foolhardy – but then so was Alan Cobham', as well as 'highly strung': 'but one allowed for that, and I used to pull her leg and laugh her out of it.'

'I always mean to write a personal letter to you,' Sheila wrote to Kaye Maclean during the pre-flight preparations, 'so this means you never get one, and I dictate madly to my secretary at odd moments! As usual we have an avalanche of paperwork for the new Record Attempt. . . . I believe they are getting along with "our company", but everything seems to take so long!'

A few days before she was due to leave, she was told that the Harmon Trophy award ceremony was to be in New York on Friday, 13 October – when she had promised to be in Toronto. The sponsorship money of the British exhibitors had already been spent on preparing the aircraft, and Sheila had committed herself to appearing at British Week; she had no option but to say that she could not be with the other three winners – astronauts Edwin Aldrin and James Lovell, and supersonic pilot Alvin White – to accept her trophy in person. 'It would have been fraud to cancel the arrangements,' she said, 'but it was heartbreaking to have to miss one of the greatest days of my life.'

She was nevertheless looking forward, among other things, to renewing her acquaintance with Princess Alexandra, who was to be in Toronto and whom she had met in London at a cocktail party at the Mansion House. Afterwards, at a private dinner for ten with 'her and Angus', Sheila found her 'enchanting and natural', as she wrote to Kaye: 'She was laughing with me all evening about what we would wear, and things like that. Then she asked if she could escape with Angus to see *Myth* over there, and she really meant it, because she asked the organizers to make sure she had a day off to do it!'

There was no surer way to Sheila's heart than praise of her beloved aircraft.

Her last engagement before the flight to Toronto was at the House of Commons, as guest of honour of the Worcester Association. She was made its first honorary life member, and was praised for her unsurpassed skill, courage and charm; in reply she admitted that flying was very lonely but had become a vice with her. Worcester's public recognition of its local heroine also took the form of commissioning a portrait of Sheila by Ernest Waldron West. In several sittings in her flat in Park West he did sketches and oils both of her, and of his impression of a storm she described over the Pacific; then he produced a big canvas in which she stood larger than life, smoking an inevitable cigarette, in front of her aircraft.

His feelings about her were mixed: 'Sheila was very attractive in many ways – you had to admire her. She had courage, and knew exactly what she wanted to do and what she was up to. But she was difficult to work with. One moment she was delightful; then suddenly she would fly off the handle – very temperamental. I was never quite sure where I was with her – she would make me feel very welcome, then she would have a spasm, and five minutes later she'd be almost kissing me.'

Sheila left London on 9 October for Shannon, which was to be her only stop before Newfoundland. Bill Robinson, who had to leave on a trip just after she arrived in Shannon, expected her to be safely the other side of the Atlantic before he returned, and deputed a fellow navigator to look after her flight planning in his absence. She was, however, grounded for four days by bad weather with Bert Goodchild, an engineer whom Doug Bianchi had sent to Ireland to supervise refuelling for her. Bert found her tension and frustration at the delay so exhausting that he telephoned Edna Bianchi: 'Edna, please get Doug to send for me,' he begged, 'I can't stand it any longer!'

On the fourth day, Bill Robinson returned from his trip to find Sheila still in Shannon. The weather was improving but was still poor, and as the forecast was not good the Met. men were reluctant to let her leave; but Sheila took matters into her own hands and took off just before 2 a.m. on Friday the 13th, dressed in green. It may have been because of the combination of possible causes of bad luck, or because of the weather conditions, or just because of her foolhardiness in setting out alone in such a small aircraft, that from the first weather ship out she received a message: 'Good luck – and we hope you live to break more records!'

For seven hours of darkness she battled against severe head winds, never more than two thousand feet above the water. Eventually icing forced her down until she was often as little as two hundred feet from 'the cold dark waves'. She was flying too low to pick up the beacon from the second weather ship, and reached such a peak of fear, caught between the sea and severe icing, that according to Bill Robinson she sent out a Mayday signal. He was telephoned at his home at 8 a.m. to be told that she was in distress; he assumed that she must either have engine trouble, or be running out of fuel, although there was nothing he could do other than work out where she might be. An air-sea rescue search was initiated, although Sheila never admitted either to this, or to having sent a distress signal.

They were the most miserable and frightened hours of her life; her only comfort was again the thought that, if she was going to be killed, it would be doing what she loved most, and in the thing she loved most, and that although her survival time if she ditched in the Atlantic would be no more than two minutes *Myth* would probably float. While she was facing what she was convinced must be certain death, her fellow Harmon Trophy winners were being presented with their awards by the President of the United States: it seemed a fitting time to die.

At last she made contact with Gander; the information that she was safe was relayed to Bill Robinson. When she saw land, Sheila had only two hours' worth of fuel. She landed after an exhausting seventeen hours fourteen minutes in the air, with another record to add to her list; but she was aware that she had only just made it. Later she wrote to Kaye Maclean: '*Myth Too* and I had a most exciting flight just above the waves.'

There was little time to rest – she had to carry on, both to keep her engagements at British Week and to create a new record from Shannon to Toronto. Forty-two hours after leaving Ireland Sheila arrived, exhausted, in Toronto, where she was met by Sir Ralph Perring. She was, not surprisingly, overwrought, and at first refused to speak to the reporters who had been waiting for her. 'I'm not going to have anything to do with anyone except you, Sir Ralph,' she said. He took her into a private room, soothed her, and persuaded her to face the press after all.

'It was quite traumatic,' Sir Ralph told me. 'She was very uptight and fraught, very nervy – a dear thing, but she required a lot of handling.'

At 8.30 the next morning he held a special meeting to decide how to cope with her. He and Sir Peter Allen, chairman of Canadian Export and a fellow organizer of British Week, decided that they must make a special fuss of her; they made sure that she had the best hotel suite, sent her flowers, and, as Perring put it, 'toned her down'. They felt that disaster had been averted, although what Sheila no doubt needed more than anything was a long sleep, followed by an hour with her hairdresser, Sandra Collins, who had been released by René to accompany Princess Alexandra to Toronto.

Sheila attached obsessive importance to her hair; the obsession may have been a legacy from her acting and modelling efforts, or it may have been part of her determination to create an image behind which she could hide. No one ever saw her looking windswept or dishevelled, even on a draughty airfield. 'Darling, my hair!' she would wail to Norman Lonsdale whenever there was the slightest breeze to ruffle it. It was a matter of personal pride never to be seen looking as if she had not just stepped out of a hairdresser's salon, even if this meant relying on a collection of wigs attached to hairbands. For Sandra Collins, being Sheila's unofficial personal hairdresser while she was officially Princess Alexandra's was 'a bit awkward': her first duty was to her royal employer, who never gave her any notice of when she would want her.

Sheila found Princess Alexandra and her husband, Angus Ogilvie, 'delightful'. 'I had long talks with them,' she reported to Kaye Maclean; 'once she was talking to me about certain philosophies, and what we find in the air, and then told me she had only talked to three other people who felt the same as us, and one of them was a Space man from USA!' She clearly found this flattering, and warmed even further to Princess Alexandra and Angus Ogilvie when they told her that they felt 'the same way that I do about masses of people around'. 'She certainly did help me a great deal,' her letter continued; 'although I am much older, it was like a mother telling me how to cope with it!'

Sir Ralph Perring found British Week 'an inspiring ten days'. The Toronto *Globe and Mail* wrote that Toronto would never be the same again; fifty thousand bottles of Whitbread's beer were sold in the

English bar, which had a special licence for standing – drinkers were normally made to sit down in Toronto.

'Canada was fantastic,' Sheila wrote to Kaye, 'but much too hard work. 3 television and radio shows a day plus a formal luncheon, reception and banquet every day! Now it seems I have to attend the men's official luncheons! The only woman and when the government wives ask why they cannot go too, the Government people say, "Oh – Sheila's not a woman – she's an institution!"' It was an anecdote which immediately entered her public speaking repertoire.

It was more flattering to be 'quoted daily' as the most distinguished pilot in the world, which Sheila attributed to being a Harmon Trophy winner and to *Myth*: 'You and I know I am not a very good pilot, or at anything,' she admitted to Kaye, 'except I love this kind of flying and have the most wonderful aircraft who never lets me down, and when I am in trouble (which is often) just takes over and gets me down safely.'

Still with her all-British wardrobe Sheila flew on to New York, where one of her first appointments was for a hair and beauty treatment at Arden's. Her clothing and cosmetic secrets had just been revealed in Britain in a half-page article by Georgina Howell in the *Observer*. The accompanying large portrait photograph, taken before her departure for Canada by Clive Arrowsmith, had captured a faraway, almost haunted, expression in her eyes, and showed the fine lines across the forehead and under the eyes caused by tension and by the intense concentration of flying. The mouth was firm and straight, but seemed equally ready to turn down disagreeably or to curve up in laughter – the deeply indented lines from the nose to the corners of the lips could have been caused by either expression, or by both.

She looked what she was – a well-groomed, over-sensitive, humorous, intelligent, but slightly dissatisfied woman in her mid-forties who was not sure whether to laugh or cry and whose chief claim to beauty was in her bone structure. Her neck was in shadow, but there too the lines were visible, although she was an experienced enough model to hold her head so that these would be stretched rather than sagging. Her shoulders were hunched forwards tensely, as if she was concentrating hard on something difficult and at the same time wondering whether to run away.

The article itself was less revealing of the personality behind the photograph, although it mentioned Sheila's gentle, umemphatic voice and described her romantic attitude towards flying. 'All my senses come alive,' she was quoted as having said.

> On the ground, I can't taste my cigarettes or smell my scent, and music is muted. Up there you experience everything as if for the first time. Colours are fantastic. Every part of the world has a different sky. I play music on my tape recorder, all kinds from 'Yellow Submarine' to Rachmaninov, and every time I cross the Equator I play Beethoven's Fifth to celebrate.

Her revelations about the cosmetics and perfumes she used were a mixture of honesty and carefully contrived acknowledgement of firms by whom she was already being sponsored in kind, or whose sponsorship she perhaps hoped to attract; a total of twenty-seven products from nine firms were mentioned, complete with prices – even for the Man's Kleenex at 1s 9d which she used 'for everything from polishing the windscreen to wrapping up rubbish to keep the aircraft tidy'. It all sounded more like something from a women's magazine than from a serious Sunday newspaper, with handy hints about the convenience of wrapover skirts – the only ones Sheila could change into in a confined cockpit – and ski or sailing clothes for draughty aerodromes.

Somehow Sheila had the remarkable ability to look as well groomed when she stepped out of the cockpit after hours of discomfort as she did at formal social functions, of which there was no shortage in New York and Washington, her next port of call. The most memorable were a dinner at the Adventurers' Club, where she shared the role of guest of honour with the elderly American air force general James Doolittle, and a reception at the British Embassy with the American 99s at which she was again the star. Sheila was, however, more excited about a visit to the Piper Aircraft factory at Lockhaven where she met the founder, Mr Piper, himself – it was very much a family business – and where *Myth Too* was parked beside an equally famous but older Comanche, *Let's Fly*, in which numerous records had been broken by Max Conrad. 'They looked like a couple of girls chatting it over,' she said whimsically, 'and I was unbelievably proud of her.'

From Washington, she sent a postcard at the beginning of November to Kaye Maclean: 'Still hectic – now en route to open the

Flying Treasure Hunt in Bahamas. Then hope to make Jamaica for a few days rest before tackling Trinidad, Natal SA to Dakar Africa and Atlantic record and home November 20th.' In the Bahamas, she was promised sponsorship by the Tourist Board for a record attempt in January from London to Nassau. This would have made up for the disappointment of not being able to try the ambitious flight round the world via both Poles of which she had been dreaming. 'It is absolutely tragic the way UK has become so slow in doing things, when we were once the GREAT pioneers,' she complained to Kaye Maclean.

Her few days' much-needed rest in Jamaica became a week, during which she had time to write a longer letter describing both the events and emotions of the previous few weeks, and the 'little bit of paradise' to which she had escaped; for the first time for two and a half years, she felt like 'a human being'. She had rushed on and off so many idyllic islands on her record flights that it was sheer luxury to have 'seven whole days freedom in the most beautiful surround-ings,' in a house called Manana which overlooked a blue-green bay, and was surrounded by poinsettias, bougainvillea, banana trees, humming birds, singing frogs and lizards, 'just like a fairy story'.

In mid-November, feeling for once thoroughly rested, she took off for Senegal – an eleven-hour 'honey of a flight' and another record. But the devaluation of the pound on the same day was considered more newsworthy in Britain, so neither her South Atlantic record, nor that between Madrid and London on the way home, received the coverage in the British press which Sheila thought they deserved. The news that *Myth*'s picture was to be displayed in the Smithsonian Museum in Washington alongside those of the aircraft of Amelia Earhart, Amy Johnson and Jean Batten only partly made up for the slight she felt she had received in her own country.

In spite of the occasional protestations of humility in her letters to Kaye Maclean, Sheila had reached the stage when, rather than being flattered by fame, she had come to expect it. One side of her therefore considered it no more than her rightful due when she was asked, in confidence, if she would accept an OBE in the New Year's Honours list; the other was as excited as a child before Christmas, and could not resist sharing the secret with Kaye and Archie Maclean. Her excitement was diluted by a three-week bout of flu, which combined with her usual depression and disorientation after a record flight to make her feel that there was, after all, nothing to look forward to. The Nassau promise of sponsorship had not materialized, and the year ahead looked dull and empty apart from lecture bookings – which Sheila accepted not for pleasure, but from financial necessity.

In the middle of December, Sheila Scott Flying Enterprises was at last formed. Elizabeth Overbury, who had succeeded Sheila in November as chairman of the 99s, was a director. 'Thank you . . . above all for the wonderful "donation" to the company,' Sheila wrote to the Macleans. 'Everything . . . seems to be under control . . . a deposit account (where your money is, and which pays the HP at the moment) and a current account of my earnings.'

She wrote them a much longer explanation and appreciation a few days later:

I hope Norman and Geoffrey [Maitland Smith, her accountant] have explained the company fully to you now. The situation as far as I am concerned is that this is my company which I asked my solicitors to form over two years ago – they then decided against it. So finally Norman and the accountants thought it up again this year! . . .

Your capital was to be used to pay the remainder of the HP over 2½ years (but at the same time providing capital for the company) while my capital was already in the aircraft, and MY actual earnings (plus record sponsorships if any) are what will pay for the upkeep, engineering, hangarage, replacements of the aircraft and my secretary. In other words everything I have will be in this company too.

I am represented by a very conservative legal firm, as well as the accountants, although they are slow!! I think you know I am not a very good businesswoman – but it is nearer to the truth to say that I don't like being one and wanted to fly! . . .

Again when you gave me this wonderful opportunity to survive with *Myth*, I handed the details over to the men again but this time very sweet, kind and honest ones, and what happens – they are too slow and miss the boat! So I am viewing them again with a very jaundiced eye!

Anyway I hope this has made the situation a little easier to understand. The one thing I would like to repeat is that I do not want you to enter into anything that is difficult, or could hurt you. The company is legally formed and must now go on – so I can still sell the aircraft and repay you, and give up the flying. Also there are still many lectures and a book to be written so the company would simply go on as a 'ground bound' thing only.

Bless you both for all your wonderfulness and sweetness to me. I cannot think why you should help me so much, and entirely without public recognition. You must be about the most unselfish people in the world.

Please take care of yourselves and have a wonderfully happy Christmas, and here's wishing us all a brighter New Year. . . .

With much love to you both, and deep appreciation for all you are trying to do for *Myth* and me.

Sheila and *Myth Too*. x x

PS. . . . All forms have been signed by me to get Alan entirely out, and the plane in my name only now (apart from Lombards).

Although she would of course have been heartbroken and resentful had the Macleans taken her at her word and put her in the position where she had to sell *Myth Too*, she felt that she had to make the offer. And her gratitude was genuine, as was the affection she felt by this time for the Macleans, whom she saw from time to time in Somerset and occasionally in London.

The 'book to be written' had in fact already been written – or rather, typed by various secretaries from Sheila's tapes – but had been firmly turned down by Collins. Through Alan Cobham she had met Gerald Pollinger, a literary agent who specialized in aviation books. Privately Pollinger was inclined to agree with Collins that the book was 'lousy' and unpublishable in its present form; after it had had attention from a series of ghost writers – whom Sheila had to pay, although none had completed the task – he offered it to Hodder and Stoughton. 'The book news is that Hodder definitely want a book by me,' Sheila told Kaye. But they wanted it almost entirely rewritten: 'Heaven knows when I can find time for this reversal – but I suppose I should be happy that a publisher definitely wants it!'

Just when she seemed about to settle into a long gloom, an unexpected opportunity for excitement presented itself: she was invited by the Fleet Air Arm to fly faster than the speed of sound in a Hunter jet. At last she was able to use her high-altitude certificate. With a Fleet Air Arm examiner to keep an eye on her, she dived from

42,000 feet to break the sound barrier. Even at subsonic speeds, being at the controls of the Hunter was exhilarating: she felt that she was dancing among the cloud tops and racing rainbows. Finally she was proudly put through 6g by the instructor, withstanding six times the force of gravity without blacking out. There was champagne on the tarmac to celebrate afterwards, and the blue Hunter was flatteringly christened *Sheila Scott* in memory of the first supersonic flight with the Fleet Air Arm by a British civilian woman pilot.

The association continued at a Ladies' Night, presided over by Admiral Donald Gibson. To Sheila's delight, she was awarded wings – two sets: jewelled ones for evening wear, and the official Fleet Air Arm version for her flying suit. This entitled her to consider herself the first honorary female Fleet Air Arm pilot. It was a romantic and flattering evening, with orchids, candlelight, a full orchestra and dance band and a proper dance floor, and a banquet. A live link-up with BBC radio in London had been arranged, and film of Sheila's supersonic flight was shown. As an extra, she was given a silver cigarette box: her addiction was well known.

It had been a full year – fuller than she could have imagined at its start. 'I am much happier than I was a year ago,' she said as the new year started. She felt that she had helped to prove both 'the happiness that could be found in the sky' and the safety of light aircraft, and had done 'something worthwhile for Britain', at the same time catching 'a fleeting glimpse of things we do not yet understand'.

9

For her investiture, on 12 March, Sheila chose as her two official companions Elizabeth Overbury and Kaye Maclean. 'I am delighted that you liked Elizabeth so much and agree with me,' she wrote afterwards to Kaye. In spite of the public recognition of the OBE, she felt as if she was spending her life on trains and in hotels, and that her only links with flying were talking about it or attending meetings or dinners of the various aviation groups of which she was a member.

After more vicissitudes with ghost writers, in May 1968 Sheila at last signed a contract with Hodder and Stoughton for *I Must Fly*. Much of the £600 advance she received on signature had already been paid out to so-called collaborators, although one after another these had dropped out – the last, a woman who claimed to work for *The Times* but whom neither Sheila nor Pollinger ever managed to contact there, had received £75 of a promised £250 but did not complete the work, and then made a breach of contract claim which had to be resolved through solicitors. It was with help from Gerald Pollinger that the book was eventually prepared.

'Believe it or not,' Sheila wrote to Kaye,

the book dull and dreary as I know it is, is actually being published by Hodders and it will still be called *I Must Fly*. Hodders have the same sort of plans for it as they put out for Francis Chichester. I am afraid the book has become awfully dull in the middle and I am not at all happy about it. . . . It is still awfully tough trying to get sponsors for the various attempts, and none of them seems to want to pay for all the expenses. It seems a little hard considering I never actually earn anything for personal uses on these attempts and, in fact, have to work very hard to fully pay for them. However, who knows, perhaps this year will see changes as you both seem to have brought me luck.

Retrospective opinions on Sheila's difficulty in obtaining sponsorship vary. Some have told me that in their view she was badly treated, and that her efforts as a flying heroine and an international representative of British aviation should have been financed by someone – although by whom, and why, is another question. Others feel that her motivation was self-centred, and cannot see why she should have expected her personal satisfaction to be financed by anyone else. I have also been told that she was not doing anything special anyway – the days of pioneering records were long since over; she should not therefore have expected the degree of public interest or the financial backing which the true pioneers had aroused. Yet others felt that it was because she was a woman that she was not taken seriously.

Norman Lonsdale, who had been caught in the crossfire of antagonisms between Sheila and her sponsors, was convinced that if she had been less temperamental there would have been considerably more support available. 'She was her own worst enemy,' he told me, 'She seemed to bite the hand that fed her. Word got about that she was difficult.' Even when she had not been difficult, there were rumours of disagreements. 'Of course, she fell out with Ken Wood,' I was told more than once, 'that's why he stopped sponsoring her.' She had not, however, fallen out with Ken Wood: he had agreed to sponsor one flight as a commercial venture which had gone as well as both he and Sheila had hoped.

Sheila considered herself less difficult than hard done by. She could see no reason why she should be discriminated against – as she felt she was – other than British reluctance to give credit where credit was due. She saw herself as both an ambassadress and a latter-day pioneer. It was a rationalization of her addiction to flying – she had to fly, as the title of her autobiography implied – which did not strike her as unreasonable. Whatever she did on the ground was geared only to making more flying possible; once she had experienced the elation of long-distance record breaking, whatever the problems it brought, she could no longer be satisfied with anything else; she felt that it was her duty both to herself, and to Britain, to carry on breaking records and to maintain her status as a flying heroine.

She had two flights in mind for 1968, still with the longer-term objective of another round-the-world marathon over both the Poles – one was a record attempt between London and Moscow, for which initial Russian interest had, however, not been confirmed; the other was the one for which she had been promised sponsorship by the Bahamian tourist board in Nassau. By the beginning of April she was still hopeful that another western Atlantic crossing, continuing further down the Bahamas, would materialize.

Then the *Daily Mail* announced a novel transatlantic air race to be held the following year, in commemoration of the fiftieth anniversary of the first flight over the Atlantic by Alcock and Brown in a Vickers Vimy. It was to start simultaneously at the tops of the Post Office Tower in London and the Empire State Building in New York; competitors could use any combination of forms of transport to finish where those going in the opposite direction had started. The race received considerable publicity from its inception, and not surprisingly this attracted the interest of numerous potential sponsors – and made it even more difficult for Sheila to gain support for the independent solo efforts she was planning. She let off steam in a letter to Kaye:

> The Daily Mail Air Race has done us [i.e. her and *Myth*] great harm this year although it is not until next year. We have lost 2 sponsors out of 3, and now expect the third to give up. They only seem interested in this stupid gimmick which is only for the rich man and his brandy bottle while a paid pilot flies his private jet! How is that for bitterness on my part? However take no notice – *Myth* will win through the year somehow!

Sheila and *Myth* continued the round of air races, with one win – in the 99s' women's race at Halfpenny Green in September. On the ground Sheila raced from lecture to lecture and from meeting to meeting. Somehow she found time to devise a flying adventure game, with a vast board and various penalties and bonuses based on her own experiences. Gerald Pollinger attempted to sell it for her, to tie it in with the publication of her book, which had been postponed to November. Waddingtons replied that they did not market that sort of game and had already turned down a similar suggestion with a nautical theme from Francis Chichester. Pollinger's efforts on Sheila's behalf to interest the BBC in a play based on *I Must Fly* were no more successful: it was rejected by both television and radio. Neither Minimodels, nor Airfix, nor Meccano was interested in models of *Myth Too* because of 'the brief topicality of Miss Scott's flights', and no one wanted various articles she submitted through Pollinger.

In the summer Sheila took on a new, full-time secretary, Lana Jeffers. Lana, who was petite and pretty with long blonde hair, had just left school and had had to abandon her ambition to become a physiotherapist because she was below the minimum height of five foot two inches. With no clear idea of what it might involve, she signed on at the Brook Street Bureau as a 'personal assistant'. She was, as she admitted, 'totally unqualified and incompetent' when she was sent for an interview with a client who wanted a PA but whom the bureau had been 'unable to sort out': 'and so I found myself working for Sheila, as my first job,' Lana told me. 'Sheila said: "Let's give it a go!" and taught me how to be a secretary.'

The initiation was at times alarming. Sheila was often over-wrought and made no attempt to control herself in front of Lana, whom she nevertheless appeared to adore. Lana in return admired and liked her, but was at first terrified of Sheila's 'tantrums, stampings of feet, and tears'. She was also often resentful of the demands Sheila put on her: she found herself acting not only as secretary, but also running the flat, packing and making sandwiches – which had to be just right, and wrapped exactly the way Sheila liked – and dealing with anyone from wigmakers to engineers. Sheila's assumption that her secretary would be totally dedicated caused friction between Lana and both her boyfriend and her mother.

She was paid £21 a week, of which £7 went on rent and much of the rest on clothes: she often had to accompany Sheila to social functions, for which she was expected to look glamorous. As Sheila claimed that she could not afford to pay her during her holidays, during the two years Lana worked for her she took part-time holiday work at Christie's – and was understandably irritated when Sheila went on exotic holidays herself or bought an expensive new trouser suit.

'I never dared to be ill,' Lana told me, 'Sheila extracted total loyalty, and had total demand over one. I gave her my unquestioned admiration. She liked to feel needed, and I confided in her; she gave me advice, and was very affectionate. We had lots of giggles.' It was a strange and intense relationship; but the suspicion of people who saw them together that there was a lesbian attraction was, Lana assured me, unfounded. Gradually she lost her fear of Sheila's outbursts, which consequently became less frequent. 'She used to cry for effect, and cried and stamped at the drop of a hat,' Lana said; by the time she had worked for her for a few months, whenever Sheila started stamping and swearing, holding a cigarette and with tears pouring down her face, Lana merely said: 'Pull yourself together.' 'I felt she was more lonely than unbalanced,' Lana told me; 'and she was resentful because she'd made a great sacrifice for Britain and had nothing to show for it.'

Sheila treated Lana in many ways both as the mother she had never had, and as the daughter she would never have: she was by then forty-six, and although she had plenty of men friends there seemed little likelihood that she would ever remarry or have a family. It was a symptom of her loneliness that she had no one else to rely on, or to be relied on by; but Lana was only nineteen, and was so exhausted by the combined burden of her official and unofficial duties that when she got home in the evenings she often fell asleep fully clothed on her bed. 'You're no fun,' complained her flatmates, none of whom had to earn their own living.

Her chief official duties were to type up endless letters approaching potential sponsors and to put together begging brochures from Sheila's longhand. The living room in the flat at Park West, which was carpeted in electric blue, served both as Lana's office and as the room where Sheila entertained. The paperwork overflowed into the bedroom, where Sheila slept on the right side of a large double bed; Lana was sure that, in spite of rumours to the contrary, Sheila never slept with anyone in the flat, as there was never any sign that the overflowing ashtray or the clothes and papers which were always a jumbled heap on the left-hand side of the bed had been cleared away – 'There was no room for a man even to get his big toe in' – and there was never anyone there in the morning. Flying memorabilia filled a small boxroom, and in the living room there were numerous awards, as well as mobiles, two Sadler balloon prints and several pictures of aircraft which had been specially painted for Sheila.

Lana's secretarial duties included farming out to her various boyfriends the questions sent in advance from quiz shows in which Sheila was to take part. She and Sheila would then go over the answers together – these sessions counted among the 'giggles' they had together. Sandra Collins was often at the flat before Sheila's public appearances, to comb out her hair and make sure that it looked immaculate. Sometimes, while this was being done, Lana was given a list of people Sheila was about to meet and had to read out any information gleaned about them from *Who's Who*.

Sheila's sittings for a portrait by June Mendoza provided some respite for Lana. June and Sheila had met at a social function, and had felt an instant rapport: Sheila always knew immediately whether or not she was going to like someone – she believed that people gave off positive or negative vibrations; if the vibes were negative, there could be nothing more than mutual civility; positive vibes could lead to a rapid and close friendship and understanding. The vibes from June Mendoza were good. June found Sheila attractive both as a person and as a subject, and asked if she might paint her. It made a pleasant change to choose her own subject from time to time instead of relying always on commissions. Unlike Ernest Waldron West, she found Sheila easy to get on with, and during their many sittings their mutual liking and admiration grew.

The result was a large portrait in oils which captured both Sheila's beauty and her tension, and emphasized equally her strength of character and her insecurity. It showed her sitting, but poised as if ready to escape, one hand resting on Amy Johnson's jewel box, the other holding a cigarette. The globe presented to her by the BWPA after her round-the-world flight was the only object in the background, offset to one side so that it served as a symbol without diverting the attention from the subject. As in the *Observer* photographic portrait, Sheila looked as if she might as easily laugh or cry, and there was no attempt to disguise the lines on her forehead and from nose to mouth. Her hair was as she often wore it, swept back with a hairband and curling upwards from just above her shoulders – the style copied in the wigs on which she relied when she had to appear in public immediately after a flight – and the lighting emphasized her bone structure. June kept the portrait, although it would have been a better indication of Sheila's personality in the National Portrait Gallery than the photographs which they commissioned of her.

At the beginning of October Sheila received a letter from Hodder and Stoughton, not about her own forthcoming book, but about one on which another of their authors, John Anderson, was working. It was to be called *The Ulysses Factor*: 'In this he is considering, in depth and from a somewhat philosophical angle, the reasons why people, like you, do the things you do . . . and hopes, by means of a careful analysis of the achievements of explorers and adventurers, to answer a number of puzzling questions about twentieth-century man (and woman).' The same letter was also sent to John Ridgway, who in 1966 had crossed the Atlantic with Chay Blyth in an open rowing boat, and to the mountaineer, explorer and diplomat Eric Shipton.

Sheila accepted an invitation to lunch with Anderson with unfeigned enthusiasm. 'I truly believe in what you are doing,' she wrote, 'if one did not experience certain compelling factors, one certainly would not be able to go on with my sort of attempts. It would be a once only! This is a lunch date I truly look forward to (so many of them are for duty!)' After their meeting, she wrote to him again – he had become 'Dear John': 'I think you are a very special person yourself. . . . Again thank you for inviting me, and for all your interest. Am afraid I talked too much!'

J. R. L. Anderson was an adventurer in his own right, as a yachtsman who had made and written about a transatlantic voyage under sail in the wake of the Vikings. Sheila felt that her inclusion in a book about the great adventurers of the twentieth century, alongside Francis Chichester, Thor Heyerdahl, Robin Knox-Johnston and sailor/mountaineer Bill Tilman, was the greatest possible acknowledgement.

'Her achievement in the air is almost beyond credibility, and has been sustained year after year,' Anderson wrote – although he found it difficult to assess quite what she was trying to achieve. What he called the Ulysses factor was made up, in varying degrees, of courage, selfishness, physical strength and competence, imagination, self-discipline and competitiveness – all, except physical strength, qualities shown by Sheila; but her implied desire to enter a trance-like state beyond physical fatigue added a mystical element not shown by the typical Ulysses male. Sheila felt that he understood her: 'her feelings towards her aircraft . . . are identical to those of a man towards his boat, compound of love as for a wife or a mistress, dependent love, as for a mother, and solicitude, as for a child. She considers her aircraft female, like boats, but her attitude towards them is more akin to heterosexual love, with a sense of reliance on them that a woman may feel about her husband.'

Sheila's book *I Must Fly* was published in November, with a flurry of public appearances and press, radio and television interviews. Car stickers saying 'I must fly' were part of the hype. Foyle's had a window display, and borrowed the June Mendoza portrait. Sheila did numerous signing sessions, both in London at various West End stores – including Harrods – and elsewhere. Her flying friend David Lewis rang up to say it was the best and most exciting aviation book he had ever read: a year later he dedicated his own book on the history of air racing 'to Sheila Scott OBE, in friendship and in appreciation of achievements which have imbued British sporting flying with renewed spirit'.

The exercise books in which Lana kept a list of telephone callers and messages were filled with requests for interviews and congratulations. From several of her entries it is clear that at least one article in the *Daily Mail* was less than favourable. Peter Scott, who had been trying unsuccessfully to raise sponsorship for Sheila's proposed Russian flight, was reported to have spoken to the editor, a friend of his: 'He too horrified. Perfectly sincere and genuine apologies from Editor of *Mail*. Promised unfailingly to make amends.' Jane Eustace of Hodder and Stoughton wanted to chat with Sheila about the article but 'doesn't think there is really much she can do for you'. Gerald Pollinger, according to Lana's notes, took a more positive view:

> He is really quite pleased about it, as a number of people he has spoken to say it was derogatory to you – and has aroused a great deal of sympathy about injustice for aviation and women in general! (Nobody he has spoken to has seen it in the way that you and I interpreted it!)! He says not to worry as everybody seems to have taken it in a different way – and he is pleased with it – and going to use it for publicity – (Everybody is angry on your behalf!)

The editor of the *Daily Mail* kept his word: 'Peter Scott rang again – thinks review in *Mail* today is marvellous and makes up for all yesterday's caper!'

Nevertheless Sheila felt threatened. Whenever she was depressed, whoever she felt closest to at the time was likely to receive a late-night telephone call for help. On this occasion, it was John Anderson. He took her seriously enough to write a letter of encouragement the day after she had poured out her misery over the telephone.

'Your telephone call last night distressed me greatly,' he wrote, and went on:

I can understand only too well the horrible treadmill that life has made you walk, but I am angry and unhappy that it should be so. I can also understand your rage at the tattlings of gossip-writers, but here I feel on slightly firmer ground. You are so *infinitely* more important as a human being than are the gossip-writers . . . that you really can afford to ignore them. . . . *You must know* that those who try to understand you, what you are and what you have done, either never read gossip-columns or, if they do, read them with the contempt they merit. Life, your life particularly, is infinitely more than 6 lines, or 6 million lines, of somebody else's alleged diary.

But more important than any of this is what should be your care for yourself. The utter physical weariness of endless travelling from lecture to lecture I understand, and I think it must be far worse for a woman than for a man. I have the deepest admiration for what you do, as for your courage in doing it – I think it takes more real courage to give brightly the 200th lecture when you are desperately tired but determined not to let anybody down, than to trust to your compass course in heavy weather. It is no use saying that I wish you didn't have to do these things, for you do them because you are what you are. But what I can and do say is that you must try not to let weariness and the transient worries of the day belittle to *yourself* your own achievement. You have done what few people, men or women, have come within 1000 miles – or even 1000 lifetimes – of doing. Nothing can take that away. . . . So try, please try, not to let worries about the future diminish, in your own thinking, the greatness that is yours for all times, and which nothing can ever make recede. . . . I know how next-to-impossible it is not to worry about the bread and butter necessities of life. But I also know that your sort of achievement is more valuable than all the gold in Fort Knox; and this you *have*. The snow leopard belongs to the hills and the clean sky. Let the wolves snarl at each other in the jungly valleys. Good luck Sheila.

After a month filled almost entirely with book promotion in England, Sheila left for a few days in America and Canada for more of the same. Afterwards she wrote to Kaye Maclean:

USA was busy but as good as a rest to get away from secretarial nonsense and screaming telephones here. It was so pretty with all its lights for Christmas. . . . Back into the millstream here with lectures and trains up North. Seem to be on the radio a lot recently. . . . Two repeats last week – *World at One* today. Also *Does the Team Think?* in about two weeks time. *Petticoat Line* Tuesday, *Galaxy* also sometime in the next few weeks. Do not know if I told you that it is always most important for an actor or actress to get one Variety Club luncheon, and the Guest of Honour at Green Room Club during their career. As you know I had the Variety Club luncheon after the World Flight, and you can imagine my delight to be guest of honour at the Green Room with Sir John Gielgud as my opposite number on Feb. 2nd. It seems to pay to be a 'resting actress' in this sense!!

To both Lana and Norman Lonsdale, who apart from Kaye Maclean were at the time the two people closest to Sheila and those who therefore bore the brunt of her depressions, she made occasional threats of suicide; they wrote these off as part of Sheila's melodramatic ability to create a crisis out of anything, and did not take them seriously. In public, she presented a very different image: as Lana put it, 'She was professional as far as the press and public appearances were concerned – she was glamorous, she brought glitz, she gave the public what they wanted.'

But the public, however much it admired Sheila's glamour and glitz, still did not give her quite what she wanted – appreciation combined with a large enough income to stop worrying about how to support herself and *Myth*. When the aircraft's engine was found to be in need of expensive extra work in addition to the usual maintenance, it was only through yet another contribution from the Macleans – gratefully acknowledged – that she could pay the bill.

There was a gap of a year after Sheila's New Year letter to the Macleans in the file so meticulously kept by Kaye. During that year Archie died, at the age of eighty-four, with his and Kaye's anonymity as Sheila's major benefactors intact. During the two years since their first meeting they had moved from the formality of new contacts to mutual affection. The Macleans had not hesitated to offer Sheila their advice and to state their criticisms of how she organized her affairs, and of her behaviour – they felt that she smoked and drank too much.

She, in turn, although she found their concern about her smoking and drinking habits irritating, had shown equal concern about their well-being, and particularly about Kaye's painful and disabling affliction of Dupion's contraction of the hand and fingers. Her letters had also included appreciative comments about their house and garden, an interest in their activities – although inevitably these were less interesting than her own – as well as repeated gratitude for their generosity. It is inconceivable that she did not write to Kaye after Archie's death; the letters may have been too personal for Kaye to keep with the others, or she may have been too preoccupied to file them. Although in the past Sheila had on occasion fallen out with some who had given her or might have given her financial support – Sir Alan Cobham in particular – she had remained so far on excellent terms with the Macleans and had apparently valued their friendship as much as their money.

Her hopes of retrieving her financial situation through the income from her book were, however – as so many of her financial hopes – to be disappointed. Whatever may have been her expectations as an authoress, it did not bring in a fortune, although it eventually went into profit – in other words, as far as the publishers were concerned it more than covered costs. As her agent, Gerald Pollinger took 15 per cent of her advance royalties; Sheila's income from the book was at most a few hundred pounds.

Not long after the publication of *I Must Fly* Sheila entered a new name in her diary: 'Colonel Whitbread'. They first met at a reception which was part of the long run-up to the *Daily Mail* Air Race of which she had written so scathingly. Nevertheless she was, inevitably, considering entering, although as usual money was a problem: most of the potential sponsorship had already been soaked up by entrants with more obviously commercial links. But her meeting with Colonel Whitbread, chairman of the brewery of the same name, was to be the start both of a year's sponsored flying, and of a friendship with him and his wife. As an enthusiastic amateur pilot himself – he had started flying in the 1920s, and had his own private aircraft and a landing strip at one of his country homes, in Wiltshire – the colonel appreciated her spirit of adventure and her refusal to consider defeat.

'She had a passionate determination, which was quite outside the normal,' Colonel Whitbread told me at his second country home, in Surrey. 'She didn't mind what she did to achieve what she felt she had to do for flying. She felt she'd been given a gift and damn well had to use it, and everyone had to help her.' Although at their first meeting he did not commit himself to sponsoring her, and left such details in any case to his public relations manager, John Fox, a seed had clearly been sown. During the next few months it germinated and grew and eventually bore fruit.

10

SHEILA STARTED 1969 in a state of exhaustion. Before continuing preparations for the transatlantic race, followed by further African record attempts sponsored by Whitbread's, she spent a month in Jamaica. She left detailed instructions about things to be done in her absence by Lana, who was resentful that in spite of her constant plea of poverty Sheila could have a holiday in the Caribbean while she was slaving on her behalf in London, and by 'Ivy', who was, it seems, to spring clean the flat.

Lana was to

Do bookshelf – bang each book separately and dust edges of pages; turn off central heating in bedroom & spare room (it yellows clothes); go through 'mileage book' – your ex. doubled up the amendments – it's chaos!; scrapbooks (but remember separate pages, *not* overlapping; make 2 more games – get large plastic bags to cover the games! Store pieces in separate little boxes (1 each game and rules); put in as much radio/TV as is offered March 11th onwards! – write all UK 99s personal letters re Race at IoM [Isle of Man]. . . ; send apologies to Royal Aero Club Comps Committee for not being there, owing convalescence; cancel lectures –arrange others' trains etc; hems: blue dress – collect blue and green buttons (ready Monday); check both typewriters in working order.

As if all this was not enough, Sheila also told her how to do the filing: 'By this I mean all filing now left undone to be put into correct companies. Index to above made. Remember I am coming straight back to a record attempt. Direct reference to each Record (i.e. Airport requests . . . etc) to go into separate folders each record 1) New York–Copenhagen; 2) Africa; 3) World.' Then there were bills to be paid, a wig to be returned, clothing to be taken to or fetched from the dry cleaners, post to be forwarded, a party at Oxford for everyone who had helped with *Myth* and another to be organized with Norman Lonsdale in London – 'Whitbreads could surely send a barrel or two to the Oxford party' – as well as press releases to be prepared and sent: 'Take every opportunity with open hands re press, TV and radio – See them yourself – give all information – send briefs, and thank them for their interest.' Finally, Lana was to 'TELEPHONE ME DETAILS IF WE WIN ANYTHING!'

Within a week of her return, Sheila had made a speech at the Mansion House as the first woman liveryman to reply to the toast at a City Livery Company's banquet – a distinction of which she was very proud. She had also made two lesser lunchtime speeches, and had attended her own guild's AGM and an RAeC committee meeting.

The telephone messages taken by Lana and by several occasional part-time secretaries during 1969 filled five exercise books, and included considerable discussion about the wording of a telegram and the cost and design of a cake to commemorate the first test flight in Britain of the Concorde. Sheila's initial suggestion for the telegram was 'Let the French have cake and we'll fly the flag – may your landings always be smooth and happy.' Since Concorde was a joint Anglo-French venture this was felt to be tactless, and was amended accordingly. The cake, which she presented to the BAC test pilots Brian Trubshaw and John Cochrane when they landed safely after Concorde's maiden flight, was an excellent piece of patriotic PR.

Another aviation first, which meant even more to Sheila than Concorde, had recently been achieved by Elizabeth Overbury, who had gained her Air Transport Pilot's Licence and whom Sheila congratulated by telegram: 'Congratulations on becoming Britain's first Air Transport woman jet pilot. I am proud of the best friend I hate.'

'She's my best friend – and I hate her,' was a standing joke between the two women pilots, whose spheres of operation were so different and whose friendship surmounted any occasional minor disagreement. 'I couldn't have done what she did,' Elizabeth admitted, 'and she couldn't have done what I did. I often said to her: "Keep on keeping on." ' Most people admired her, but some were rather jealous. Sheila was a very able pilot, and a very good friend to me. But we both needed space – and I think the people she antagonized were the people who didn't give her space.' Theirs was a comfortable friendship; Elizabeth was one of Sheila's few lastingly close friends. She could drop in at the Park West flat at any time and be welcome – one of Sheila's letters to Kaye Maclean was interrupted because 'Elizabeth has just come through the door' – and equally Sheila was often a guest at her house near Whipsnade Zoo in Bedfordshire.

Apart from Elizabeth and one or two other people – Norman Lonsdale, for instance – Sheila's friends seemed to come and go, changing so rapidly that many people thought she was incapable of a sustained friendship, or was so self-seeking that she dropped people when they could no longer be useful to her. She was aware that friendships which had started well were too rarely continued – not through any ill-will on her part, but because of the pressures of time and distance. It was inevitable that the people with whom she associated most closely at any time were those with whom she was involved for a particular reason; and it was an all-too-frequent cause of sadness to her to find that in her absence old friends had found new friends, and that she had become an outsider.

Her constant insecurity, too, was often a barrier. With only a few exceptions, she found it difficult to believe that people liked her for herself; she felt – probably often with good reason – that she was being used by hangers-on, and she imagined slights. It was perhaps in her relationships with other members of the British Women Pilots' Association that this was most in evidence. When Connie Fricker, a fellow member of both the BWPA and the 99s, flew with Sheila during an Isle of Wight rally she found her delightful, friendly and helpful in the air; but when they landed, and Connie wanted to join the others in a big marquee, Sheila said: 'I'm not going in there – it's full of bitches who are all out to get me.' Although there was a certain amount of resentment in the BWPA about the 99s' more glamorous image, and some understandable envy of Sheila's personal glamour and her flying heroine role, none of the BWPA members to whom I have spoken was ever 'out to get' her. They admired her, and were proud of her, but often felt that she held herself aloof. Her fame had created a barrier which meant that, although she knew many people, on the ground she was often lonely in a crowd.

In spite of all these tensions, and her initial contempt for the *Daily*

Mail 'Top of the Towers' transatlantic race as a rich man's gimmick, Sheila eventually found it 'undoubtedly the greatest fun'. She was one of 360 entrants, few of whom took it as seriously as she did. For her it was more than a race – and a light-hearted race at that, with even a chimpanzee among the competitors. Sheila used it as an opportunity to try for several more records in both directions, and the publicity given to the race itself was a useful boost to her own PR efforts.

Lana was roped in to help not only with the advance secretarial work, but with the preparations for the first part of the race during several weekend practice runs which she found 'enjoyable and often hilarious'. Sheila persuaded Aston Martin to lend her a car, two drivers and a helicopter with pilot to take her first by road from the Post Office Tower to Battersea heliport, and from there to London Airport. With the help of several of Lana's friends, they got this part of the race down to a fine art. Sheila was enjoying herself. She had little hope of winning, as on the long Atlantic crossing *Myth* would be up against very much faster twin-engined aircraft; but she was determined not to be last, although she told herself that 'we are in it for the fun'.

Just before Easter, her pleasure was suddenly and unexpectedly marred when she was sent a tape recording of a seance: a medium warned her that her engine was spluttering – 'phut, phut' – and stopped over the sea, 'just like Amy Johnson's'. This was taking the frequent comparisons made between Sheila and the pre-war flying heroine too far. Amy Johnson had ditched in the Thames estuary in 1941 during a flight with the Air Transport Auxiliary: her aircraft had been seen to plunge into the sea, but her body had never been recovered.

Although Sheila did her best to ignore the warning, telling herself that the tape was 'negative thinking' and that she should not be superstitious, she sent it to Lord Donegall, who had once conducted what she termed 'a great psychic research' as a newspaper correspondent. His letter to her, after he had listened three times to the tape, is the only indication of what was on it, although she kept recordings from all her flights, television and radio appearances and lectures.

'I do not know whether the medium is a professional or not,' he wrote. 'Probably she is a professional, I think, as the clap-trap phraseology is the familiar pattern.' Although he thought that the

people who attended the seance were almost certainly all sincere
believers, he pointed out that mediums, like journalists, had to
'produce an extra special rabbit out of the hat, once in a while, in
order to prevent the circle from losing interest'. After a detailed
analysis which demolished the authenticity of the 'message' point
by point, he told Sheila: 'Frankly, I wouldn't give this seance
another thought. Whatever may be the explanation, neither Amy,
nor any other "spirit", had *anything* to do with it. Of *that*, I am quite
sure.' He signed himself 'Yours most cordially, Don', and added a
PS inviting Sheila for a drink.

Sheila took comfort from his opinion, although she considered it
prudent to authorize a thorough check of *Myth*; she later claimed
that as a result several little things were found and put right which
individually might not have been serious, but together might have
led to a ditching. Had she received the tape when her mental
balance was as precarious as it had sometimes undoubtedly been, it
could well have had a serious effect; but she was making fewer wild
claims about 'them', and she was able to do as Lord Donegall had
suggested and treat the so-called warning with contempt – even if
she did keep her fingers mentally crossed.

There were innumerable details to attend to before the start of the
race. They included a quick sitting for a charcoal portrait by an
artist called Zsuzsi Robosch and an interview with actor-writer
William Wordsworth for a book he was preparing about outstanding women.

The hair tinting and wig experts at René's were having difficulty
with one of Sheila's wigs: 'Gordon would like a cutting of your hair
to ensure getting a good match,' Lana wrote in the telephone
message book. 'Says he had a lot of trouble getting the "red" look
out of it.' Further frantic messages about the wig were interspersed
among those about the cars, helicopter and aircraft Sheila would be
using at various stages of the impending race, and about insurance
and charts.

A week after Gordon's request for a sample of hair, he resorted to
lending Sheila a wig: 'The other one is still not right yet – he quite
honestly thinks that it will never be the correct colour,' Lana recorded.
'Says that it is very yellow now and that hair like that (it is Eurasian
mixed with Nylon) just will not take any new colour – but will try and
get it wearable for 4th May [the start of the race] – but doubts it will be
any good – says you may borrow one I have left on your bed.'

The next problem was arranging enough money for the three weeks that Sheila planned to spend in New York between the transatlantic race and her return record attempt: it was in the days of a £50 British travel allowance. 'Barclays rang to say that the Bank of England are querying why Sheila has to stay in NY for three weeks,' Lana wrote. 'I said she hopes to do television etc and stressed it was necessary to have some considerable rest after flight.'

Although Sheila was entering the transatlantic race without a sponsor – Whitbread's promised support was for the record attempts she was planning later in the year – she was adopted by the Navy as their unofficial entrant. As the BBC had chosen her as one of the entrants to follow on film, she was guaranteed maximum publicity. Everything was going well, but as an extra precaution she took with her a horeshoe from one of the Whitbread Shire horses to bring her luck.

She had elected to do the Atlantic crossing at night, to ensure daylight as she approached the American coast. This allowed her to stay in bed listening to and laughing at radio reports of the antics of her fellow competitors with an earlier start. There was only one hiccup in her carefully laid plans: the sticky red American super de luxe de-icing fluid which had been smeared over *Myth* was industriously washed off at London Airport by a foreman who thought the aircraft needed a good clean. Doug Bianchi gave up his Saturday morning to replace it.

Sandra Collins had been summoned to do Sheila's hair so that she would look her best for the BBC television cameras. By the time she arrived Sheila was in her usual last-minute flap, exacerbated by the haunting memory of the seance warning. 'She seemed terrified of going,' Sandra told me. 'She kept on saying she wasn't ready, everything seemed to be wrong, she didn't expect to come back.' Spontaneously, Sandra, who was expecting her first baby, hugged her and said: 'But of course you're coming back – you're going to be a godmother!' Sheila had never been asked to be a godmother before. 'I was as thrilled as though it were my own child!' she commented. Her depression vanished as she set off to join the noise and apparent confusion at the Post Office Tower.

Then it was 'GO, Sheila!' helter skelter down in the lift into the waiting deep blue Aston Martin – just in case one broke down, and to lead the way, two had been provided. A London taxi driver – the best possible navigator – sat beside the chauffeur. The motorcycles of a team of white-helmeted Royal Marines screamed through the cheering crowd to provide a surprise escort as Sheila was driven at top speed to the waiting Jet Ranger helicopter – her PR handouts had not forgotten to mention that she was Britain's first female commercial helicopter pilot, although she had never used the qualification.

At Heathrow, it was on and off the scales and into the cockpit – *Myth*'s engine had already been started up. As Sheila made her fastest take-off ever, Raymond Baxter's excited commentary from the control tower broadcast *Myth*'s every quiver to the nation. . . . Then Sheila and *Myth* were alone again with the sky, flying in late afternoon sunlight between the brooding outline of thunder clouds which seemed to have parted to let them through. Sheila talked to *Myth* about their life together: 'One moment full of doubt, unsure, dark and threatening, and yet as suddenly full of soft happiness like an iridescent cloud.'

She landed fifteen minutes ahead of schedule in Shannon, where Bert Goodchild was waiting to fill *Myth* with 'the thick green liquid that is her life blood' – Sheila was in lyrical mood as she reported on her progress into her tape recorder. With a wave to the television cameras, and to Bert, she was again secure in her little cabin: 'The familiar smells of gas wafting gently with the aroma of bananas, and I touch the velvety smooth control stick as I check the elevators. My cockpit lights are warm and golden. . . . Just like an actress, I take three huge gulps of steadying air. . . . We almost lumber forward, *Myth* awkward at first, with her unaccustomed weight.'

Slowly, carefully, because of the extra fuel needed for the long flight, Sheila and *Myth* left 'the bonds of the sticky tarmac'. She felt more 'gloriously free' than any Pilgrim Father and mused that the air traffic controller must be handsome as he had a 'nice furry Irish voice'. The night was magical enough for fairy princes, although there were only 'the three of us, old nanny Engine, *Myth Too* and me'.

Soon the magic of the night evaporated as *Myth* iced up. Sheila was forbidden to fly low to avoid the ice because there were so many aircraft which were out of radio contact flying in the opposite direction. Then she too was out of contact as she sat huddled in a shawl trying to keep warm. 'Is there an outside world, or am I the only one left?' she wondered as she flew on through the darkness. Fear grabbed her as she heard the bang-snap-crash of ice flying off the propeller and the engine started to complain, but was banished when almost at the same moment she made radio contact with her mother ship, HMS *Nubian*, and then saw her searchlights. Through *Nubian* she requested to fly lower and was granted permission. She talked to *Myth*, and to Buck Tooth, the toy rabbit, who as usual grinned back inanely.

Edging carefully down through fog, she found pack ice. She was flying so low that for a few horrified seconds she was looking up at a 'magnificent giant iceberg'. As she swung away from it she was aware of 'the icy joyless arms' that awaited her if she allowed her concentration to lapse for even a second, but felt less afraid than awed. In Gander, Newfoundland, where an extra flurry of snow and a sleepy airport manager greeted her, she was told almost accusingly that she was four hours early. Then it was up and on again, over Nova Scotia and south towards Boston and New York. First the Canadian, and then the American, controllers kept up a steady stream of flirtatious chat to stop her from falling asleep.

At La Guardia she was so tense with cold and concentration that she could hardly move, but the high-speed antics of the start of the race had to be repeated in reverse order. She was hauled into the waiting helicopter, only to tumble out of it and into an Aston Martin within what seemed mere seconds. Out of the car, into the elevator, out of the elevator – slam into a wall: wrong way, try the other. The BBC camera crew filmed and shouted encouragement simultaneously. Stop the clock: twenty-six hours fifty-four minutes and twenty seconds tower to tower, a new light aircraft transatlantic record, beating her own, although that could not be positively confirmed until the end of the race week. Champagne – 'but I'm drunk already! I'm happy, happy, happy!'

She was too happy, and too drunk with excitement even without the champagne, to sleep. The usual post-record red roses from the Royal Aero Club greeted her in her hotel room, as well as a fragrant basket of bath oils, foams and lotions from Elizabeth Arden. Telephone calls and telegrams poured in. Bob Webb, who had done her flight planning, mock-grumbled that he had been woken every two hours to be told her position; there was a signal from the Admiral and another with love from the 250 sailors on board HMS *Nubian*.

In its ecstatic coverage of its own race, the *Daily Mail* allocated more space to Sheila than to any other individual entrant. Under a headline 'How I beat the ice fury', it told how 'lone flyer Sheila Scott arrived exhausted in New York . . . after two days without sleep and a nightmare struggle to keep her iced-up plane airborne.' Sheila, patriotically dressed in a red, white and blue trouser suit and tam o'shanter, gave the credit for her survival to her aircraft: 'In any other plane I would not have been able to do it. But this plane holds sixty-seven world records.' She had just brought the total to seventy-two with the various categories she had broken, including Ireland to Newfoundland in under twelve hours, knocking more than five off her own previous time. 'I stayed awake without drugs,' she told a reporter in New York. 'I feel as if I have been flying for three weeks – I don't know if I will ever sleep again.' 'We were all convinced that she was on tranquillizers with one hand and pep pills with the other,' John Blake told me – a suspicion without foundation, as far I have been able to ascertain, although not a surprising assumption given the gruelling targets she set herself. Her pre-flying drug history was known to no one in aviation, although it was suspected by a few.

Back in London, Lana was fielding and making telephone calls on Sheila's behalf. She gave information to reporters, carried on with plans for the party in Oxford, accepted an invitation for Sheila to judge a beauty contest at a hunt ball, booked various interviews and lectures, and ordered '2 gross biros (£3.13.6) with your name and *Myth Too* in gold (blue and gold) . . . good for publicity'. Instead of the three weeks Sheila had planned to spend in New York she had to do a return trip to London – by commercial airliner – to be presented at a *Daily Mail* race reception to the Duke of Edinburgh and to receive her £1000 first prize for a light aircraft piloted by a woman. She was not to be late, Lana warned in the message book: 'Prince Philip has another engagement that evening so they want to lose no time in getting on with the ceremony.'

Then it was back to New York and off for the next, unsponsored, run of records. By the end of May Sheila had clocked up half a dozen more records between New York, Goose Bay in Canada, Reykjavik, Copenhagen, Prestwick and London. She was planning to start the round of South African records at the end of June, and had already received £2000 of Whitbread's £5000 sponsorship, when it was decided – after discussions about the possible weather conditions – that this should be postponed until September.

In June, Sheila was invited to be the first person to land at

Lympne after it was rechristened Ashford Airport – a change prompted by the problems caused by the spelling of the name. Lympne, which had been requisitioned for the government in 1919, had recently been acquired by Eric Rylands for Coachair Services, the firm which employed Elizabeth Overbury. Its fiftieth anniversary as an airfield seemed a suitable time to rechristen it. 'Americans used to say: "If you can pronounce it, you can't spell it, and if you can spell it, you can't pronounce it,"' explained Eric Rylands, who had known Sheila throughout her flying life. Edward Heath, Conservative leader in opposition, was invited to conduct the ceremony, to which he brought considerable pomp and publicity. Sheila was then supposed to land with a flourish of even more publicity.

It was an exceedingly windy day. Sheila, elegant in flared white trousers, wore a wide-brimmed hat which incorporated a scarf so that the wind would not be able to ruffle her hair as she taxied into sight and came to a stop in front of a cheering crowd. She had in fact come only a few hundred yards along the ground: because of the strong cross wind the engineers had pushed her aircraft to the end of the runway, out of sight behind a clump of trees, during what Eric Rylands termed 'the hoo-haa with Heath'. It was nevertheless considered justifiable, in the interests of historical and mutually beneficial publicity, to pretend that she had indeed been the first person to land at the newly named Ashford Airport.

During the next few months Sheila felt that she was flying through an everlasting summer, and that it would go on forever – although the flying was inevitably interrupted for pressing social and professional engagements on the ground. But she was for once on a relatively long-term high, and thought – and hoped – that her life was moving ahead positively and according to plan. For several weeks, as she planned her second South African trip, she remained happy, busy and optimistic about the future.

Shortly before her departure to South Africa, Sheila was interviewed by a journalist called Gordon Winter who promised that his article would be syndicated throughout the world. She had no reason to suspect an ulterior motive, although when Winter hinted at a secret mission in which she might be involved in South Africa she was both intrigued and alarmed.

Gordon Winter's career as a journalist had started when he emigrated to South Africa after serving a twenty-one-month prison

(Inset) Sheila's mother, *née* Edyth Kenward

Studio portrait of Sheila as a teenager

Sheila as a VAD, with Peter Korda, 1944

Sheila and Major Rupert Bellamy: wedding photograph

Shakespeare in repertory at
Windsor

First publicity still as an
actress

Sheila's first aircraft, Thruxton Jackaroo, *Myth*

Sheila and *Myth*

Sheila with the Brantly
helicopter with which she
gained her helicopter licence
in America

In front of statue of pioneer
aviators Alcock and Brown,
at London Airport, before
taking off on 1966 round the
world

GREAT SCOTT

LOOK WHAT LANDED AT THE MIRROR!

(Above) After Sheila's 1966 world flight *Myth Too* was suspended in front of the *Daily Mirror* building

With Sir Alan Cobham on arrival at London Airport after 1966 round the world flight

(Above) Sheila with Norman
Lonsdale

(Below) Sheila and Dr Edward
(Teddy) Sugden

Sheila and Mr William Piper,
of Piper Aircraft Corporation;
Kennedy International
Airport, New York, June 1966

Kaye and Archie Maclean,
anonymous benefactors

With General James Doolittle and Lowell Thomas, Adventurers Club Dinner, New York, October 1967

Presentation by H.R.H. Prince Philip of Guild of Air Pilots and Navigators' silver Award of Merit at the Mansion House, London, November 1966

Celebrating London–Cape Town and Cape Town–London records with sponsor Ken Wood at London Airport, 196

Champagne on the tarmac wi the Fleet Air Arm after breaking the sound barrier in the Navy's Hunter jet

Arrival in Toronto, October 1967, after breaking London–Canada records

With Princess Alexandra during British Week in Toronto, October 1967

Myth Too, Piper Comanche

Testing arctic clothing before flight over North Pole

Portrait of Sheila by June Mendoza

Sheila and Chief Engineer Les Baston with *Mythre* at CSE

1972 Biggin Hill Air Show, before take-off across the Atlantic; members of the Girls' Venture behind Sheila and Alex Torrance of British Caledonian Airways, who have spread a chart out on the bonnet of the car which had just been presented to Sheila

Piper Comanche *Myth Too* and Piper Aztec *Mythre* in the air

Flood damage in *Mythre's* cockpit

Pre-flight publicity pose: Sheila liked to see herself as a later day Amelia Earhart or Amy Johnson.

sentence for burglary in England. He had been thrown out of South Africa ostensibly because of his sympathies for the black majority and the subversive white liberal minority; but his journalistic activities, both there and in London, were in fact a cover for his role of police informer, and his deportation had been a ruse to enable him to expand his work as a spy for the South African intelligence service, BOSS. With ruthless self-interest, he had exploited the goodwill of those he had apparently befriended in South Africa and London. His ability to inspire trust in his victims was extraordinary. In 1969 he infiltrated a plot to rescue Nelson Mandela from the island jail where he had been imprisoned since 1962, and was appointed leader of the London end of the plans. The instigator from the South African end was a man called Gordon Bruce, who for the purposes of the plot called himself alternately Henry Morgan and Charles Metterlink; he had, according to Winter, been on Pretoria's political files for some time as a member of the South African Progressive Party.

Sheila had met Gordon Bruce in South Africa in 1967. He had, he told Winter, liked her, and felt that her attitude towards apartheid was such that she might be persuaded to take part in the Mandela rescue. 'She is a wonderful woman whose heart is in the right place,' Morgan said, according to Winter's later account. 'But don't rush her – she might be nervous.'

Sheila, of course, knew none of this when Winter interviewed her for his syndicated press article. He left her flat feeling confident that she would cooperate, and although he revealed nothing else he told her that she would be contacted in South Africa. His superiors in BOSS were delighted, as were his ostensible collaborators. Both appreciated the international publicity that could be gained through the involvement of someone as well known as Sheila. The idea was that she would meet Mandela on a remote landing strip on the Cape after he had been enabled to escape from Robben Island. The genuine rescuers assumed that she would then fly him out of South Africa, and that everyone concerned would be bathed in a righteous glow of international approval; the fact that Sheila would never be able to enter South Africa again, and would be in considerable danger, did not enter their calculations.

As Winter later revealed, General van den Bergh, the head of BOSS, saw it rather differently; he appointed a warder on Robben Island to liaise with Winter so that the first part of the plan would go without a hitch. Mandela would be shot – thus solving the problem of what to do with him – during a dramatic recapture as he was about to board Sheila's plane. Sheila would then be taken to court in a massive show trial; her safety up to that point would be ensured; but afterwards it might well have been a different matter, depending on her attitude at the trial and the public reaction to it.

For once, there seemed to be remarkably few snags during Sheila's pre-flight preparations. Instead of feeling cheered by this, she was alarmed. Gordon Winter's whispered hint of conspiracy had cast a shadow.

'The blonde actress is oddly worried,' her press officer, Robert Snoxell, revealed. '*Myth Too* is flying too well.' After a final test flight from *Myth*'s base at CSE Oxford, Sheila explained: 'Usually there's a snag of some sort which we overcome at the last minute. This time, although the weather was bad, *Myth Too* behaved perfectly and landed like a dream. I suppose I'm just superstitious, but it worries me a bit.'

But there was after all a final snag the next day to reassure her. Sheila was already at London Airport when her carefully laid plans to make her first stop in Benghazi – where she had been promised a camp bed at the airport, ground assistance with paperwork and refuelling, sandwiches and fresh coffee – had to be aborted because of a Libyan coup. After an hour's delay she took off instead for Malta, serenaded by two buglers from the Royal Marines School of Music: they played a 'Salute to Sheila Scott' composed in her honour and the Fleet Air Arm's 'scramble' call.

'Sandwiches wrong temperature,' a BUA radio operator reported to Lana when she relayed a message after Sheila's arrival in Malta. 'Chaos at Malta,' Sheila told Lana, 'except for RAF PRO who spent all night sorting things out and trying for Khartoum but very late & without com with Libya'. She was beginning to think that she would have to abort her second African flight for much the same reasons as she had had to make a second start on her first.

As it happened, the problems were sorted out in time for her to take off for Khartoum the following day. From there she sent Lana another message, via BOAC, with the comment that it was 'not for publication': 'Thank heavens I am in Sudan and what a difference from last night everything beautifully arranged and will even get some sleep. All quiet when I flew over Benghazi. I wish I had gone there. Taking off around 1 hours Nairobi. Love and thanks to all.'

Forty-eight hours after leaving London she arrived in Nairobi, having established another record.

From there she participated a week later, with more enjoyment than success, in a two-day East African Safari, with a co-pilot on crutches. The caption under a press photo of the two of them in front of *Myth Too* reported that 'Alan Coulson . . . continued the race, although injured in an (non-aircraft) accident at Malindi'.

A fortnight after her arrival in Nairobi Sheila added yet another record to her collection, from Nairobi to Cape Town. Her time in South Africa had been planned well in advance, with several guest of honour appearances, a visit to a game reserve, a trip down a gold mine and to see a native war dance, and a guest cottage at her disposal in Johannesburg.

When she went to her hotel room in Cape Town to change before a reception, she found a letter from Gordon Bruce on a chair. She tore it up and flushed it down the toilet. It was followed in Johannesburg by several telephone calls from men with South African accents. Their conversations were monitored, as were all her telephone calls and movements while she was in South Africa. By this time she clearly had some idea of what the secret rescue involved, as she apparently told Bruce that she was having second thoughts about getting involved in something so dangerous, and felt that her liberty was at stake. 'I must be honest with you and explain that flying means everything to me, and I can't really risk involvement in anything that might jeopardize that,' she is claimed to have said.

According to Bruce's report to Winter, she nevertheless promised to think about it until she returned to London; Winter would then contact her. She did indeed think about it, and the more she thought about it, the more frightened she became. All her old, long-forgotten nightmares of being watched and followed returned. Although she was not then aware that she was indeed under constant surveillance by BOSS, she was sure that someone was keeping uncomfortably close tabs on her. South Africa seemed suddenly to have changed from the sunny, friendly, welcoming country she had loved to a place full of menace and dark shadows in which 'they' were lurking.

She telephoned Norman Lonsdale, who only half believed her story. 'I don't like the sound of it,' he told her. 'There's something wrong. Keep out of it.' This conversation too was monitored, and reported by General van den Bergh to Gordon Winter: 'I forecast that Miss Scott will withdraw,' he told him. 'I base this on a monitored conversation she had by telephone with a man in Britain who apparently helps finance her flights.' Winter was ordered to keep away from her, and so never contacted her again.

Sheila was aware that she had become unwittingly and unwillingly implicated, in however small a way, in something dangerous, although she did not know exactly what. The suspense of not knowing whether she was still considered to be an accomplice, or whether her involvement was known to anyone else, preyed on her mind. ' "They" are after me,' she said to Norman more and more frequently after her return to England. He dismissed this as 'just Sheila being Sheila,' as did anyone else to whom she voiced her fears.

It is a measure of the seriousness that she herself attached to the episode – which anyone else might have been able to treat more lightly – that she did not mention it to any of her South African friends. It gave a focus to her paranoia, from which she was afterwards never able to escape.

11

SHEILA HAD TWO and a half months after her return from South Africa to prepare for a race which she called the biggest thing in air racing history for thirty-seven years: the first race from England to Australia since 1932. It was to start just before Christmas and finish in the New Year.

The search for sponsors was on again: the money she earned from lecturing was rarely more than £100 a week, and her company was still on the verge of insolvency. Almost everything she needed for the Australia race and for her subsequent continuation round the world was either lent or donated. Her eventual list of sponsors in kind included nearly fifty names, from Tupperware – which provided a leak-proof plastic container into which she managed somehow, with considerable agility, to urinate in flight: one of her favourite anecdotes was about the time it was whisked away and filled with sandwiches – to various suppliers of navigational equipment. The only thing missing was money; at almost the last minute Geoffrey Edwards, a friend who had made a fortune as an arms dealer in Saudi Arabia, came to her rescue with a loan of £4000.

It was on the fashion angle that her pre-flight publicity concentrated. Sheila was reported to be 'battling against time . . . her capsule wardrobe (designed by Sheila herself) sharing blame with flight planning for keeping her up late'. For a few weeks Angus Stewart of the International Wool Secretariat and Sheila were thrown together while they worked on the all-wool outfits donated by the IWS. He found her reliable and straightforward, but 'intensely private, with a whole series of nettings about her': 'flying was back in the egg, her refuge. She had a lot of doubt in herself, so she took up a lot of time . . . you always knew she was isolated. . . . Success is very expensive, and she was caught in the web of her own fame.'

As far as her clothes were concerned, Sheila knew exactly what she wanted, and why, choosing styles and colours – violet, mustard and yellow – for maximum impact in black and white press photographs and resisting the image of gentility which others wanted to create for her. Her ideas were eminently practical; the inability of dressmakers to understand them caused her intense frustration: 'We'll make the clothes this way, Miss Scott' – 'But then I won't be able to get into them in the cockpit.' She put together a folder of sketches, apparently with the intention of marketing her designs under the trade name of 'Plane and Pretty', with accompanying capsule luggage and an organizer diary almost identical to the filofaxes which appeared on the market nearly twenty years later.

As 'Britain's only honorary Naval Airwoman' Sheila was again adopted by the Royal Navy as its unofficial race entrant. The Fleet Air Arm headquarters at Lee-on-Solent and the Naval Air Station at Yeovilton sent her good luck messages. The frigate HMS *Nubian* once again promised to keep watch for her in the Persian Gulf area, the Commander of the Far East Fleet in Singapore was to lay on a special reception, and the Navy in general would keep in touch with her and cheer her on all the way. 'This is a great honour. . . ,' she responded, '. . . even if I cannot pull off the win, I am determined to do well for the Navy.'

She was one of only four women to enter the race, in which there were only two other solo entrants, both men; the rest were all flying in crews of two or three, and could therefore share the chores both in the air and on the ground. Sheila knew that exhaustion was likely to be her greatest handicap; it undoubtedly contributed to the problems she encountered and the navigational errors she made during the race.

It started badly for her: she was running late, because of a last-minute hair appointment. This antagonized the press and almost caused her to miss her take-off time at Gatwick, where she caused a rumpus at the final briefing and wanted the start postponed because one of her navigational aids was not working. 'How do you expect me to start an air race without ADF?' she asked John Blake angrily. It was not the first time she had voiced complaints at a race briefing; as usual, the attitude taken was 'Shut up, Sheila, and get on with the race,' although not in so many words.

Several aircraft were forced out of the race, and there were two fatalities during the first leg, which was beset by alternating snow and thunderstorms. Two of the RAF Red Arrows aerobatic team, Terry Kingsley and Pete Evans, were competing in a Machetti, accompanied by civilian pilot Arthur Gibson, owner and managing director of an advertising agency and a keen aviation cameraman – he went 'for the hell of it and to film'. They realized they were out of the running after losing time in a storm over Italy, but decided to carry on for fun and to try to finish within the time limit.

Within the first few hours, Sheila's autopilot and avionics were out of action. 'There had', she claimed, 'to be something extremely odd for so many things to be wrong on a perfect aircraft.' In addition to her technical problems, she felt that there was an atmosphere of ill-will towards her over the radio from some of the other competitors.

After Athens, the first compulsory stopping point, the snow and thunderstorms gave way to intense, shimmering, hazy heat. Sheila stripped off her woollen long johns and shoved them behind her seat. On the way to the second control point, at Karachi, the race was gradually sorting itself out; the first few to land would have an inevitable advantage. Sheila monopolized the control tower with questions while she circled. The competitors waiting impatiently for their turn to land were irritated because she appeared to be 'using the control tower as if it was her own personal PR'. Eventually the captain of an official Australian entry lost his temper: 'Aw, shut up you Pommy bitch!' he burst out over the radio.

When she landed, Sheila found to her surprise that hers was only the second aircraft to check in. In her single-minded dedication to her own cause, she was convinced that some of the other competitors were deliberately trying to make her lose the advantage she had gained by blocking her way in the queue to refuel. On the ground, even more than in the air, she felt the extra strain of being a solo competitor.

The publicity which she had so eagerly courted rebounded on her at every refuelling stop, when all she wanted to do was make a quick turn-round and grab some food and sleep; but everywhere there were reporters eager to talk to her, as she was considered the star entrant, whether she felt up to it or not. Everyone was under pressure, and many of the others resented the preferential treatment which Sheila received from the press. She was aware of the resentment, and began to feel that the forces of evil, in human form, were plotting against her.

In Singapore she claimed that someone had cut her aerial, and in spite of the support she received from the Navy she was again convinced that she was being deliberately obstructed. She showed her irritation, and such details were relayed and magnified. A rumour that she had either lost her money in Singapore, or that it had been stolen, and that she had therefore asked someone for a loan, reached Australia as a story that she had demanded £10,000 in cash from the Singapore Aero Club. She had as usual told reporters about her financial problems, and her need to earn £10,000 a year to support herself and *Myth*.

When she left Singapore, she was still well in the running for a fast time to Darwin. The women's prize would automatically be hers provided she finished in the allotted time – and of that there seemed little doubt. She almost dared to feel confident that she might both win another prize, and beat the England–Australia women's record of just under six days set in 1936 by Jean Batten.

Then she found herself again without communications, in thick cloud. Her throat was too dry to eat her sandwiches and bananas, and when she tried to drink coffee it splashed over her face and hair. The glucose tablets she chewed for energy tasted unpleasantly sickly and powdery, and made her throat even drier.

As she thought about the advice she had been given about how to avoid possible thunderstorms over Timor, she no longer knew whether it was Timor, or perhaps Sumba, or somewhere else, ahead of her under the blackest part of a storm. It is difficult enough in any conditions to spread large maps out in a tiny cockpit – almost impossible with one hand when the aircraft is bucking about and the autopilot is not working. Amy Johnson and Jean Batten had not had autopilot, Sheila reminded herself. She was only a few hours from Darwin, and the record: 'There has to be a way,' she said aloud. She had been flying for the best part of three days without sleep, but she felt less tired than desperate, annoyed and removed from herself, almost as if she was listening to and watching someone else.

Her instinct told her to fly low, but the cloud forced her too low, with virtually no forward visibility as the rain beat against the cockpit. She put on her life jacket and clutched her Sarbe beacon, which would bleep for two days if she ditched. The possibility of death was so real that it seemed both inevitable and right that she and *Myth* should meet it together. 'We've tried, and we've failed,' she told *Myth*, 'but at least we've tried, and that matters most.'

She was lost. Later, she attempted to record her feelings as she waited to die and assessed her life. Her mind dwelt first on the unhappiness of the last few days, in which ruthless and malicious competition had apparently destroyed the camaraderie of air racing, and on the loneliness of her life on the ground. She felt that she had become for most people no more than a name, and had been robbed by her fame of the right to normal personal feelings.

Then, banishing self-pity, she reflected that she had experienced more than most, and remembered 'the incredible and beautiful times in the air', the spontaneous gestures of goodwill from strangers in the street, the friendship of Kaye Maclean and Elizabeth Overbury, the unstinting practical support of the engineers at CSE and BUA, the last-minute help with finance from Geoffrey Edwards. She told herself that they believed in her, and that she could not give up without letting these people down. Most of all, she felt that she had a duty to *Myth* to survive.

She forced herself to sit up straight and relax, peering blindly over the sea. Her only relief from the stiffness which made her entire body ache was to do minute isometric exercises, and to vary her position from time to time with a small cushion. Her brain felt unnaturally clear and alert, and she was aware of the mingled smells of her leather seat and of over-ripe bananas; she was convinced that she was thinking faster and more clearly than ever, with an unusually vivid sense of her own identity and of the potential of the human mind.

Then she started to hear inexplicable voices and electrical crackling over the radio; she thought, but could not be sure, that first a woman, and then two men, were talking to and about her, and that someone was trying to guide her with a series of messages in Morse. She tried in vain to make radio contact; her slow, laborious Morse was more successful, although she could make little sense of the replies. There was an atmosphere of unreality and an increasing sensation of electrical energy in the aircraft; Sheila was convinced that she was being led as she followed the course indicated by 'a mysterious signal' on her radio compass.

She heard the woman's voice only twice: 'Sheila, you must pray before you die,' and then: 'Oh, do be careful, Sheila. Keep still,' when she was circling in an attempt to climb above a cloud. Rejecting the possibility that she was hallucinating, she decided that she was having a genuinely mystical experience.

She was not sure whether to consider the later snatches of conversation as another example of something extra-sensory, or whether she was really hearing the voices of two men.

'You don't think you are going to get her out of that?'

'I don't care, I still want to find her.'

The men discussed various headings. Sheila signalled frantically in Morse, but received no reply.

Then there was silence for a while. She was still following the mysterious radio compass signal, flying low under a thunderstorm, when she heard more conversation.

'She seems to be in a coma.'

'That's the way I want her, nice and easy, relaxed.'

'It's a great situation. There's a huge Cu Nim [cumulo-nimbus cloud] sitting at the side of her.'

Then, ahead of her through the storm, she caught a glimpse of a long, low shape on the horizon. 'Ship or island?' she signalled in Morse.

'Ship.'

She thought about ditching beside it; but it was not a ship – it was an island, one of a group stretching one behind the other, but none big enough to land on. She circled each one, looking longingly at palm trees, and eventually sighted a beach on which she thought she might be able to put *Myth* down. As she flew backwards and forwards trying to judge her approach, she saw what she thought were rocks. When she realized that they were sharks, terror of being eaten alive overwhelmed her and she rejected the beach as a landing place.

'Can you save her?' she heard over the radio.

'We don't know yet.'

'Is it the Navy?' she asked in Morse.

'Let her think it is.'

'She was dedicated to flying, and now she has given her life for it. This was the last photograph of her with her secretary in London before the race take-off.'

'I am not dead yet,' Sheila protested uselessly. 'There are two hours to go. I am alive and can hear you. This cannot be death if I can hear you.'

Then the same man's voice said that Sheila Scott was battling for her life. It must, she thought, be some reporter filing two stories to cover all eventualities.

She was almost out of fuel, and could still see nowhere to land, but made a last, desperate attempt at Morse: she did not want to disappear without trace, as Amelia Earhart had done in the Pacific.

Five minutes later, to her relief – although she was sure she was beyond saving – she heard her message read back, with the remaining fuel time.

'We could save her,' someone said.

But Sheila was sure that she was about to die; she hoped that she would have the dignity not to scream like an animal in pain. Drowning was, she had been told, a pleasant sensation – but what about the last moments of waiting while the aircraft filled with water and sank, or as she lay injured in the dinghy? Would the sharks get her first? If they did, she knew she could not remain dignified, but would certainly scream out in terror.

A gleam of light diverted her attention from the horror of death by shark. Sun on the water, she told herself. Or a mirage of hope. No – it was land. The cloud had lifted enough to reveal a sheer volcanic mountain. Not much hope there, but she turned towards it – to find that beneath the mountain there were flat, sodden paddyfields.

'*Myth*, we may get a bit hurt, but we won't drown and we won't be eaten by sharks,' she said aloud. Paddyfields meant people, and people meant life. Then, better still, like a miracle she saw first another aircraft, and then 'the most comforting, beautiful, long piece of ordinary concrete' – a runway.

'Sheila, air race number 99 okay, runway in sight,' she signalled in Morse.

At first, after she had landed and taxied off the runway into long grass, the airfield was deserted and silent. She struggled out of her lifebelt, but was too weak and exhausted to make any further movement. Then she and *Myth* were surrounded by men in uniform, who dragged her roughly from the aircraft. She had, she discovered, landed on an Indonesian military airfield outside Makassar. The light which had caught her eye and saved her life had been the rotating beacon on an aircraft which had been waiting for the usual bad weather of the afternoon to lift.

For once, she was past caring about her appearance during the inevitable questions and explanations. *Myth* was brought to the apron to be kept under surveillance. This involved a long procession of villagers who treated the unexpected entertainment as a fiesta. Gradually Sheila began to recover, although not enough to enter into any festive spirit. A message was sent to the race organizers to say that she had landed safely, although she was told that no other communication was possible except from the town, an hour's drive away.

She spent the night at the house of the commandant, whose wife spoke fluent English. Although she had had virtually no sleep for nearly three days, was running a temperature and felt as if she had been drugged, even in her dazed state the race was still uppermost in her mind. Now that she knew where she was, she was determined to continue as soon as possible: Darwin was only eight hours away, and the coveted record could still be hers, she calculated as she fell asleep. By the time she woke, feeling ill and her face puffy from insect bites, daylight was streaming through the window and her planned early start had been missed.

Myth stood forlornly in torrential rain, with stray dogs nibbling at her tyres: a telex later sent by Sheila mentioning this was garbled so that it was widely reported in the press that frogs were eating the tyres. She felt that this made her look ridiculous.

That evening she talked for hours to two American missionaries, who berated her about her suicidal foolhardiness in wishing to continue without having her faulty equipment repaired; she could hardly expect a second miracle, they pointed out. After questioning her about the strange events of the previous day's flight, they told her that her over-tired brain had rebelled and caused aural hallucinations: she could not believe it was that simple.

Next day, tearful and with a headache, she succumbed to their efforts to organize spares and was reminded that it was nearly Christmas. She wrote a long letter to Lana, which was to be shown 'if anything else happens' to Teddy, Elizabeth, Les Baston (the chief engineer at CSE: Sheila considered him one of her greatest friends and supporters) 'and/or whoever you think fit'.

The people here are so very kind to me, and perhaps I have been given this respite to show me there are really kind people still (the unkind remarks in the air from one or two pilot crews was unbelievable . . .) I have never known pilots do such dreadful things – I still cannot believe I was flying in a race – international sport. The people at every stop were wonderful to me though. I was desperately trying to break the record to Darwin in less than 3 days, and would have made it, but there is something dreadfully wrong with *Myth*. . . . I am desperately afraid she was nobbled.

The letter continued with details of her problems after leaving Singapore:

After several hours I was lost and at one time believe I was about 4 hours from Australia. . . . I think I must have become only semi-conscious because the last two hours in the sky I kept hearing voices. . . .

Then everything became very strange . . . voices seemed to come through the aircraft electrics – I still do not know if this was real or delusions. . . . Please do not think I am crazy – perhaps it was all telepathy or the strange things I have found before in the air. . . . Perhaps they were trying to stop me being frightened, before I died. Please find out if these really were people to do with the race. Thank them and say they helped. They sounded very wonderful people.

I also want Les Baston to know *I know* that there was nothing wrong with *Myth Too*. Someone must have chopped the aerial down to 70ft and put the drogue back on – that cannot be accident – and how could it be the long distance things only that were wrong at first? They must also have tugged at all the wires under the panel and loosened everything. How else could things just fall apart? This all too obviously led to short circuiting. . . .

You all know what I believe in (although I hope it won't be sharks and it will be quick if I do not make it) and flying gave me the only real happiness lately. Lana and Elizabeth, Teddy and the boys in the hangar also did, but most of the ground most of the time was unbelievably lonely for many years, and some people very strange and non understanding. I felt such a failure particularly as I was given such great chances to succeed but always seemed to lose them. Life could have been so happy all the time but there was no one to advise me, and I always made mistakes about people and things, and yet my intuition is good. . . .

Bless you all who tried to help me and *Myth*. . . . I still think it's better to write this letter to you all so no one (those that surround me) can feel it was their fault – although I am afraid some unthinking stranger may have done something. Certainly the aircraft was never in this condition after it had been prepared as I flew it myself. I wish there were an answer – but there is no other answer is there? . . . There is torrential rain now, but I cannot think what else to do except try and fly on in the race, and at least finish what we aimed to do – arrive there! After all I chose this life, and still did not want to retire from it. . . .

My love to you all whatever happens. Sheila and *Myth*.

The use of the telex system which had been banned on her arrival was eventually offered to her, with as much cooperation as she could have wished for as telex followed telex. There was even, to her delight, a telephone call from the editor of the *Daily Mail*: one of his reporters had, he told her, worked with British United Airways for three days to track her down.

An Indonesian Air Force radio engineer gave up some of his Christmas leave and managed to get Sheila's VHF set working. She was preparing to take off for Australia at last when a telex arrived from the Red Arrows team offering to reroute to give her an escort to Darwin. Sheila accepted enthusiastically, and added an optimistic PS to her letter to Lana.

Arthur Gibson and the Red Arrows had been told in Singapore that Sheila was having trouble with her avionics, and had decided that as they were in any case already out of the running they would go to her assistance. Later in the day they arrived in Makassar. At supper that night, they were served what looked like huge fried lobsters.

'We're in enough trouble as it is without inviting dysentery,' Arthur remarked.

'It would be insulting to the people who've looked after me so well to refuse,' Sheila whispered to him.

It was Christmas Eve; they briefed for a take-off in the morning. Sheila's Comanche had double the endurance of the men's faster Machetti, so they would have to land on Timor to refuel before attempting to approach Darwin.

In London, Lana Jeffers was summoned that day by the BBC to Bush House to be interviewed about Sheila's disappearance. She was so obviously nervous that she was given a large tumbler of whisky to calm her nerves, but the only thing she could think of was that Sheila had told her to mention the International Wool Secretariat on every possible occasion – which she proceeded to do. Outside the glass wall of the studio she could see the producer frantically signalling 'No!' to her.

On Christmas morning in Indonesia, the two aircraft were given a grand send-off at dawn by all Sheila's new-found friends. She had rarely flown in formation, and only in good conditions while she was being filmed. Her eyes watered in the bright early morning sun as she concentrated on keeping the Machetti in sight. It was not long before the clear skies once again gave way to thick wet murk. They flew only thirty feet above the sea; spray leaped up to meet them and ragged patches of mist merged with the waves.

They should have been able to pick up a radio beacon on Timor, which was shrouded in fog; when they failed to do so, both the men and Sheila realized, as Arthur Gibson put it, that they were in serious trouble. They could not, as they had flight-planned to do, land at Kupang, on Timor; Sheila still had enough fuel to continue, but the men needed to refuel the Machetti. Although they were impressed with the way she had kept up with them, they felt that they would all have a better chance if they separated. Sheila could hardly make out their final message over her radio, which was again playing up, but had also come to the conclusion that they would have to fend for themselves: in better weather, she would have enjoyed the high-speed low-level formation flying.

As Sheila turned west away from the Machetti, she fought to keep control of *Myth* in the violent turbulence around thunderstorms. She attempted to look for the other aircraft, which she knew would soon be out of fuel; but although she flew frantically backwards and forwards there was no sign of anyone or anything – only a jagged coastline, with a few scattered palm trees, and the angry swell of the sea. She turned south and climbed, away from the land.

At last, after struggling with worse conditions than she had ever known as she edged round to the northern side of Flores, she landed on Sumbawa's long grass runway. By then she had convinced herself that the Red Arrows must have ditched. Incoherently, sobbing as she spoke, she tried to explain that it was an emergency, that her friends were missing, that they had probably been killed. But there were no telephones or telex system in Sumbawa, where the only communication was by Morse – and even that worked only when the weather allowed. The Indonesians refused to be infected by her panic; if she had landed safely, they said, then surely her friends must have been able to do so too.

Nevertheless they agreed to send a Morse message. It was several hours before the reply came that everything possible was being done to find the Red Arrows team. Sheila spent the evening with the only European in the area, a seventy-year-old German doctor with an Indonesian wife, and the night at the local resthouse, a dingy hut which offered neither comfort nor privacy. Although she was too ill and miserable to eat, she recorded her feelings, blaming herself for the fact that all three men might be dead because they had escorted her: 'I feel utterly helpless, and more shocked than I've ever felt in my life.' On any other occasion she would have appreciated the romance of the tropical night. It was still Christmas Day, but there was nothing to celebrate. Her towel smelt, and she had only two packets of cigarettes left.

The only ray of comfort next morning was a visiting card from the Air Vice Marshal of the Indonesian Air Force, who wished her 'Happy Landings' and promised that fuel would be sent. Then 'Your friends are safe in Australia,' she was told. They had landed on a beach, where the local people had provided them with fuel, and their subsequent safe arrival in Darwin had been reported in a radio news bulletin. Sheila felt weak with relief, although she was sure that everyone around her wanted to say: 'I told you so.'

It was with a 'glorious sense of freedom' that she at last took off for Bali, leaving behind her a 'black cage of clouds and emotions'. In a new modern hotel in Bali she was given bacon and eggs – her own choice – and a dessert full of raisins and currants with a candle stuck in it to make up for having missed her traditional Christmas pudding. She treated the normal mod cons of the hotel with the excitement of a child with a new toy, turning switches and knobs on and off, and soaking in a long, scented bath. The greatest luxury of all was to be able to chain smoke without risking running out of cigarettes.

When she arrived at last in Darwin next day she felt happy and excited, until at a press conference she had to face questions which she construed as accusations that she had deserted the other aircraft, and that neither she nor *Myth Too* was fit for the race. She was appalled at what she considered the unfairness of the attack. The chairman of the Aero Club restored her confidence in Australia by staying up late to change her oil and plugs, but Sheila had seemed so apprehensive that a message was sent from Darwin to Peter Lloyd, the Australian race chairman: 'Request it imperative you meet her on Aerodrome upon arrival Adelaide, as fears for safety of aircraft and safety of her life.' Although Sheila had been careful not to use the word sabotage, she had made it clear that this was what she suspected – and if she was right, every precaution had to be taken. She was still the star of the race, in spite of the difficulties which had prevented her from being one of its leaders, and if anything happened to her in Australia it would rebound on the race organizers.

On the way next morning to Alice Springs, the last compulsory stop before Adelaide, Sheila encountered a new problem: the dial which should have registered manifold pressure was not working, although there seemed to be nothing wrong with the engine. At Alice Springs a break – or rather, according to Sheila, a clean cut – was found in the manifold pressure pipe leading to the dial.

Sheila became even more convinced that she was the victim of a plot when at Alice Springs she received a message from Peter Lloyd: 'Have message will meet you on airfield in DCA [Department of Civil Aviation] yellow vehicle with Snook. Your plane will be secure in hangar. Police in attendance don't fear for your life glad you are nearly here.'

As he later explained in a letter, he had endorsed 'near as possible exclusive use of hangar for the safe custody of *Myth Too*'. He had also suggested, as her arrival would inevitably lead to large crowds, 'that a request for additional Police be made with particular protection for your own person, in view of the extraordinary statements being published world-wide claiming sabotage to your aeroplane and allegedly attributed to you'.

In Adelaide, Sheila was ordered to stay on the runway until the official car arrived, an instruction which she considered 'very odd'. A large plain-clothes policeman wedged himself in the door of the aircraft; Beverley Snook and Peter Lloyd sat on the wings, as she was escorted off the runway by several cars. She was then, as Snook put it, 'bundled off, for her own safety and peace of mind'. It was not at all the way she had wanted to arrive, although he thought it was 'all a bit of a laugh'.

During the following press conference Sheila felt that she was again under attack.

'Is it true that you believe your aircraft was sabotaged?' she was asked.

'I personally did not use the word sabotage,' she replied. 'I had a very good and very well-equipped aircraft, which had flown all over the world many times, and which had been a hundred per cent perfect on test flight.'

'Is it true that you asked for police protection?'

'I did not ask for police protection. I don't know who did, or why, but I certainly did not want it.'

'Is it true that you deliberately gave up the race four hours out of Darwin, because you could not win it?'

'In fact I was doing well in the race up to that time.'

'Did you not think that you could cash in on the publicity by coming in at the last moment?'

'No.'

'Why did you enter the race if you did not expect adventure? . . . Was it not irresponsible to enter the race in an aircraft which was not properly equipped?'

There were many friendlier questions, but Sheila was left with the impression that, whatever she said, she would be misquoted.

In his efforts to straighten out the muddle, Peter Lloyd explained both to her and to the press why she had been given police protection on arrival in Adelaide. 'In answer to a number of press enquiries about you and statements allegedly to have been made about you, I told the *Adelaide News* of the . . . arrangements . . . including your message as told to me supposedly from you in Darwin,' he wrote, 'and added that, as you were one of the greatest living English women fliers, I was determined that you would receive every possible consideration and courtesy and be accorded the best in Australian hospitality, but that I did not agree that you had chosen the most prudent route which is purely a matter of opinion.'

Although he finished his letter by urging her to 'relax and enjoy yourself, fly brilliantly and safely to Sydney and take out the Ford Prize of $5000 which everyone is hoping to see you win', the rift between them was never fully breached. 'Like you, I too have been subject to a good deal of pressure from the press,' he pointed out, 'and a great deal of personal concern about your safety. . . .'

The suspicions of sabotage were never investigated: to most people, they seemed too far-fetched to be believable. 'We all knew Sheila lived in a world of her own,' John Blake told me, 'although she was never out to be boss or push herself. Although she was always blaming the equipment, and implying that someone else was to blame for it being faulty, she did not do this on purpose. She merely said the first thing that came into her head because she was so tense, and would burst out with her woes to the press.' That she had equipment failures on the Australia race cannot however be denied; many of her problems were traced to technical failures which could occur on any aircraft, particularly in such adverse and strenuous conditions; others can almost certainly be attributed to pilot error through exhaustion.

The second part of the race, from Adelaide to Sydney, started on 2 January. To Sheila's delight, *Myth Too* was performing beautifully. She immediately overtook two other Comanches, and then saw no one until several aircraft converged above Griffith, which was a compulsory stop. The weather was again bad, with torrential rain which forced the controller to close the airport while several aircraft were still circling. Those with enough fuel – including Sheila – were diverted to Narrandera, thirty miles to the south. Once again there was confusion in the press reports: Sheila was said to have force landed at Narrandera.

Although later it was possible for the diverted aircraft to reach Griffith, the weather continued to be so bad that they were then marooned there for two days. Sheila spent most of the time in bed. Griffith was a small town, but she had nothing but praise for the way it coped with its unexpected guests – only to be reported as having said that it was 'a bum town': no doubt another misinterpretation, but one which did nothing for her reputation in Australia, and which she again considered part of a conspiracy to blacken her name. 'It was all so untrue and petty that I should have been able to laugh if off,' she admitted; but she was so far beyond laughing that she considered suicide.

She took off from Griffith in tears. Her competitive instinct, never dormant for long, reasserted herself in the air. By the time she landed in Sydney her depression had vanished, and so had the cloud of criticism which had hung over her since she had landed in Australia. She handled the subsequent interviews with aplomb, and did not allow herself to be drawn into anger even when she was asked: 'Sydney thinks of you as a prima donna. What do you think about that?'

Nevertheless the prima donna image was difficult to discard during the rest of her time in Australia. Margaret Kentley, an Australian 99er who had flown in the race with her son, voiced her opinion that Sheila expected privileges, and even claimed that she had wanted the rules of the race bent for her. There was undoubtedly also an element of jealousy of Sheila's glamour and of the publicity she attracted, and perhaps also of the bouquets of flowers with which she was greeted. Nancy Bird Walton, Australia's most famous pioneering aviatrix and a fellow 99er, told me that Margaret had made Sheila feel so unhappy that she would not go out in Sydney: 'She so greatly resented the special treatment Sheila received along the route that she considered her a publicity seeker – which of course they all were.'

Nancy took no notice of Margaret Kentley's criticism; nor did Bryan Monkton, with whom Sheila had for several years had a relaxed and affectionate friendship. Monkton, a commercial and record-breaking pilot who had served in the Royal Australian Air Force during the war, had been astonished when he first met Sheila to discover that 'this woman who had achieved so much in a predominantly man's world could be so utterly feminine – and attractive. . . . She could cry, be jealous, even slightly catty at times – but all in a nice feminine way.' The Sheila whom Monkton knew best was, as he put it, not 'the famous aviatrix', but 'the other Sheila, the warm, feminine, caring person – a good and loyal friend'.

Sheila felt particularly in need of friends after the Australia race. Her outings with Bryan on his fifteen-ton, forty-foot cutter *Utiekah* were an idyllic escape from the pressure of publicity. It was her introduction to sailing, although she had often been to the London boat show, and according to Monkton she took to it readily, showing considerable potential nautical ability.

The Red Arrows made a good story of their part in Sheila's adventures when they returned to Britain. 'You know what job I got?' Terry Kingsley joked. 'I had to lug the bloody wigs across the sand!' In spite of the rumours that Sheila had deliberately led them astray and abandoned them to almost certain death, there was, I have been assured, no animosity towards her on their part.

12

SHEILA LEFT *Myth Too* in Australia until June before continuing on her way round the world in a relatively leisurely manner across the Pacific and America, finishing with a New York–London record attempt. 'I expect some of it will be fairly tough,' she admitted, 'but unless I give myself something to beat I don't feel I've achieved anything. All the same, I shall make it as comfortable as I can in the conditions.'

Across the Pacific she was, for once, not trying to break records, and so could relax. Even a delay of several days while a coral runway was being repaired did not upset her. She sent postcards to Kaye Maclean. Fiji was 'the most wonderful place in the world', the Fijians 'happy and very wonderful', 'the country glorious', and the people she met were 'real friends'. 'I cannot begin to tell you the peace and happiness I have found amongst the gracious & happy Fijian people. We are carrying their greatest honour – the whale's tooth. I know now the South Pacific is where I belong. It's here I could write the real book. Bless you my dear and remember you are not alone.'

She made a tape recording of the dawn ceremony during which she was presented with the Tabua, the sacred whale's tooth, by Fijian chiefs in their traditional costume. Both she and the chiefs sat cross-legged and bare-footed on woven ceremonial mats. The only modern intrusions were the proximity of the airport, and her quiet, soft question: 'Can I smoke now?'

One of her new 'real friends' was Prince William, Duke of Gloucester. She had just washed her hair one evening, and was about to have supper alone in her hotel room, when there was a knock on the door. 'The Duke of Gloucester would like you to have dinner with him tonight,' she was informed. 'I can't possibly – my hair's wet and I'm not dressed,' she protested. But the Duke's

equerry was insistent, and she gave in. The evening together was the
first of several meetings: she and the Duke, who shared a fanatical
interest in flying, had, as she put it, 'a lot of fun together'.

From Tarawa Atoll, in the Gilbert and Ellice Islands, she
enthused again by postcard: 'I have found what is for me – heaven
on earth. Complete happiness and freedom and great love from all
the South Seas people. I cannot bear to leave – I must return – here
no commercial tourism. My room looks onto a turquoise blue
lagoon with flame red sunsets, and silhouettes of palm trees.'
Honolulu was almost as idyllic, 'much of it still like 100 years ago',
but Sheila could not linger because of 'all the duty things ahead in
USA and Canada'.

In New York she was expecting to be met by the 99s. Instead an
employee of BOAC, June Eggleston, was told by her boss: 'Go down
to the hangar – there's an English woman coming in in a private
aircraft. See what you can do to help her.' 'Sheila arrived looking
immaculate,' June Eggleston told me. 'She knew how to stand and
be photographed from the best angle, and smile.' Doing what she
could to help included taking Sheila to stay in the flat she shared
with a friend. June was struck by her 'quiet undramatic courage – a
Battle of Britain type', and felt that she had 'two distinct characters:
one on stage, dramatizing, flirting with photographers; and one very
private, sitting on the floor, washing up, shopping'.

June described how when Sheila took off from New York she 'did
her bit for the cameras', and then reverted to her private character
as they walked together down the hangar. They exchanged their
'private signal' – thumb up with the right hand – as she taxied
towards the runway.

She arrived at Gatwick on 3 September, having completed what
she had set out to do – another round-the-world flight, finishing with
a new record across the Atlantic. As she arrived two hours ahead of
schedule, before the television cameras were ready, she was told:
'You'll have to go up again and make a second landing so that we
can film you.' Among the people who had met her was Sandra
Collins with her daughter Tabitha, who was by then fifteen months
old. Sheila adored her god-daughter: 'I'll take Tabitha with me,' she
said, but then realized that if she had a passenger – even such a small
one – it would be obvious that she was not being filmed as she
returned from a solo flight.

Sheila had left Lana Jeffers in charge of her affairs in London while she was away. Whenever there was not enough money to meet bills in Sheila's absence, Lana resorted to using Sheila's emergency telephone number – Teddy Sugden's at his Half Moon Street consulting rooms.

'I need some money,' she would say.

'Yes, my dear, how much?' Sugden would ask.

'Do you think I could have £100 to pay so-and-so until Sheila gets back?' she would ask tentatively.

The money was always readily forthcoming.

During Lana's second year as Sheila's secretary she had found her more balanced, calmer, and generally less erratic and easier to work for. She took little notice when Sheila whispered: 'They're trying to get me,' and assumed that she was referring either to other people in general, or to the other competitors in the Australia race. As Lana had had to deal with the rumours and innuendos during and after the race, and as Sheila had told her nothing about the South African episode, she thought neither that Sheila was behaving irrationally, nor that she might possibly be in genuine danger.

Lana had often been lonely and bored while Sheila was away. She left in September, to take up a position with Hill Samuel's shipping and insurance group which trebled her pay. She had always been too embarrassed to ask Sheila for a rise, although she had dropped hints in the telephone message book: 'The girl from the agency says she will not be able to come unless the rate of pay is improved.' Sheila, who had always assumed that Lana worked for fun rather than from financial necessity, kept in touch with her, and complained from time to time that a new secretary was 'hopeless' or 'clueless'.

At last Sheila thought that she might be sponsored for the flight she had been dreaming of for so long, round the world again and over the North Pole. She was pinning her hopes on a big advertising company, Saward Baker, and met Lord Erskine, a professional photographer, amateur pilot, gourmet and its managing director, several times at a Japanese restaurant in the Hilton Hotel. But although Lord Erskine had meetings and discussions with various clients, he failed to gain enough support for the project. One of the firms he approached was Ovaltine; the managing director, Colonel Trevor Jones, was abroad at the time, so it was not until later that he was told that the approach on Sheila's behalf had been turned down. 'I would have jumped at it,' he told me when I met him and Lord Erskine at the Special Forces Club. 'It would have been ideal – good clean sponsorship.'

Sheila spent Christmas with the Whitbreads at Warren Mere, a twenty-bedroomed house in Surrey which had been extended by Lutyens, with grounds designed by Gertrude Jekyll – the first joint Lutyens/Jekyll project. It was a quiet Christmas, with only the Colonel, his three children by his first marriage, his second wife Betty and the three children of their marriage, and Sheila. She appreciated the family atmosphere and no doubt also the attention of the Whitbreads' six staff, including a butler.

It was a brief but welcome respite. In the New Year, Sheila resumed her efforts to earn enough to keep herself and *Myth*, and to find sponsors. Although every firm which had expressed interest had backed down, an Adventure Trust was being formed to back her polar flight, which would, it was felt, be 'a good thing for Britain'. 'We're on!' Sheila announced ecstatically.

Finding yet more records to break or to create was, as she put it, 'the catalyst fusing wider knowledge' which she claimed that she found through flying. This knowledge, she explained, incorporated both involvement with 'people of all nationalities, colour and belief' and an 'awareness of an energy, a vibration like a sound, an actual force . . . the philosophy of the sky'. In the sky she felt that she was 'on the very edge of understanding'.

In her attempts to probe beyond the elusive edge of understanding, she made a note in her diary of 'books to get': *Intelligent Life in the Universe*, J.B. Priestley's *Man and Time*, Einstein's *Knowledge and Wonder*, *A Trip to the Fourth Dimension* and, on a less intellectual level, *The Spirit of St Louis*, Charles Lindbergh's account of his first Atlantic crossing. Even with such a demanding reading list, on the ground Sheila felt that her energy all too often evaporated into what she called 'a cabbage-like lethargy', the lethargy of depression.

There was no time for lethargy or depression once plans for the polar flight had been set in motion, although the project was to be kept secret until nearly the last minute in case anyone else decided to steal her glory by doing an anti-clockwise round-the-world flight over the North Pole first. Sheila's competitive instinct was always very much to the fore: she wanted to be first, and she wanted to be best, and she wanted this to be known. The need to prove herself, both to herself and to others, undoubtedly stemmed to a considerable extent from her feeling of rejection as a child. It was as if she was saying to the mother who had abandoned her: 'Look at me! I am somebody – I am worth something after all!'

The first decision about the forthcoming flight was the most difficult one: to abandon *Myth Too*, with which Sheila had by then accumulated ninety-four world-class records, in favour of a twin-engined Piper Aztec. The Piper Comanche did not have the necessary range for a long flight over the Arctic, nor would Sheila have received official acceptance of such a flight with a single engine, as a forced landing or a ditching would almost inevitably mean her death. She felt sad, and as guilty as if she was letting a friend down, that she could not use *Myth Too*; but at least, with the sponsorship she had been promised, she could keep her. For once she thought she had no financial problems.

The Piper factory in America agreed to cut the delivery date on a new Aztec from months to weeks, and CSE said they would modify it equally rapidly. The Fédération d'Aviation Internationale accepted her record bid, and Sheila booked a seat on a commercial airline to America to finalize details of her new aircraft, and at the same time to accept an invitation to Cape Canaveral to see an Apollo rocket launch.

Then her financial backing evaporated. Her sponsors considered the polar flight too dangerous, although they would still consider backing something less ambitious and less likely to result in her death.

Sheila sought the advice of the engineers at CSE. Les Baston said what she wanted to hear: 'Girl, you must do what you say you'll do. You always have. Somehow we'll all do it.' He and his colleagues had never doubted that Sheila would succeed in anything she set out to do, however long the odds against her; but even their encouragement could not clear the hurdle of how to finance the flight. Sheila sat alone for hours in the dark in *Myth Too*'s cockpit; *Myth*, she convinced herself, felt part of the new flight, and so she could not abandon her. She continued with her plans as if she still had the backing of her sponsors – time was short enough as it was, and she could not afford any delays if she was to leave, as she intended, on her birthday at the end of April.

It was Kaye Maclean who again came to her rescue. Sheila outlined her problems on the telephone. A few hours later, Kaye rang her back: 'You must keep your word. You cannot end your career with a broken word. I have sold some shares, enough to start you off. You must raise the rest, as that's all I can do.' Sheila did not reveal the amount of the loan nor its source; but it was enough, with what she could raise herself with a bank overdraft, to put down a £14,000 deposit. Kaye was about to leave for a two-and-a-half-month holiday; Sheila made an entry in her diary: 'Kaye sails on *Canberra* (Southampton) send flowers etc.'

At the end of January, Sheila flew to America. She wrote to Kaye from New York, on Cape Canaveral notepaper:

I got over here just in time to meet the astronauts (the ones left on earth!) & watch the launch to the Moon. It was fantastic – the power is unbelievable until you actually see and feel it! It was a super way to see it in the astronauts enclosure, & Alan Shepherds daughter stood next to me, so I felt part of the family as it were! . . .

The new aircraft is on the way to the UK, & equipment is being assembled from all over. There are many problems & hard tough deals but I think we are winning though heaven knows how we'll be ready in time. I cannot express my gratitude to you for being given the chance to go on – & every time someone throws a spanner in the works – I remember you & what you have done for me & battle a bit harder!

The biggest spanner in the works had, according to the same letter, been thrown by the British Board of Trade, which had exempted aircraft from import duty but had forbidden any commercial interest. The ban included all advertising by sponsors. 'Really it makes me sick,' Sheila complained,

How on earth do they think any of us can do anything worthwhile for Great Britain without commercial help? As usual the Americans have allowed me enormous discounts (without which I could not afford the equipment) & yet I am not allowed to let them advertise in return!! Of course it's not on . . . So it goes on – but I am deeply interested by all the new techniques in flying preparation I have ever done (& VERY few others can ever have done it!) . . . Well, my dear, by now you must be glamorously brown and healthy. Here it is below freezing and often snows! . . . Have fun – and don't worry! . . . Again thank you my dear for your most fabulous gesture, & generosity. I also do not know why you do it for me, but you have been the most wonderful friend a record attempter could have, & I hope I live up to your trust.

Although Kaye may have responded with an explanation of her continuing support, as Sheila kept none of her letters her reasons can only be a matter of conjecture. Patriotism? Vicarious pride in achievement? A wish to do something worthwhile with her money while she was still alive? Affection for a semi-daughter? Whatever the motivation for her generosity, she was by no means the only person who believed that Sheila could and would do what she set out to do, or who liked and admired her enough to want to help her. In spite of Sheila's reputation for being 'difficult', and for biting the hand which might feed her, the majority of those who sponsored or worked with her admired her professionalism as much as they did her courage and tenacity.

It was while Sheila was at Cape Canaveral that her polar flight gained a new and unexpected dimension, during a light-hearted conversation with astronaut Phil Chapman and Dick Hoagland, who was covering the Apollo launch for CBS. The two men had met in a school classroom, at a meeting of an organization called Committee of the Future for which Hoagland was a consultant; they shared a concern about the lack of grassroots appreciation of the implications and significance of space exploration.

'I want you to meet a remarkable friend of mine,' Chapman told Hoagland when they met again, at Cape Canaveral just before the launch of Apollo 14. The friend was Sheila. The three had dinner together that evening; among the topics of conversation was Hoagland's plan to take night photographs of the rocket with some new experimental film developed for NASA by Charles Wyckoff for use on the moon.

'You'll need a really good camera,' Sheila commented. Her own Nikon was better than the camera Hoagland had intended to use, and she insisted on lending it to him.

Hoagland went offshore in a twenty-foot boat to photograph the ceremony of lighting the rocket. The scene was, he told me, 'ethereal', with the beams of eighty searchlights, the 386-foot rocket like a 'huge blazing candle', and behind it the stars. To keep the camera dry in the surf which rocked the boat he wrapped it in his jacket, and when he returned to land he rushed up to his hotel room

to leave it on the bed before excitedly telling Sheila and Phil
Chapman what wonderful pictures he had taken.

While they were talking in the bar, his room was broken into and
Sheila's camera was taken. She was more concerned about the loss
of the film than about the theft of the camera, but Hoagland felt so
guilty that he immediately started thinking of ways of making it up
to her – 'like getting her a satellite'.

Next day, Sheila went with Hoagland and Chapman to watch the
launch. They took the old road along the Cape, and stopped at the
museum which housed replicas of all the earliest rockets. While they
walked on past the old gantries, they talked about what Sheila
planned to do: the idea of tracking her by satellite was discussed.
Sheila took the conversation less seriously than either of the men. By
the time she arrived in New York to stay with June Eggleston, only a
couple of days later, Phil Chapman had already discussed the
feasibility of such an idea with Chuck Cote at the Goddard Space
Center outside Washington.

Cote was in charge of a programme known as IRLS – an
Interrogation Recording and Location System originally designed
to measure tropical winds; the Nimbus satellite designed for it was
still in operation and had successfully tracked buoys, balloons, elk
and polar bears. The idea of testing it for the first time with a
human, and with such a fast-moving object as an aircraft, immediately appealed to Cote and his team. Sheila was told in New York
that her flight might be used for a satellite tracking experiment, as
well as to provide potentially useful biomedical and environmental
information.

Although Cote was enthusiastic, it was not until Dick Hoagland
decided to nudge NASA into making a decision that any positive
plans were made. He sent simultaneous telexes to the head and
deputy head of every department he could think of, on the principle
that anyone who thought someone else was giving the proposal
serious consideration would be shamed into doing so too:

> The application of near earth space satellite technology to the
> solution of many grave problems facing the world community is
> currently not fully appreciated by that community. It is in this
> context that this request is made. Miss Sheila Scott plans an early
> April solo flight round the world. In her small twin engine Piper
> Aztec D she plans three major attempts. Equator to equator, first

woman solo across the North Pole, and shortest time Australia to London. Her complete itinerary follows. Leaving Nairobi Kenya, Benghazi Libya, London United Kingdom, Tromso Norway, across the North Pole to Point Barrow Alaska, Fairbanks Alaska, Anchorage Alaska, Cold Day Adak, Midway, Wake Island, Tarawa Atoll, Guadalcanal Rabal, Darwin Australia, Singapore, Madras India, Karachi Pakistan, Athens Greece, London United Kingdom. This attempt to be completed within a month affords several unique opportunities for cooperation between NASA and herself. Several environmental and bio-medical experiments are planned which will increase basic scientific knowledge of the planet as well as human endurance. The request is made, therefore, for co-operative use of Nimbus-4 and the IRLS experiment as well as a data package to relay this environmental and bio-medical telemetry from the aircraft during all portions of the flight. Miss Scott because of a great problem of precise navigation in the Arctic is requesting the co-operation of NASA for a positioning experiment using IRLS and Nimbus-4. This affords an obvious opportunity for an aircraft positioning demonstration over the Pole as well as a unique solution to Miss Scott's problem of verification for the FAI of her actual flight over the geometric Northpole. Finally it is a search and rescue facture to consider IRLS representative of a very practical solution in the event of an unforeseen emergency during the attempt particularly during the 18 hour polar segment. Technical feasibility studies conducted by Goddard indicate all this is quite possible. Because of severe time limitations I am as Miss Scott's representative requesting urgency in your decision. This is an opportunity which should receive serious consideration.

The ruse worked, and began a partnership in which an American government organization was giving support to a foreign national – and a female one at that – in official cooperation with the British.

Permission was granted in the middle of March, with various provisos. The experiment was to be endorsed by a suitable British government agency, such as the Ministry of Aviation; no funds were to be exchanged between NASA and the UK sponsoring agency; Sheila was to assume responsibility for installing, and returning, the necessary equipment; and data provided by the experiment was to be made available to NASA and the UK sponsoring agency.

The Royal Air Force Institute of Aviation Medicine in Farn-borough telexed its agreement by return, and enlisted Sheila as a guinea pig in investigations into the sleep patterns and problems of long-distance pilots which were being conducted jointly with BOAC and the Institute of Sports Medicine. As she had to have official government clearance, it would appear that her fear of security repercussions because of her unwitting near-involvement in South African politics was unfounded. The only slight reservation was about her psychiatric and medical background, of which senior aviations doctors were, in spite of her secrecy, aware; but as she had shown no sign of reverting to drug or alcohol abuse – she drank no more than most people, and never during a flight – and had demonstrated considerable psychological stamina on her previous long flights, it was not felt that this constituted any risk.

Hoagland was less successful in interesting CBS, which employed him as a freelance, in Sheila's venture; but with the idea that she might interest *National Geographic* in an article, he arranged for her to have some of Charlie Wyckoff's limited experimental film stock. He considered Sheila 'a very very special person to recognise the unusual; she really had a big picture perspective, and made the transition from aviatrix to global scientific pioneering – she saw instantly how she could serve mankind'.

Sheila's new aircraft arrived at CSE while she was still in America. She was determined to keep the name *Myth*: as Myth 2 had become *Myth Too*, so Myth 3 became *Mythre* even before she saw it. 'My first glimpse of *Mythre* was without wing tips, ailerons flapping in the breeze, & a great gaping hole where the cabin should be!!' she wrote to Kaye Maclean.

Just like 1966 they could not wait for me to return to see her in all her glory – but she seems a nice girl, & I think she may have the same aura that *Myth Too* has. The engineers took *Myth Too* to meet her on arrival in this country & I have a super picture of the two aircraft nuzzling & a kiss! Today I am off to RAF Manby for ground training in 'celestial meridians' and such high faluting things!! Thank heavens for the Services (& I am thinking of Archie) they are seeing me through whenever it is possible. Sorry I am going on about my flight (but it is now day and night work & my head is full of it) please forgive any selfishness, dear Kay. *Mythre, Myth Too* & Sheila are remembering that you started this

& made it possible. Archie is maybe pushing for us too as so far we got the Mini Loran [a long range navigational aid] for free (£4000 worth) and a syndicate is paying for the insurance (at least £3000). Maps & charts being given . . . Thank you, my dear, & I do hope you are as happy as can be on your world trip.

She had still not won the battle with the Board of Trade. 'They allowed the aircraft in less £7000 customs,' she told Kaye, 'but will allow NO ONE to advertise in any way either during or AFTER my flight – which puts an end to my commercial help.' A British postal strike was equally blamed:

Who could have thought that such a thing could happen & put my whole flight in jeopardy? It's finally put paid to sponsors as I cannot get the screeds to them (except for very few) however all help is good and there is much help in kind (although not cash!) and we are even blessed by the Government! Minister of Sport will give and host the send off party for press two days before flight at the Ministry of Environment (did you know we had one!)

It seemed to Sheila a lucky omen that the call sign of *Mythre*, G-AYTO, was a variation on the letters of *Myth Too*'s G-ATOY. A moth was painted on the tail, below the intertwined flags of Great Britain and America symbolizing the cooperation between the two countries and Sheila's pride in representing both. Elizabeth Overbury added a message: 'Nil carborundum illegitima.' The CSE engineers were, as Sheila told Kaye, 'being wonderful and working overtime to get the massive engineering jobs done in time' – but with additional equipment from NASA to be installed, and the international complications, it was soon clear that the original take-off date was impossibly optimistic.

Help in kind was given by many people, from the RAF instructors at Manby to the Royal Navy, from friends who gave up their free time to two secretaries, Fiona McGinley and Jackie Williams. At the Institute of Aviation Medicine, Sheila's survival gear and Arctic clothing – which made her look like a cross between a polar bear and an advertisement for Michelin tyres – was tested in a pressure chamber in which she was taken down to minus twenty degrees Centigrade. Her heart rate was monitored by remote control as it would be during the flight, with a result which surprised the experts: instead of going up slightly on take-off and considerably more on landing, as was usual with male pilots, hers showed only a slight increase on take-off, none on landing, but shot up when she was talking on the telephone. Her claim that she felt relaxed while she was flying, but found life on the ground difficult, was borne out.

At CSE in Oxford it was, according to instructor Tom Carpenter, 'sometimes chaos' during the preparations: 'Everything was rushed, things were running late. Sheila was chain smoking and chivvying. She sometimes drove the engineers up the wall, but they all had a lot of time for her although her neurotic approach was sometimes hard work.' There was little time for Sheila to familiarize herself with the twin-engined Aztec, although 'she took to it well enough' during the fifteen hours she flew it with Tom. Tony Marchant, a CSE engineer, had more opportunities to fly *Mythre* than Sheila did, often using the aircraft to fetch her. Her only real test flight was to Norway with Lieutenant Commander Chris Allen of the Fleet Air Arm. Sheila was surprised that *Mythre* did not perform as well as *Myth Too*. This was put down to the difference in weight and shape.

An agreement between Sheila Scott Enterprises and Lombank Ltd was signed on 22 May. Lombank agreed to a hire purchase agreement on the £36,000 outstanding after Sheila had paid the deposit on the £50,000 aircraft, with *Myth Too*, on which there was still over £9000 hire purchase to repay, as collateral.

Sheila staked everything on the success of the flight, and on somehow making it pay; if she defaulted on the monthly payments of nearly £1300, Lombank could take both aircraft. She did not have to make the first payment for five months, while she would still be paying for *Myth Too*. This would, she hoped, give her time to make money out of a book about the flight, and to sell the film of the polar leg she was planning to make with a borrowed video camera. She also anticipated, with unquenchable optimism, that her success would attract considerable sponsorship for her next venture, over both the North and South Poles.

The possibility of failure was banished firmly from her mind as the last few days of preparation drew to a frantic close, although she found it difficult to ignore a feeling that something was wrong with *Mythre*: 'She looks a beautiful aircraft, and maybe she is,' she told herself firmly. Her misgivings were, she reassured herself, no more than apprehension at setting out in an aircraft with which she did not yet have a close relationship – and that would surely have been remedied by the time she reached Nairobi, the starting point of her great adventure.

13

THE DAWN AIR at Gatwick was crisp and cold. It was just over a month after Sheila's original take-off date, which was to have been her birthday at the end of April – a month into which, even by the standard she had set herself before previous flights, more had been crammed than had seemed at first possible. 'Given the difficulties she met, most people would have abandoned the project,' Phil Chapman acknowledged, 'but she just kept going, overcoming failures of people and equipment only because of her remarkable will to succeed.'

A television crew was waiting to film the departure of 'Britain's ambassador in the air', as one newspaper called Sheila on the morning of her take-off for Nairobi. She was gratified that even at such an early hour several of her friends and helpers had turned out to say goodbye. *Mythre*'s cockpit still felt strange, but comfortingly self-contained, as she did her pre-flight checks – which for the first time included attaching the wires of an astronaut's harness to a portable electro-cardiac box slung over her shoulder.

As soon as she was in the air, she began to relax. Although her flight would not officially start until she left Kenya, the green light indicating that the satellite was interrogating the aircraft flashed on while she was over the Mediterranean. Sheila pressed the black 'ready to test' button and did her various experimental tasks: she checked the battery in the heart box recorder, noted the inside and outside air temperatures and the pressure altitude, wrote a brief description of the terrain below her which would later be checked against the satellite readings, and filled in her biomedical reports. Although there was no direct communication between them, the men at Goddard would know where she was, a comforting thought although as yet she did not need any comfort.

As she approached her first stop, Benghazi, she was tossed

169

around on the edge of thunderstorms and anxiously recalculated her speed and fuel. *Mythre* was not performing as well as she should have been, and was averaging only 100 m.p.h.: Sheila's estimated flight times had been based on an average speed of 175 m.p.h.

She had permission to stay in Libya, where a strict curfew was in force, for only an hour. Because the flight had taken so much longer than anticipated, it was almost dusk when she arrived. By the time her tanks had been filled ready for the next long leg to Nairobi, it was dark and the wind had changed. Rather than risk a cross-wind take-off with full tanks on an unfamiliar airfield, she decided that she would have to stay the night: the immigration officer reluctantly granted permission for her to sleep on a camp bed in the airport office.

She dreamt that she was taking off alone, and that her aircraft pitched and crashed on the runway, bursting into flames. Her sleep was further interrupted by a new immigration officer who insisted on interrogating her in his office, and on the way back to her camp bed she had to fight off an amorous approach. She spent the rest of the night in the control tower with three Egyptian air traffic controllers.

Her nightmare was still haunting her in the morning until one of the ground crew she had met the night before gave her a cheerful wave: she felt that her dream was broken because she was not after all alone. The take-off was, however, almost as bad as she had dreamt, lacking only the final crash and fire. She struggled to centralize the controls to keep *Mythre* straight and level as, heavy and clumsy with the extra fuel, the aircraft bucked repeatedly and threatened to stall. At least in the daylight she could see the humps on the runway: had she taken off in the dark she was sure that her dream would have come true. Once again she felt she had been given some form of extra-sensory guidance.

At last *Mythre* was off the runway, but only just; for twenty miles Sheila felt powerless as the aircraft climbed slowly, grudgingly, a foot at a time. It was a bad beginning to a long and demanding flight. *Mythre* continued to under-perform as Sheila struggled in humid heat through flailing sand. She made an unscheduled landing at Khartoum, and minutes after she touched down the airport was closed as a sandstorm turned day into night.

When she was able to take off again she had to contend with both midday thunderstorms and *Mythre*'s continuing lack of power. The most she could coax out of the aircraft was 95 m.p.h.; when she tried to gain enough height to clear the mountains ahead the stall warning light came on, but she did not have enough fuel to return.

At Goddard Jack Effner, who was in charge of reading the data relayed to NASA by satellite, was aware that Sheila was having problems and had backtracked by the time she landed on a Sudanese military airfield on the Nile. Although she had every reason to fear a bureaucratic delay she was treated like an honoured guest, and instead of sleeping spent several hours drinking ceremonial tea before at last being allowed to rest.

It was midday before she received permission from Khartoum to fly on, and then only provided she landed at Juba to clear Sudanese customs, making her route to Nairobi even longer. Over Entebbe in Uganda, the thunderstorms again began to build up. Sheila realized that yet again she would have to land without permission.

Idi Amin's Uganda was not the best country in which to arrive unannounced; fortunately she knew the air traffic controller, Terry Murphy, who was able to ease her way although not without some difficulty. He greeted her by name as she flew into radio range, and shushed her when she landed and announced that she was Sheila Scott and was on an important world flight. 'Oh, she's just a tourist in a private aircraft,' he told the Ugandan commander as he arranged for *Mythre* to be hustled out of sight before it became known that she had American space equipment on board and was taken for a spy.

Next day, after what felt like a tourist flight, Sheila at last reached Nairobi, where all formalities were waived and she handed *Mythre* over to the engineers of Wilken Aviation while she enjoyed three days of freedom and sun – a much-needed rest after the previous few months' gruelling work of preparation. When she spoke to Chuck Cote and discovered that he knew all about her route changes, and their reasons, she felt almost as though the satellite had crept into her brain. The information obtained from a carbon dioxide sensor, one of the various monitors fitted on her aircraft, was already being analysed: it showed unexpectedly high air pollution over the Libyan desert.

She had to wait in Nairobi – not too reluctantly – until she received a message that the weather pattern for the Arctic looked good enough for the polar attempt. The long return to London was little better than the outward flight: *Mythre* continued to perform badly, and there were more delays as this made further maintenance stops necessary.

In Malta she was told that there had been a break-in at her flat and that 'a few trophies' had been stolen. She flew on feeling miserable, but not aware of the extent of her losses. Fiona MacGinley had prepared a provisional list for the police, but had not wanted to alarm her.

Fiona's list included eighteen cups, one silver and one gold cigarette lighter, a silver cigarette box, several silver ashtrays, and a gold and amethyst ring given to her by Norman Lonsdale after the first round-the-world flight. She had sold most of the rest of her jewellery to raise money. Worst of all, the Akai video tape recorder which she had been lent to film the polar leg, and which was so advanced for the time that it was not yet available on the British market, had been taken, along with all her video tapes. At least she still had the Arctic gear – the suitcases which had held it had been emptied and used to carry the loot away.

Sheila felt that her whole career had vanished. 'Everything of any value to me had gone – jewellery, trophies, hundreds of little things which had been given to me all round the world, the only tangible memories of all my races, all my flights, all my records.'

Uncharitably, several people have told me that they never believed Sheila had been robbed; like the boy who cried wolf, she had so often been melodramatic about minor problems that they no longer took her tales of woe seriously. She reacted outwardly more calmly to the robbery than to many less significant everyday disasters, although inwardly she felt desolate, and was convinced, because of what had been taken and what had been left untouched, that the burglars were people who knew her and her flat well. Real or imagined, this was an injustice which she could neither forgive nor forget. It preyed on her mind until she saw the break-in as part of a plot against her which would not be abandoned until she had been destroyed. Nothing was ever recovered, and the break-in joined the long list of unsolved London robberies.

While Sheila dealt both with the formalities of being the victim of a robbery, and with those essential for the continuation of her flight, the two days she had intended to spend in London became four; by then, although the weather in the polar region was as good as could be expected, she was blocked by fronts over the North Sea and Norway. If she could not leave within the next twenty-four hours she knew that she would have to abandon the project for the year as the summer thaw, which would bring fog, had already started – and she feared that this would mean giving it up for good.

When at last she was given clearance to leave, with a forecast that the bad weather between London and the Arctic would dissipate by midday, the delay and the break-in had demoralized her so much that she felt apprehensive even about taking off from London Airport. An impatient air traffic controller grumbled at her hesitation. As she lined *Mythre* up alongside a BEA jet which towered over her, its captain wished her 'Good luck, Sheila,' over the radio. She felt she needed it, and the promise that 'We are with you' from the control tower. Her fear was changed by the familiar smells of the cockpit and the sun glinting on the tarmac into a feeling of exhilarating freedom. Nothing which lay before her could be worse than the strain she was leaving behind. But her mouth was dry with apprehension about the frozen wastes she was to fly over.

As soon as she was clear of London and had established the course given her towards the North Sea, she attempted to switch to autopilot: again, inexplicably, as with *Myth Too* on the Australia race, it was broken. She radioed a message to Field Aviation in London, asking them to make sure there was an engineer at Bodo in Norway to repair it. The idea of flying without autopilot over the Arctic Circle, where even the smallest navigational error could be fatal, appalled her. She flew on, through murky cloud over Scotland, across an unfriendly North Sea, and over Stavanger on the south-west coast of Norway.

Her sophisticated Sperry autogyro compass, designed to avoid the magnetic pull of the Pole and act as a simple direction indicator, was steady; but the standby compass was already reacting erratically. As her only polar navigational aid she had an astro compass, for which the sun had to be visible. NASA's green light reminded her that the team at Goddard was willing her to succeed, and that she was not as alone as she felt. *Mythre* was flying smoothly as she approached Bodo over the bonfires with which the Norwegians celebrated Midsummer's Eve, and although it was 10.30 in the evening the sun was still high.

To her dismay, there was no one at Bodo who could help with the autopilot. Someone – Sheila referred to him only as 'a remote and irresponsible British gentleman' – suggested that she should return to England; but she took no notice. Although it was frustrating not to be able to join in the midsummer celebrations, her time was filled with last-minute telephone briefings from Goddard and with trying, in vain, to rest: in spite of her exhaustion, she was too keyed up to sleep.

As *Mythre*'s air speed was still so much lower than had been expected Sheila's flight plan had to be modified, with the help of an RAF flight lieutenant, Eric Stafford. They decided that instead of the original direct grid course she should fly a single-heading pressure pattern, to take advantage of wind strengths and so make the actual distance flown shorter. This involved a flight track curving first to the left, then towards and over the Pole, before swinging towards the Alaskan coastline.

Before leaving Bodo, Sheila unloaded everything she would not need on the polar leg – the RAF's Dominie was to fly it back to London for her. It was not cold enough on the ground for all her five layers of Arctic clothing, but over her bulky underclothes she put on a cashmere trouser suit, a donation from Pringle's which matched her aircraft livery and made her feel at least vaguely feminine.

She was waiting for the weather data about wind strengths at all pressure levels, which she would need to fly her new course, when fog rolled down the mountains and across the fjords. Andoya, where she was to land to refuel, was still clear, but was an hour's flight away. Sheila felt desperate: the warmer it became the more fog there would be, and the less chance of making the flight at all. When even the RAF flight was cancelled she glared at the fog, but it refused to lift except for a few seconds at a time, and each time rolled back even thicker than before. Another day was lost, and there were more telephone calls to tell everyone who needed to know about the change in plans.

The next day started clearer, but with a threat of fog later. Sheila felt that she could not bear even another hour's delay after six months of anticipation. Eric Stafford had worked out a new pressure plan with the bonus that the wind was expected to be stronger. In the cold air, *Mythre*'s airspeed and rate of climb had improved. 'No problems today,' Sheila thought happily – apart from the broken autopilot and scanty navigational aids; but if it had been easier to fly over the Arctic in a light aircraft, it would already have been done.

The Arctic Ocean beneath did not look alarming, as she had expected, but serenely beautiful, dark blue-green round lazy delicate iced cakes. The military runway at Andoya stretched out to the sea beside breathtaking mountains of green forests and snow. She thought of the explorer Nansen, and wondered whether trolls could have been ancient space robots.

The RAF's blue Dominie had arrived before her. Its crew, and the Norwegian Air Force personnel stationed at Andoya, assisted with the last-minute preparations and took her for a meal at the hotel in the little fishing town. She was to take off at 1 a.m., to enable her to make full use of the sun with the astro compass and to fit in with the timing of the satellite passes. All her spare time at Andoya was needed for franking and stamping four hundred specially issued polar covers – arranging these had been one of the most complex parts of her preparation, and page after page of her telephone book had been filled with messages about how to comply with all Post Office regulations.

Finally, she donned her layers of Arctic clothing – silk long johns, vest and socks, several layers of woollen garments including two more pairs of socks, the outsize turquoise Pringle trouser suit, with a lightweight anorak and a Himalayan survival duvet ready to struggle into in the air. Anti-icing paste had been spread liberally over *Mythre*, who sat tail down, nose up haughtily, with the weight of the extra fuel.

Sheila felt awkward and clumsy in her bulky clothing and her heart was thumping as she climbed into the cockpit, after shaking hands with each of the men who had helped her and seeing in their eyes that they thought she needed more than good luck to survive her self-imposed ordeal. Eric somehow squeezed in beside her while she checked her three watches and chronograph – all agreed to the second – then plugged herself into the heart box and recorded the time, and made the last pre-flight check of setting the Sperry autogyro compass.

'For heaven's sake turn back if there is anything wrong – anything at all,' Eric said anxiously, 'Don't press on. We'll be here all night. Good luck!'

The NASA green light flashed on reassuringly just as Sheila was taking off, at 0113 GMT on 25 June. She had her last glimpse of trees for several days, and was then wrapped in cloud. As she flew, she talked to *Mythre*: 'Please keep climbing – please, please, climb!' It seemed an eternity as at only twenty feet a minute she reached 7000 feet. The red stall light flicked on as the aircraft lurched. To follow her pressure pattern she was supposed to be at 10,000 feet, but

Mythre was clearly not going to reach the required height until her load of fuel was lighter.

At least the sun had reappeared, so Sheila could set up the astro compass, which was on a sliding bar across the front of the instrument panel. She needed four sun readings at four-minute intervals to start her plot, but when the sun came and went behind the clouds she had to start again. The magnetic activity near the North Pole was affecting the radio, but from time to time she heard snatches of conversation. 'Too little speed out of Norway . . .' referred, she assumed, to her and *Mythre*. Then: 'Jeepers! Not a woman out there on her own!'

'But I'm not on my own,' she told Buck Tooth, who as usual was grinning inanely behind her.

She coaxed the aircraft to 9500 feet, but the airspeed was only 130 m.p.h. – not enough to reach Barrow in Alaska at the rate the fuel was being used. It was bitingly cold, but she dared not use any fuel for the cabin heater, and her electric gloves and socks overheated so rapidly that she decided not to use them unless the only alternative was frostbite. Instead she pulled on a fourth pair of socks and wrapped a knitted shawl round her head.

Without realizing it until her jaw started to ache, she was clenching her teeth with tension and concentration. Her arms and legs, too, were painfully stiff. 'Relax!' she told herself, changing her position by pulling a cushion under her and doing exercises to stretch her jaw and neck. She had been in the air for seven hours – only seven hours, she told herself.

When she tried to make contact on the radio she could get only a Russian signal – which she assumed meant that she must be well to the right of her course. By then, according to her flight plan, she should have been near the Pole, but even with the decrease in weight as the fuel was used her airspeed had not improved. She glanced in the outside mirror on the port engine. Was that something hanging down?

A closer look revealed that the door encasing the nose wheel was half down – which explained the loss of airspeed. She activated the gear mechanism: the amber light indicating that the gear was up and locked blinked at her.

'Poor *Mythre*!' she said aloud. 'So that's what was wrong with you!'

Nevertheless the airspeed still did not pick up. Without the unlikely miracle of a strong tail wind, she realized that she would run out of fuel long before she reached the Alaskan coast – even if that was where she was heading: she was not sure – she might after all be heading for Russia. She was out of radio range, and the sun had gone in, but the beauty of the shadowed, glittering world of ice below her was so unexpectedly intense that she could not feel afraid. The sight of pack ice indicated that she had passed Spitzbergen. The wheel came down again, and once more she reactivated the gear mechanism. But from the continuingly low airspeed she suspected that the door was still not fully closed.

Ahead she could see puffy green-tinged clouds, and behind them more solid cloud which looked almost like glaciers and mountains. Or – were they, could they be, mountains? If she was making a true track of her pressure pattern path, they should be the mountains of Greenland; but she had persuaded herself that she was off course. The only radio beacon anywhere near where she now thought she might be was at Nord.

'G-AYTO to any station,' she called on the HF radio frequency.

'Nord here, Tango Oscar,' a deep voice replied. 'Where are you?'

'I'm estimating, repeat estimating, 84 North at flight level nine zero, but it is only an estimation. I was unable to pick up Bear Island and Spitzbergen beacons earlier today but now I can see glaciers ahead of me.'

'That's not surprising – those beacons are usually overcome by a stronger Norwegian one. Have you got my beacon?'

'I'm already tuned to your frequency, but one needle points one way and the other the other way! Do you have very high snow-covered mountains with low cloud below them?'

'It's all snow here! We have mountains, but clear skies. It's lovely sunshine here. You must come to Nord – there's nowhere else for you to go. Where is your radio compass pointing now?'

'I have two and they're pointing in opposite directions.'

'You'll have to choose one needle to follow and trust it.'

Sheila chose, and as she flew on, over glittering sea and ice floes, not knowing whether she had made the right choice but trusting to luck and to her guiding spirit, the NASA light came on. She punched all the test buttons: wherever she was, someone would know. There was an emergency button which would activate rescue services, but she was not yet ready for such an extreme measure of desperation.

'There are twenty-seven men here, all waiting to meet you . . . We have nine thousand feet of runway .'

This made Nord sound so big that Sheila looked for a village as she followed her chosen compass needle. As the mountains came closer, she saw a long, dark slope – a runway? – but no houses; then a tall mast and a few low huts came into sight. Nord! – it had to be Nord. She could see the men of Nord waving from snow-covered roofs and watching through binoculars. On the ground, she was surrounded by blond, suntanned, bearded Danes in parkas with fur-edged hoods. They greeted her with hot food and coffee in their mess, and told her that Nord was a Danish weather station, built in 1952 with the help of the United States Air Force and four hundred miles across constant snow and ice from the nearest village.

Sheila was allocated a room in one of the several huts, each with a dozen rooms and a shower, and then taken to the radio hut, where telex messages were sent to England and to the Goddard Space Center. Communication between Nord and the rest of the world took time, which she filled in with much-needed sleep: she had been awake for over forty hours and felt safe and comfortable under a quilt, although the Arctic sun streamed all night on to her.

A day passed with no return messages. The time was spent tinkering with the aircraft as if it was a normal day at its home base in Oxford. The timelessness of life at Nord was relaxing. On Sheila's second day there, telexes began to pour in from Goddard; she replied 'with love from me and twenty-seven men thousands of miles from nowhere without a chart'. In spite of the frustration of being delayed yet again, she was happy, and joined enthusiastically in the weekly Saturday night party.

The next day deluged the Nord operators with more telexes, some from Britain, some from Goddard. Meanwhile, messages were flying backwards and forwards in London to and from her secretary, whose telephone book was soon full of questions she could not answer and queries about what Sheila wanted anyone to do, and how she thought anyone could do anything: some people thought she should return, some that she should backtrack to Bodo and start again from there, some that she should fly direct to Barrow.

Sheila's replies to Goddard were sent from 'twenty-seven Danish Santa Clauses and one Mother Christmas'. 'We'll have you in our stocking any time,' Goddard answered. The light-hearted banter by telex masked the deep concern felt by Chuck Cote and his team, which had been joined by Lee Field from the United States Navy at Patuxent. When they were told by a radio operator in Greenland

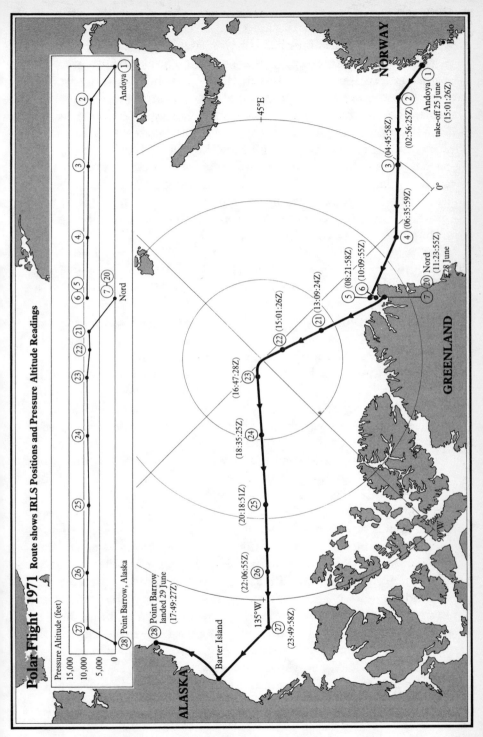

Polar Flight 1971 Route shows IRLS Positions and Pressure Altitude Readings

Pressure Altitude (feet)

15,000
10,000
5,000
0

where she was, they thought that she would pack it in; later the suspicion crossed their minds that she had planned the diversion for extra publicity. As soon as they realized that she was as determined as ever to carry on, they stayed up all night working out a new flight plan for her: at three in the morning Phil Chapman, a pilot as well as an astronaut, sent the others to raid various offices at Goddard for charts, information on atmospheric tables, and nautical almanacs.

Because of the time it took for telexes to reach Nord, several arrived after the departure times they suggested. Eventually 'the longest telex ever', according to Chuck Cote, reached Sheila with the new flight plan, complete with sun angles and a specific take-off time to coordinate with spacecraft orbits.

Half sadly, half feeling she would burst with suppressed excitement, Sheila hugged each of the bearded Danes goodbye. *Mythre* was waiting nose up, her tanks having been laboriously filled by hand pump from barrels.

'We have lift-off for the Pole,' Sheila said as *Mythre* climbed with renewed confidence, her nose wheel safely locked out of the way. She felt as if she was flying through the gates of heaven in the calm air above what she described as 'this wondrous wilderness of beautiful shapes and colours – the very essence of primeval glory'. Once again she seemed to be two people, one the observer, the other the doer, both very aware of her remoteness and of 'the collective positive thought' of the team at Goddard.

The clear weather and euphoria were short-lived. Although her undercarriage had retracted without problem after take-off, once again the nose wheel kept dropping and she repeatedly had to recycle the mechanism. The slow airspeed that this caused was at least less of a problem as she had more than enough fuel, provided the head wind did not exceed the forecast ten knots. The sun had soon disappeared, hidden first by grey tentacles of cloud and then by rain, which turned to hail. Sheila felt trapped between the ice below her, and the severe icing which kept her lower than she would have liked. It was bitterly cold in the tiny cramped cabin, and she complained to *Mythre* and Buck Tooth about the discomfort of the many wires sprouting, it seemed, from almost every part of her anatomy to the various recording boxes.

It was only by timing herself and keeping as closely as she could to her course that she could judge when she was approaching the North Pole. When the mist parted for a few minutes, the carpet of ice below her reflected the colours of a rainbow and looked as if it, rather than she, was moving. She felt suspended in space, not sure if she was on course; there was too little sun to take readings with the astro compass, and the radio compass was behaving as wildly as she had known it would so near to the Pole's pull of gravity.

Sheila pushed aside her doubts as she counted down with no one except herself to hear: 'Pole minus twenty minutes. . . .'

The outside air temperature rose to minus two degrees Centigrade, and the cabin became almost warm. At what she estimated was the time for ninety degrees north, the cloud parted to reveal a small, smooth-looking hill of snow among the jumbled, awe-inspiring jungle of ice. Sheila claimed the snowy hill as her North Pole, and opened the storm window to throw out a Union Jack for Great Britain and a paper Snoopy for America. They were whipped out of her hand by an icy blast which made her gasp.

'We're here – I'm on top of the world!' she shouted aloud.

'Say again.'

It was the operator at Nord. Sheila had not expected anyone to hear her.

'I am on top of the world. Operations normal. Tango Oscar is at ninety north,' she replied. There was no answer, although she repeated her message exuberantly again and again.

Doubt crept in. Perhaps she had mistimed it. She carried on for another twenty minutes to make sure. Cloud and ice enveloped her. She felt that she was struggling for survival. Had she come this far, only to perish when no one would ever find her body or the wreck of her aircraft?

The wheel was down again: it stayed up for only minutes at a time. Her confidence that she had more than enough fuel turned to panic as the ice built up: she realized that what had seemed a relatively short, thirteen-hour flight could take seventeen hours. Fate, she reflected, was making her pay for her 'relaxing moments of pride and triumph'.

At last she could turn twenty degrees to port, still half convinced that she had missed her target. The NASA light flashed on – 1750 hours. She did her mental acuity test carelessly, and concentrated even harder than usual on completing the rest of her tasks accurately; but she was lonely and frightened, her eyes were burning and her back aching after thirteen hours in the air, and she was rapidly losing her confidence.

Chuck Cote gave me the Goddard side of the story: 'When Sheila was at the Pole, everything else stopped for the team; there was nothing on our minds except Sheila's safety. From Nord, she flew straight for the Pole – there was no way to get a straighter line than shown on the data. She went over, made a left turn, then went off course. Then she came in south of target – she was supposed to come into Port Barrow, was detected by radar at Barter Island, then followed the coast in: she was almost out of fuel, and we wondered how she'd make Alaska.'

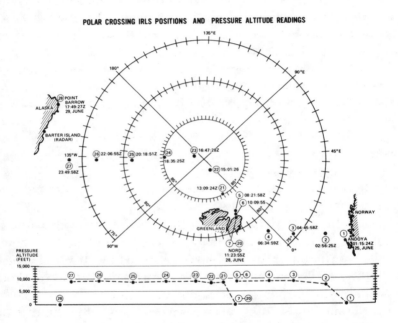

POLAR CROSSING IRLS POSITIONS AND PRESSURE ALTITUDE READINGS

Sheila was wondering the same thing when, after an hour or two of relatively comfortable flying, the weather again closed in as she approached what she knew must be the coastline: but Barrow was stormbound, she was told over the radio, and she must head instead for Barter Island. From Barter, she was informed unwelcomingly that there was a blinding snowstorm and a strong crosswind across the single dirt runway. The next radio messsage indicated that the weather at Barrow was clearing – so she changed course again. She had had enough and wanted the flight to end, and responded irritably to NASA's winking light, her mind on whether her undercarriage would work.

At first, as she let down for Barrow, the right wheel remained retracted; she pulled the emergency loop under her seat which would shoot all wheels down together if the mechanism failed. To her relief, this worked; the emergency services which had been rushed into place below her would not be needed. As she drew to a stop on the runway, in her anxiety about *Mythre* she almost forgot that only a few hours earlier she had flown over the North Pole: she leaped out, wires trailing, and threw herself on the ground under the aircraft's belly to see if there was any damage.

She was soon pulled out, congratulated, welcomed, photographed, given champagne; but it was not until Chuck Cote said over the telephone: 'You went right over the top! How do you feel?' that she believed she had really done it.

'Top of the world!' she replied. 'But are you sure I really flew over the Pole?' The information relayed by the satellite, analysed at Goddard and entered on a huge display board – which ten years later was still there – left no doubt. As Chuck Cote put it, when Sheila landed safely at Barrow 'the sigh of relief from NASA was heard around the world': their first tracking experiment with a human being had been a success.

Sheila was convinced that she had again been guided by some supernatural power or force, some undefined but extra-sensory influence, during her flight across the top of the world. 'How else could I have flown right over it without any normal aids at all, and in a very sickly aircraft?' she asked. 'I am certainly not a brilliant pilot so my navigation guidance did not come from within, though the concentrated thought of the team monitoring the flight at Goddard may have accomplished it for me; or perhaps it was something even stranger – perhaps the answer is simple, a sort of mental wave like a radio wave, but we have lost the sense that makes us aware of it.' Sailors or fishermen might call it instinct or a sixth sense, the sense that led tenth-century Vikings, for instance, from Greenland to the coast of northern America and back with no navigational aids; some might call it luck – but an uncannily accurate form of luck.

The engineers at Barrow set to work to sort out *Mythre*'s problems. Their findings that the hydraulic tubing had been severed by an aileron cable were later explained in a letter: 'The tubing was located on the left side in the belly of the aircraft where an aileron cable passes through the wing fillet on the way to the aileron bellcrank. The hole is very small but under pressure it will leak all your fluid very quickly' – which indeed had happened. For once, Sheila did not mind when she was told that she would have to stay an extra day while the damage was repaired; it gave her time to explore the Naval Arctic Research Station and the neighbouring Eskimo village of Utevik, and to renew her strength after her ordeal over the North Pole.

A note in the telephone message book at Sheila's London flat recorded: 'Serious damage found on plane. Sheila was not just being temperamental.' The Americans at Goddard had never doubted that, if she claimed there was something wrong with the aircraft, she knew what she was talking about. Their respect for her professionalism was not marred by the sourness so often shown towards her in Britain. 'Sheila always kept her poise,' Chuck Cote told me. 'She was always logical, always had a way out – nothing ever defeated her – she always knew it would be OK. We had become a part of each other's lives, and mentally together.' The Nimbus satellite continued to report back, and the NASA team to follow Sheila's progress, when she continued after Barrow to Anchorage and then San Franscisco and on round the world, but there was not quite the same shared excitement and anxiety once the polar leg had been successfully completed.

Sheila spent several days in San Francisco waiting for spares – her autopilot was at last to be repaired – and dealing with the press. A press conference to be held the day after her arrival was cancelled, apparently because of confusion about who was responsible for it. Dick Hoagland had assumed that NASA's PR department would handle such matters, while NASA thought he had organized it. Although there was nothing that Sheila's secretary could do from the flat in Park West, she dutifully recorded messages: 'All the press converging and being turned away. What should they do? Told Hoagland trying to save conference – keep press there. NASA reply – no conference this end', 'Dick Hoagland will see that UPI will put it out.' Eventually a reference to the pollution which Sheila's sensor had detected over the North Pole found its way into the press.

By the time she left San Francisco, Sheila had amassed a cumulative sleep loss of sixty-six hours over the twenty-four days since she had left Nairobi; the figure was based on her average of seven and a half hours' sleep a night in London. Nevertheless her mental acuity tests showed she had an unusual ability to function coherently and efficiently even after several days virtually without sleep.

The next fortnight was relatively leisurely, with no more than eight hours in the air on any day and with little loss of sleep as she flew from San Francisco to Honolulu, then to Canton, just below the Equator. There she was able to claim her 'first flight' from Equator to Equator over the Pole – it had been slower than she had hoped, but it was still a first.

Her next stop was Fiji, where she was guest of honour and one of only two Europeans allowed at a traditional celebration in her honour, and attended a Hindu healing ceremony during which young men in a state of trance walked unscathed and unafraid through fire. They had had two weeks of abstinence and meditation as preparation, and told Sheila that anyone with sufficient faith – any faith, not necessarily theirs – could meditate and do the same. She ascribed this to what she called 'the power of positive thought', in which she was a firm believer. Her religious instinct had been strengthened through her adventures in the air; the God she believed in was 'an overall power, but as an actual force, more a scientific thing – could we but learn to communicate via another dimension of intellect'.

The islands of the Pacific had always had an equally philosophical and relaxing effect on Sheila, so once again it did not matter that she was held up in Fiji for four days waiting for aircraft spares to arrive from Australia. Then she flew on to Queensland, where she was at first treated stiffly, with a formality she had not expected from an Australian flying club but which she put down to the unfavourable publicity she had received during the Australia race; as the evening wore on, the stiffness was gradually relaxed until everyone was uninhibitedly singing bawdy flying club songs.

She spent two days in Queensland, and then, after an eight-hour flight across Australia, another two days in Darwin before breaking Jean Batten's thirty-four-year-old record from Australia to England. To do this she flew as nearly non-stop as was possible, stopping only briefly in Singapore, Madras, Karachi, Bahrein and Athens. In Singapore she managed to sleep for two hours on a stretcher in the airport office, and in Madras she snatched another hour's sleep. It was no wonder that by the last leg, from Athens, she was so tired that she could hardly think. She felt again as if she had become two people, one watching while the other, lethargic and lacking in concentration through exhaustion, treble-checked every action.

The only stimulant she normally allowed herself on a flight was coffee – with cigarettes to relax her tension. But, faced with several more hours in the air before she could allow herself to collapse, she took an amphetamine tablet: it kept her awake, but even so she felt that, had she had another leg to fly after London, she would have been incapable of carrying on.

Geoffrey Edwards provided a lavish reception at London Airport, where the spectator viewing gallery was packed when Sheila returned in triumph but exhausted. Apart from flying over the North Pole, and once and a half round the world, she had broken the coveted five-day Darwin–London record by one and a half days. In addition she had cooperated in various scientific experiments which she hoped would serve a long-term purpose, and she had again, in spite of numerous setbacks, achieved everything she had set out to do.

Life on the ground was even more of an anti-climax than usual. In spite of her exhaustion, on her first night at home the effect of the Dexedrine tablet prevented her from sleeping. Her flat, with its accumulation of letters to be answered, bills to be paid and engagements to be accepted or refused, was depressing; she still felt that it had been desecrated by the robbery. For a week, according to the table drawn up from her 'sleep diary', her sleep was disturbed, and she suffered from 'cyclical swings in mood from "very high to very low"'; in fact it took her far longer than that to readjust and to regain her usual ability to sleep. Her moods continued to swing erratically – one moment she felt again on top of the world, the next equally low.

Several letters between Sheila and Arnold Miller, president of Theta Sensors in California, hint at the disappointment they shared that more was not made of the experiments conducted during the flight: 'I, too, am heartsick over the way things were left for all of us,' Miller wrote in October. Six weeks later, Sheila wrote:

Needless to say, nothing – absolutely no replies from Dick Hoaglin [*sic*] and still no photos from Charlie Wycoff [*sic*]. I think Dick must know by now the incredible amount of money he cost me, and I suppose feels there is nothing he can say. The only odd thing is the deathly silence from Phil [Chapman]. . . . It has not helped with Whittingham here too having let the whole team down so very badly, but life has a way of smoothing things out given enough time.

Dr Peter Whittingham was the RAF doctor in charge of the sleep control experiments; he had suggested that Sheila should abandon the flight at Nord, and had so far not publicized the findings.

It is difficult to see how Dick Hoagland had lost Sheila a 'considerable amount of money'; a number of people have told me that he let Sheila down badly, but have been unable to say how. The camera stolen while it was in his possession had been replaced; no money had been made by anyone out of the cooperation he had suggested with NASA, but there had never been any question of paying Sheila, however useful her findings – which of course were not legally hers, but theirs.

Hoagland considered NASA grudging and unimaginative in the lack of recognition given to Sheila's research role. 'There is now an agreement between the United States and Russia which, using space instrumentation, has saved at least a hundred lives. This stemmed directly from Sheila,' he told me. 'Her flight illustrated a whole bunch of satellite possibilities. NASA's search and rescue operation followed from this. The sensor, which was about the size of a silver dollar, presaged the whole flap over the ozone layer, and led to worldwide data about global pollutants.'

Two British aviation doctors, Frank Preston and Denis Cussen, later wrote a paper entitled 'Sleep patterns in a lone global pilot' for the American *Journal of Aerospace Medicine*. It paid tribute to Sheila's stamina:

> The sheer immensity of the task undertaken by Miss Scott in the flight . . . and the resultant total sleep loss incurred leaves us full of admiration for people of her calibre. Unlike the airline pilot who is carefully cosseted by ground crews wherever he flies and has all the routine of flight planning and meteorology removed from his shoulders, the lone record-breaking pilot has to carry out these duties on his or her own, in addition to supervising refuelling and daily maintenance on aircraft. In addition, there are other pressures such as shortage of money, material support, lack of navigational facilities, poor air-to-ground communications and the ever-present press and news media who may intervene on essential rest periods.

In a foreward to Sheila's second flying autobiography, *On Top of the World*, Phil Chapman wrote: 'Sheila Scott is a truly remarkable woman, an inspiration to all who know her. Her contributions to aviation and to the preservation of the individual human spirit of exploration and adventure are almost unparallelled in our time.' He quoted a line from Tennyson's 'Ulysses' which he felt described her perfectly:

> . . . strong in will.
> To seek, to strive, to find and not to yield.

14

FINANCIALLY, THE POLAR flight was again a disaster. Sheila returned to debts of nearly £20,000 in addition to the money lent to her on HP for the purchase of the aircraft. The theft of the video camera meant that she had no film to sell: she had been banking on making 'several thousand pounds' from this, although no film or television company had given her a firm commitment. No one wanted to buy her story, although many were ready to interview her and write their own synopses for newspapers and magazines.

The renewed round of public appearances and lectures was hardly likely to bring in enough money to pay the instalments on the aircraft, let alone the bills which it had run up; but Sheila was still looking obstinately ahead, to a circumnavigation which would take in both Poles. As a male pilot was already planning precisely this, in a Piper Navajo, a larger and faster aircraft than either of hers, she felt that she had no time to waste. As so often before, she talked vaguely of 'great possibilities of help', but was realistic enough to accept that she would have to sell one of her aircraft. It was the single-engined Comanche which would, she decided reluctantly, have to go, as she could do more with the twin-engined Aztec.

Myth Too was sold to Max Coote, to be used by the Lodge Flying Group at Elstree. '*Myth*'s new owners have turned out to be unbelievably nice people! Isn't it incredible that she should have found them?' she wrote to Kaye. 'I think her story will be a happy one now. Max Coote is the head of her group & he distributes model aircraft! He is a very very kind man (married alas – the sort of man I need – !).' In December 1971 she paid off the outstanding £9000 loan on *Myth Too*; but she still had to meet the monthly repayments on *Mythre*, and could afford to fly only when her expenses were paid: for landing on a racecourse to present prizes, for instance, or to fulfil an occasional filming commitment.

She embarked on a ground-based adventure: learning to drive. On a car provided by the British School of Motoring she was a public guinea pig for Roy Spicer, motoring correspondent of the *Daily Mirror* and a newly qualified instructor. At the beginning of September she wrote to Kaye Maclean, who had recently come out of hospital after one of many operations on her hands for Dupont's contraction: 'It's splendid news that you are driving again. I am starting officially tomorrow but I drove . . . along country lanes last week-end, and it was riotous – every car that approached was a "major epic"! Ough – I hate them – I'd MUCH rather be flying.'

Sheila told Kaye that 'the two major advertising firms in this country' were showing an interest in sponsoring her next major flight, but added: 'as they need 6 to 9 months notice for promotion, I fear it will be too late.' Her letter went on:

> I am doing the duty things necessary around the country as long as I can (unpaid of course) & sit jointly as Guest of Honour with Chay Blyth with HIS enormous sailing pictures behind us – and a glossy book of his sail on the table in front of me – but no aircraft! How cruel can people be? But never mind, I give him a huge kiss and tell them I think he is wonderful, & try not to care when he says he has been given FOUR cars, etc, etc.

When Sheila mentioned to Chay Blyth that she was having driving lessons, he found it, he told me, 'particularly amusing that she had flown around the world in complicated machines and yet did not even possess a driving licence. . . . Ford thought it was equally interesting when I told them and subsequently lent her a car.'

Eventually, in a blaze of publicity, more nervously than she had ever done anything in public, Sheila passed her driving test. Later the same day, in Liverpool, she was one of the team in a charity version of *Any Questions*, organized complete with David Jacobs by a professional fund-raiser, Jeanette Dexter. Jeanette attached a torn-up L-plate to the bouquet presented to Sheila at the end of the evening.

Sheila found it ironic, and irritating, that although no one had ever offered to buy her an aircraft, car manufacturers vied with each other to provide her with a car. Her various secretaries took several messages about cars. Towards the end of November, one of them wrote: 'Would SS mind waiting till Monday before checking up the British Leyland car?' A month later, Sheila was informed that 'British Leyland want to sort out matter of car', followed after a few days by: 'BLMC want Marina back for servicing and insurance.'

She again spent Christmas with the Whitbreads, and at the beginning of January made several guest appearances at the London Boat Show. In spite of her lack of nautical experience, she had made a rash announcement that she hoped to enter in the 1973 yacht race round the world. This was taken seriously enough for Chay Blyth's publicity agent to write to her: 'It occurred to me that you may be interested in taking a sponsored yacht – i.e. a boat financed by a commercial company – and if this is the case I may be able to arrange such a yacht for you.' Footballer Stanley Matthews later spoke to her about possible sponsorship for 'the 73 yacht race'. Sheila's complaint that it seemed that there was money for the asking for anything to do with cars and boats, but not aircraft, seems to have had some justification. The interest in sponsoring her to sail, but not to fly, argues equally against her suspicion that potential sponsors were put off because she was a woman, and the suggestion that there was no interest in anything which was not breaking completely new ground. Yet another car was promised in January, a Capri which was to be delivered from Ford within the next two weeks.

Still no one wanted to sponsor a round-the-world flight across the Arctic and the Antarctic. As Sheila already had the aircraft this would have been no more costly than sponsoring her to sail round the world – and comparatively safe, since she was already an experienced round-the-world pilot who had coped with Arctic flying conditions, but her total practical knowledge of sailing had been gained during a few day sails in Australia and Fiji.

Her financial position was becoming increasingly alarming, and early in April she entered negotiations with Dan Air at Gatwick about the possibility of chartering *Mythre* to ferry flight crews. Sheila wrote:

I am well aware of the problems of some part positioning aircraft, and hope you will understand if I say my aircraft is the most precious thing to me, and I would not allow her to be operated except with the fullest equipment that I can provide her with, and by pilots of some considerable experience. . . . I suggest a male pilot with some airline experience as its chief pilot, as I myself have *much* to learn about the ways of airlines.

Her proposals included 'a further backup of one to two Aztecs (appropriately equipped and approved by you) sharing maintenance periods of G-AYTO'; the three Aztecs were to be flown by a chief pilot and three back-up pilots, 'including Sheila Scott if acceptable', and she suggested an hourly hire charge of £34 with a considerable reduction for contract work.

Before there was time to take this any further Sheila received an invitation she could not resist, to visit an exhibition called Transpo 72 in Washington – which would also give her the opportunity to meet the men from Goddard at last, and to add more records to her total of one hundred. She accepted, brushing aside yet again the problem of finance, and wrote excitedly to Kaye Maclean:

Kaye Darling, – The miracle has happened – we are off on a record attempt 3 WEEKS today!! On absolutely zero finance this end – just begging people to put fuel in, etc, but we are still in the land of the living sky! Plans are: we take off from the final day of the Biggin Hill Air Show (Sunday 21st) in the middle of the air show with star billing (& you can see it live on ITV) for Iceland! Then we are attempting a direct record flight through the middle of the North Atlantic to Washington Transpo DIRECT! *Mythre* and I are flying for our lives – at least we've revived interest & who knows we might really win for keeps. Heaven knows how to do the three months work unaided in 3 weeks, but somehow – we'll do it.

Sheila's transatlatic flight was given advance publicity as 'a double commemoration flight . . . on the 45th Anniversary of Charles Lindbergh's solo Atlantic crossing and the 40th Anniversary of Amelia Earhart's solo Atlantic crossing'. There was a hint of desperation in the press handout prepared for take-off day:

Sheila . . . is literally flying for her life. Her life is flying and unless a sponsor can be found to help to finance her record attempts she will be forced to sell her aircraft and stop flying. Unless a sponsor can be found immediately she not only loses her aircraft but must abandon all hope of her South Polar Flight planned for later this year.

Sheila flies solo in every meaning of the word. . . . Her only revenue is from her lectures and public appearances which fall far short from the type of finance needed for world record attempts.

Sheila has given Britain over 100 records, and the South Pole can be ours too if only a sponsor can be found. . . . Sheila has given everything for Britain. Surely Britain can do something in return and help her put the 'Great' back in Great Britain.

The insurance on *Mythre* had so far been provided free by a specialist aviation company, Oakley, Vaughan and Clarkson. Sheila had not been sent a renewal notice and assumed that the company's sponsorship was still in force. It was not until a few days before the start of her flight that, purely as a matter of routine, her secretary asked for the up-to-date policy so that Sheila could take it with her – only to discover that the firm had been taken over and that the new owners did not feel able to provide free cover.

She was already in enough financial trouble without suddenly having to find £3000 for insurance; the previous week, Lombank had agreed to a three-month moratorium on HP repayments, to allow her time to sort out her finances. Although her secretary was eventually assured verbally that Sheila and the aircraft were after all insured, she set out without her insurance documents.

Max Coote took *Myth Too* to the Biggin Hill Air Show, as well as a replica complete in every detail, including all the signatures and good luck messages. Sheila became sentimentally weepy when he presented her with the model there. She discussed her insurance difficulties with Coote, who was not convinced that she was properly covered and undertook to look into it.

The Capri promised by Ford was presented at Biggin Hill, to ensure maximum mutual publicity. A few minutes before she was due to take off Sheila sat in her new psychedelic green car chatting to Vincent Mulchrone, aviation correspondent of the *Daily Mail* and an ex-fighter pilot. 'Anything that happens to me in the sky is fair enough, and worth losing my life for if necessary, but it's the ground I fear,' she told him.

Nevertheless she had good reason to fear the sky on the Atlantic crossing, which was so rough that in the turbulence three of her ribs were broken and considerable damage was inflicted on the aircraft. 'Yes the flight WAS very tough,' she wrote to Kaye, 'but nevertheless we DID fly together which is the important thing.' She arrived in

Washington, as planned, in time to join in Transpo 72 and to visit the Goddard Space Center. 'The NASA & Naval people are as great as I believed & everyone seems pleased with us,' she wrote to Kaye. 'It seems that London is the place where I get caught in a hopeless cage! . . . I am trying to do the lectures here to keep us a few weeks (& get help for the South Pole) I will be staying with my friend June Eggleston near New York some of the time. Slowly come home via Canada and Iceland in July.'

Meanwhile Max Coote and Jean Duffy, who had been left in charge at Sheila's flat in London, thought that they had sorted out the confusion over her insurance. 'Well, I had a talk with Mr Crouch of Oakley, Vaughan re the insurance and you are covered for third party as arranged by Max (a copy of which you should have) and also Lombanks got on to them re the aircraft and requested them to insure it, which they did, so it seems that you are covered all round,' Jean wrote at the beginning of June, and in another letter, with no date, she reassured Sheila that 'you are *fully covered*', although she had not paid the premium.

Sheila, who had not flown *Mythre* in America until she was certain that her insurance was in order, relaxed and made the most of all social and publicity opportunities. *Mythre* was being overhauled after the Atlantic crossing. 'I am desperately trying to get help,' Sheila wrote to Kaye Maclean, meaning as usual financial backing, 'but I am afraid I am in too deep. Every other kind of help & future experiments is being given – undoubtedly more than any woman pilot before me, so who knows what fate has in store!'

By the time the letter reached Kaye, fate had dealt Sheila the cruellest blow of all: a hurricane swept the west coast of America, leaving a trail of destruction which included the Piper airfield at Lockhaven – where Sheila had thought *Mythre* was safe, but which was flooded. An aerial photograph shows aircraft scattered at random like wingless dragonflies, their wings, and in some cases also their tails, invisible beneath the floodwater. On 26 June Sheila made an entry in her diary: 'The news of *Myth* was awful.' It was two days before she was able to reach Lockhaven to inspect the damage.

From the outside, *Mythre* looked mud-streaked but unharmed. It was not until Sheila opened the door to the cockpit that she realized that hers, like all the other aircraft on the field, had filled with thick, stinking, clinging, liquid mud. Everything, including Buck Tooth, was sodden.

From the Gralyn Hotel in Washington, Sheila wrote a desolate letter to Kaye:

What is there to say for I expect by now you know the news of *Mythre* being drowned by Hurricane Agnes along with ALL Piper aircraft factory's new aircraft. When I went to see her – she smiled at me in the sun as it caught the flags, Union Jack & Stars & Stripes so proudly on her tail still. Inside was ghastly. All the houses around were in pieces and it was a terrible sight. The Americans will be given help by the Government – but I am a British Citizen & so do not qualify. The insurance will pay off the banks but I do not get a penny! Have to pay for borrowed stuff & lost £1000 in personal belongings. However that is nothing compared to the emotional crisis – I don't think I have ever cried like it in my life. I cannot understand why the aircraft went without me. It was the hour & the day one year later when I made contact with earth after flying over the North Pole without communications – uncanny – and we survived all those oceans and a muddy river defeated us.

I have no future – no nothing now whatever the outcome (all aircraft can be rebuilt – if they do I am probably not allowed to fly the world in her – only ordinary flying & that would not allow her to be resold at her correct value & so I would end up owing the banks while someone else owned her!)

People here are trying to help. This hotel does not charge me at all. I am trying to fight back by trying to get 100% sponsorship, lectures, anything, but time here is limited to do it in. I don't think I shall find help in the UK do you? Even though the General Public seem to want to help – the Press are only interested in boats (& the sailors still have their boats!)

I am not meaning to be depressing for I really am fighting but every morning I wake with another heartbreak & loneliness. There has always been a *Myth* to work for & I am lost without. There is nothing to come home for. On the other hand I do have some friends on the credit side so I am trying to smile – but it is a bit of a crooked one!

I do Canada for a few days (& a firm there is paying expenses & with Embassy laying on TV shows to tell my story) then back to this hotel until all the many legal issues are settled. The Insurance Company should be sued but they damn well know I cannot afford lawyers!

Three months ago a documentary film was to be made of my life & the two aircraft. Some help was probably forthcoming for the South Pole – it all seems like a dream now. I expect there is a reason for being the first in the world to hold 100 records & first over the North Pole Eq to Eq & yet is the rest of life being a nothing – but as yet I cannot see where Fate is leading me.

Bless you – my dear – take care of yourself. You have been wonderful to us, and life will take care of you for it, I am sure. I am sorry we failed you.

For the first time she signed off with love only from Sheila – in the past she had always added *Myth*'s love.

Telexes, telephone messages and letters made the legal and insurance position seem even more complex and confused. One of the telexes from the insurance company in London ended: 'We regret and sympathise with you . . . any future venture make sure that you have somebody to take care of your insurance problems correctly.' As two employees of the company had given telephone assurances that she and the aircraft were insured, Sheila had assumed that this was the case.

Early in July Max Coote wrote Sheila a four-page letter outlining the position as he saw it. Although Lombank's interest of £35,000 was fully insured, it appeared that Sheila's instruction for cover for the total value of £50,000 had been ignored since she had not sent the premium. It was, although Coote did not spell this out, ultimately Sheila's responsibility to make sure that she was covered.

'All you can do is let the insurance job proceed and press on with getting sponsorship leaving the rest to sort itself out,' he wrote. 'Then, when you get home . . . with luck plus a fair amount of pressure there is a chance that Clarksons will put right any damage actually done by Hewitt's action or lack of it, though I cannot at this juncture see them being prepared to cover you for free as Hewitt did in the past.' Hewitt had been Sheila's contact both with Oakley, Vaughan and Clarkson and with Clarkson Aviation; she had relied on him as her broker to make sure that she was covered. 'I only wish I could give you better news but there it is. . . . If I hear anything else I will keep you posted but in the meantime do have some fun and don't worry too much.'

Several of her friends in America advised her to sue Piper's; but Sheila felt that they had enough on their plates and would treat her fairly, and refused to do so – even if she had been able to afford lawyer's fees, she would have been reluctant to take them to court.

Lombank's loan was paid off on the £35,000 hull insurance, leaving Sheila with 'the BITS of *Mythre*' to herself, as she put it to Kaye in a letter from the Gralyn Hotel in Washington. It was, in the circumstances, surprisingly cheerful: 'I have been lucky to get a glimpse of wondrous things. The sun is shining through my window (my room is just like a students – up at Oxford or somewhere – old wooden shutters – huge fireplace – how you would smile to see it – but here I can study many things).'

She felt compelled to stay near her aircraft, even when it was in pieces, until its fate was decided, and whiled away her time at the Gralyn by continuing with her second autobiographical book. She had made tape recordings on all her flights since *I Must Fly*, with the idea of writing another book, and had almost finished the first draft before leaving England for America. Lana Jeffers had been persuaded to type it up from Sheila's recordings; by the middle of April they had between them completed three chapters. Sheila was an untidy writer – 'I know it's here somewhere,' she would say as she searched heaps of apparently unrelated sheets of paper.

Among various organizations which invited Sheila to speak to them was one called the Bald Eagles; it was at one of their luncheons, at the end of August, that she met Eleanor Friede, editor of Richard Bach's book *Jonathon Livingstone Seagull* and herself a pilot. Sheila, who identified to a considerable extent with the seagull who wanted to fly, gave Eleanor her uncompleted typescript; a week later, she was told that Macmillan would like to publish it in America. Sheila was jubilant.

When she returned to England in October for the first time since the hurricane, Gerald Pollinger dampened her enthusiasm by pointing out that one way or another she would be in breach of contract: Hodder and Stoughton had an option clause for all rights on her next book in the contract for *I Must Fly*, and could therefore stop Macmillan publishing the new book – for which she had already signed a contract in America. After some negotiation the obvious compromise was reached, whereby Macmillan had American rights and Hodder and Stoughton UK rights. For the British edition Sheila received an advance of £1000, an honourable increase on her previous advance.

Given her financial problems, it seems incredible that she

persisted with plans on paper for an 'Adventure Flight – Equator to Equator via Antarctica', to start in November; but there was just a chance – a remote chance – that her optimism might be repaid and that she might find a sponsor. Her adventure description stated unrealistically that work on rebuilding the Aztec was expected to be completed in September, although 'another twin engine aircraft could be leased if necessary and allowing approximately six weeks for the aircraft to be prepared and for its test flight'.

The stated aims of the flight were

> to be the first woman to fly Antarctica solo; and over South Pole (starting and finishing at Equator thereby establishing an FAI world class record); to continue with small scientific experiments such as performed by NASA/Naval Air Test Center/General Instrument Corporation via satellite Nimbus and IRLS equipment. . . ; to find and film adventure and compare environment of both sides of the world below the Equator as seen from a woman's eye for future story, lecture and film use; to further develop personal philosophies particularly that travel (and modern technology as used in space) promotes friendship and peace amongst all people when one communicates directly with them.

She had worked out a brief outline for filming, including 'Trinidad, a fabulous visual and aural start'; 'Chile – Punta Arenas: positioning . . . for the ultimate challenge of Antarctica'; 'Tarawa, the Pacific atoll one dreams with coral runway among palm trees'.

Instead, her only travelling was between America and Britain, by commercial airline. On either side of the Atlantic she was obsessed with her determination to retain and rebuild *Mythre* at all costs, and accepted any paying public appearance with alacrity, if not always with enthusiasm. As part of her enforced economy drive she dispensed with secretarial help, except on an occasional part-time basis. She spent more time in America than in Britain, and in her efforts to obtain a loan from the Small Business Association, which was making money available to American hurricane victims at 1 per cent interest, made Phil Chapman a director of Sheila Scott Flying Enterprises.

Towards the end of February, she had just returned from America when she went to Brighton to give a Wednesday evening lecture to a group of Conservative women. Talking about her flights and her aircraft was painful, but so far she had always managed to do so without giving way to her great sense of loss and emptiness. On this occasion she was so exhausted that, ten minutes before the end of the lecture, for the first time in her life she dried. Although she was clearly in a state of nervous collapse, instead of putting her up in a hotel and calling a doctor her hostesses allowed her to return to London by train. When she reached her flat, she gave way to despair and stayed there without seeing or speaking to anyone for the next two days.

At some point between then and Friday evening, she took an overdose. A well-known publisher called as arranged to take her out for a drink on Friday evening. He was as aware as were all her friends of the depths of depression into which Sheila had sunk after the loss of her aircraft, and when she did not answer the door he feared the worst. He fetched the porter, who unlocked the door. They found Sheila unconscious. Beside her were three empty pill bottles which had contained Seconal, Mogadon and Paracetamol: how many of each Sheila had taken it was impossible to tell. Presumably the unnamed publisher did not consider her in any imminent danger as, rather than calling an ambulance, he telephoned his personal assistant and asked her to stay in the flat for the night; she slept on the sofa in the sitting room.

Early on the Saturday morning, Lana Jeffers was woken by the telephone. 'I'm ——'s PA, and I'm at Sheila Scott's flat. I expect you know why I'm calling you.' Although Sheila had often threatened suicide, Lana had never taken her seriously; nevertheless she knew immediately why she was being summoned. The publisher's PA had found her telephone number in Sheila's address book.

Lana went straight round to the flat, and called a doctor – not Sheila's usual one, as he was away for the weekend, and not, for some reason, Teddy Sugden. Sheila was by then conscious, but in a very disturbed state, and at first did not recognize Lana, who had 'a trying day'. At one point Sheila got out of the front door along the corridor outside the flat, dressed in a thick, fleecy dressing gown. Lana held on to her and pulled her back into the flat, where Sheila plunged into a bath of cold water clutching a humidifier. Lana managed to unplug it.

While the publisher's PA tried on the telephone to find a nursing home or hospital which would admit her, Sheila and Lana sat facing each other. Sheila's arms were already covered with cigarette burns, and unflinchingly, still staring at Lana, she stubbed cigarette after cigarette out on her skin or with her bare feet.

At last a bed was found for her at Bowden House, a private psychiatric nursing home in Harrow. It was late in the afternoon when Lana and Sheila arrived there. Sheila commented on the fact that there were pictures of aeroplanes on the walls of the corridor. She was put to bed, and after giving brief details to a psychiatrist Lana left her. The next day, when Lana went to see her, Sheila said belligerently: 'Whoever put me in here will have to pay the bill.' They never talked about why Sheila had attempted to kill herself. Lana did not feel up to going into it, and Sheila did not mention it.

Although Lana now had a demanding job with Hill Samuel, Sheila assumed that she would 'run the network'. During the following weeks she kept her busy, ringing her at frequent intervals with instructions like: 'Tell Colonel Whitbread I need a case of white wine.' When Colonel Whitbread visited Sheila, he was shocked to find her 'quite mentally deranged' and did not expect her to recover.

'I first met her in early March 1973 when she was admitted to the clinic following an overdose of tablets,' Dr Colin Herridge of Bowden House told me. 'She had previously [before she started flying] been here under the care of Dr William Knapman for difficulties associated with alcohol abuse, but I have no details of this. . . . She saw her whole livelihood as finished and hence the overdose.

'When she was admitted she was very muddled and confused and it was thought that she might have some organic brain disease, but her consciousness gradually cleared and it became apparent that the muddlement was due to the aftermath of the drug overdose. For a time she was very histrionic and difficult to approach, and then it became apparent that she had intense paranoid feelings which were on occasion of psychotic intensity. Thus, she felt that there was a global conspiracy to prevent her having any success in life, and at times she wondered whether she was under unwilling hypnosis. Unfortunately, she could not be persuaded to accept treatment after the initial few days in the clinic. She was very suspicious about medication and also became disturbed that the nursing staff were somehow tied up with the persecution which she felt. It was decided there was little point in keeping her in the clinic when she took this attitude, and she was therefore allowed to discharge herself. It was accepted that her real-life situation was a very difficult one and that she was a histrionic lady of basically hysterical/dissociative pre-morbid personality.'

Sheila went to stay with Freydis and Tim Sharland, who gave her the use of a flat which they had prepared for an aged aunt at their house in Lane End, near High Wycombe. Their friendship, and the country air, helped her to recover. While she was there, she drafted a company report for Sheila Scott Flying Enterprises for the year 1972/73:

This should have been SSFE's most successful year – partly recouping from benefits of past several years endeavours (& losses). Apart from usual lectures/radio/TV/new books an Adventure Flight was planned to South Pole & both sides of world with a film being made (when it was expected to pay off aircraft mortgage) and magazine contract. NASA & US Navy were prepared to give full assistance & permissions had been partly obtained. Agnes Hurricane both destroyed aircraft, & used up book earnings etc to attempt to save aircraft, and lost film, magazine rights, & second book income. It is hoped aircraft loan will now come through, and aircraft can be loaned to university MIT, Boston, in order to repay US mortgage.

The aircraft was found to be morally insured but technically not. It was decided by Lloyds representative & Lombank & SS to try & rebuild aircraft. Work started in USA but three months later (October) Lombanks decided to terminate the mortgage. The work to date ($24,551) was paid for by Aviation General of Lloyds & Lombanks given the change out of Breach of Warranty, and the cleaned up pieces of aircraft alloted to me. I tried for many months to raise a loan from the SBA Hurricane Victims Fund in USA, etc (as all other victims helped; I was a British subject). Eventually I got Catlin Aviation to start rebuilding aircraft (as it could only have any value other than scrap value as a flying aircraft). Meanwhile I got a contract both sides of the ocean to write a book. This enabled me to fight for the aircraft both sides of the ocean, and so SSFE survived another year!

An appeal launched by the London branch of Zonta to raise money for Sheila's aircraft received such a poor response that a few months later it was closed. The committee returned all the cheques to the donors for which it had addresses, and sent Sheila the remaining grand total of £27.

In April she finished her second book, the American version of which she called *Barefoot in the Sky*. The title she had chosen for the UK edition, *On Top of the World*, must have seemed particularly ironic: it was less than a year since she had been both literally and metaphorically on top of the world, and in the intervening time she had plumbed the depths of hell. The last few paragraphs of the book give some insight into her state of mind: 'Perhaps I may have to start my life all over again, and maybe do it right next time!' she wrote, explaining that she had discovered through her long solo flights what it was to be alone, and by doing so had learnt that this was 'but an infinitesimal part of understanding'.

With her aircraft, she claimed to have fought 'mythical giants and devils', but was only just begining to understand 'that there can be many other areas and vehicles in oneself':

> One can always go on discovering more and it possibly requires far more discipline and courage to do it this simple way. Discipline to prevent your imagination going wild and to stick to the aims you have set yourself; courage is required in all sorts of ways, sometimes in such homely ways as when and whether you should be leaving your room or deserting your studies to please others, or equally whether in reality you are learning from these associations, or whether your mutual negative emotions make both you and them worse.

She felt that it required courage 'to keep yourself on the accepted sane path, for if you let your imagination run wild, insanity will be said to have crept in. I do not believe that those who recognize and are truly striving to understand inexplicable chances and happenings are peculiar.'

She was not yet ready to admit that her horizons had been limited. As she was still considered Britain's flying heroine, and was guaranteed to ensure publicity for any event she attended, she was invited to participate in a variety of functions. Among the most enjoyable was the first International Tour of Britain organized by the British Racing and Sports Car Club, in which she acted as co-driver for the champion British woman racing driver Alison Davies in a Fiat 124ST.

There were, however, few opportunities to fly, although in October she added First Woman to Fly Concorde to her list of achievements when she was invited to join Brian Trubshaw on a publicity demonstration flight. The following month, her book was launched with a flurry of publicity. Paper aeroplane menus graced the table at the launch lunch. The reviews were almost without exception favourable, with comments like 'exciting, sometimes moving, and always readable, it reveals a courageous, sensitive – and truly feminine – spirit'.

15

WHILE SHE WAS still fighting to retain her aircraft, Sheila appeared on the television programme *This Is Your Life*. She hated it. It seemed almost like an obituary to her flying career, which she was not yet ready to admit was over. If it had not been that she was fetched by a friend, Kay Bird, she would have refused to participate. 'Sheila had been conned into going to Elstree, where *Myth Too* was being repainted,' Kay Bird told me. 'I was in the green room when the producer rushed in. "Kay, I want you to do the pick-up," he said. "Sheila can be a strange person, but she gets on with you. Tell her we won't be mentioning her marriage or her stepmother." ' Halfway to the studio, Sheila insisted on going first to her flat. 'I want to get my rabbit,' she told Kay, who was afraid that she intended to lock herself in.

The recording was tense and difficult. Sheila felt that all the wrong people had come along – like a large contingent from the British Women Pilots' Association, whom she called 'dreadful little women', although individually she was on good terms with many of them – and few of those she really cared about, like the engineers at Oxford: they had been invited, but did not feel that appearing on television was 'their thing'. Afterwards she refused to speak to her father, who she felt had let her down by not helping her to pay for the repairs to her aircraft.

'For God's sake rescue me,' she said to John Blake. He took her and a Fijian chief, one of the few people whom Sheila was genuinely delighted to see, to the Steering Wheel Club, where the six-foot-six chief's formal Fijian attire of a grass skirt and bare feet caused some consternation.

'Sheila was very strange after the show,' Kay Bird told me. 'She kept saying "They don't really care about me." ' Sheila felt that she had been abandoned by many of those who had claimed to be her friends; she had spent so little time at home for the previous two years that many had lost touch with her, and others found her constant tales of woe off-putting.

She did not feel that she belonged anywhere, although she was tempted to settle on the American side of the Atlantic – perhaps in Canada, where she told a reporter on the *Toronto Sun*, Joan Sutton, that she would like to be able to buy a farm. Canadian men, she said, were terrific at making a woman feel like a woman: 'and if you doubt that,' she added, 'come and live in London for a while'.

'In some ways, Sheila Scott is a paradox,' Joan Sutton wrote.

One has only to read the story of her life . . . to realize that she must be strong-willed, determined and adventurous. Yet, one's initial impression is vulnerability. She's obviously apprehensive about the impossible quality of any interview – revealing oneself in 30 minutes to a complete stranger is a high price to pay, even for the promotion of a book. She is self-conscious about her appearance, concerned about being photographed before going to the hairdresser. She is also quick to pick up ESP-type vibrations about the interviewer's feelings. 'I've already done one interview in Toronto,' she said, 'where I felt waves of dislike, before I even said anything. . . . I'm still afraid of being hurt – physically and emotionally.'

The article talked of her flying career as 'almost a philosophy of life', 'a love affair' – and an expensive one – with 'moments of almost complete fulfilment'.

In May 1974, Sheila and Phil Chapman signed an agreement which assigned to him, 'by way of a donation and for no consideration . . . a certain Piper Aztec Aircraft, PA-23 series 250, serial number 27-4568, and all equipment, accessories, supplies and appurtenances thereto'. As far as he was concerned, although legally this made the aircraft his, he was still looking after *Mythre* for Sheila. As soon as the repairs to the aircraft were completed he flew it from Lockhaven to Bedford in Massachusetts, where apart from one trip to Baffin Island it languished in a hangar.

Sheila announced her decision to sell *Mythre* the following month, when she claimed that she was returning to the theatre. 'I have had a television audition and there are plans for an acting job in the theatre,' she said. She was apparently hoping that she would play herself in a dramatized version of her life, but nothing came of the idea. She still took second place in the public imagination to Amy Johnson, although the two heroines of the air were linked in the press when Sheila was invited to Hull in July to unveil a long-overdue statue commemorating Amy. The Mayor of Hull paid her the kind of tribute she liked: 'It is fitting that the memorial to the greatest airwoman of her era should be unveiled by the greatest airwoman of this era.'

For Sheila it was, although she could not bring herself to admit it, the end of an era when *Mythre* was sold for $45,000 to an acquaintance of Phil Chapman's who operated a bush service in Churchill, Alberta. It was in his view a fair market price, although Sheila thought he should have been able to get more. She was incensed when the state of Massachusetts claimed 5 per cent as sales tax, and had little patience with the lawyers who took months to retrieve the money. As far as she was concerned the state had no moral right to the tax, and the law was therefore an ass.

Although Kay Bird gained the impression that Sheila received only one small payment from the sale, and made strenuous efforts both personally and through her solicitor to chase up the rest, Phil Chapman has assured me that he never laid hands on any of the money. Sheila had, as he put it, been so beaten down by fate that it had made her not entirely rational – although he did not consider her exactly irrational – and was 'getting a little frantic' about the time it took the lawyers to get the sales tax back.

Sheila was fifty-four when *Mythre* was sold – a reasonable enough age to give up testing herself with gruelling long-distance records; but she was neither resigned to being permanently grounded, nor did she have the energy to carry on fighting. She felt that she was right back where she had started.

There seemed outwardly no reason why she should not make a reasonable living in one of a number of ways, but she did not feel qualified to do anything except fly, and made no attempt to gain employment. Elizabeth Overbury did not think she would have been given work in British aviation: 'With the odd people who said she was difficult, who would have employed her? There were people in aviation who disliked her and put about rumours. Everyone is so delighted to run Sheila down – yes, she did have her faults, but don't we all? She did things which you and I could not have done – a hundred and seven world records in a very short space of time. She was not appreciated as herself; she may have been her own worst enemy inasmuch as, with her actress attitude to life, she expected to be admired all the time, whereas the average pilot just mingles in and if the light doesn't shine just continues to mingle.' But Sheila had become too well known to mingle easily, and felt abandoned when the light stopped shining on her.

The charity work into which she threw herself was only partially satisfying; she felt caged, and was too nervous on stage to enjoy the RSPCA benefit *Any Questions* shows in which Jeanette Dexter invited her to participate. She was more relaxed with children than with an adult audience, and described a children's visit to the RSPCA Animal Hostel at London Airport to Kaye Maclean: '. . . would you believe it with all the animals by the thousand that they handle, all they had were hundreds of dear little monkeys en route for heaven knows what, so they had to put up with me telling them about Polar Bears at the North Pole'.

A few months later, she told Kaye about another charity occasion:

> I was allowed to take ten children from the Eastend school to the Royal Tournament – two of them sat in the Royal Box with me in the interconnecting box! They were THRILLED, but you can probably imagine the scene with me smuggling in the sweeties and coca cola to keep them quiet. The place rang with embarrassing cries of 'Sheila what's that', and you can hardly tell kids who've never been to such places to shut up because they are in the Royal Box. Anyway my better nature won, and so I let them, as I reasoned we would not have been invited in if somebody had not understood.

As founder of the British 99s Sheila continued to support their activities, and for their tenth anniversary celebrations enlisted the organizational help of Jeanette Dexter. For the first time, Jeanette became aware of the antagonistic attitude towards Sheila from the British press; it was only because Princess Alexandra – Sheila's 'favourite royal' – and Angus Ogilvie were present that the event was given any coverage.

Among Sheila's many half-formulated projects which came to nothing was a film about flying, in which Jeanette was to have participated as a pupil; but she was not, as Jeanette put it, 'enthused about anything': 'she had immense talent, but was lacking in confidence, depressive, pulling herself and others down. She wanted something which wasn't there.' Kay Bird spent many hours in Sheila's flat working with her on the script, which was mentioned in a letter to Kaye Maclean after a weekend in Somerset:

> Thank you for a lovely weekend. It was marvellous to see you – and wonderful to be in such beautiful surroundings. The view from Archie's window really is fairytale – a little like your love for each other – for I've always thought it was one of the real romances between you two. – I am so enjoying my flowers (and the eggs & cream! Tonight I'm serving them to a girl friend who's helping me with a sort of script – so she'll enjoy them too!)

She felt disorientated and lost in London, but rejected the suggestion made by South African friends that she should settle there. Nevertheless she spent much of 1975 in South Africa, where she was lent an isolated cottage near Durban with a large black dog for company and protection. Her excuse for going there, and then on to Rhodesia, was to undertake research for a book on pioneer women aviators including Beryl Markham, retired Kenyan race-horse trainer, *femme fatale* and transatlantic record-breaking pilot of the 1930s.

While she was in South Africa, Sheila came into contact with a non-denominational non-political non-profit-making organization called World Unity Trust. Its spiritual beliefs, incorporating elements of both Buddhism and Christianity, corresponded closely with her own religious instincts. The Johannesburg chairman, Cheryl Lea, told me her impressions of Sheila: 'Sheila . . . showed a real interest in the spiritual principles which form the basis of our work. We talked deep into the night . . . and I was struck by the intelligence and breadth of her approach to life. She believed firmly in life after death and in reincarnation. She appeared to have read widely and eclectically about these subjects and was convinced that we are responsible for our own destiny, that our actions and attitudes make us what we are, and that karma exacts that toll which we have ourselves evoked and likewise accords us our rewards.'

'I feel as if I have heard all this before,' Sheila told Cheryl, 'it is all so natural for me to accept what you say. I believe everything you are telling me, it is touching chords somewhere deep inside of me and being put into words by you.' All her previously inexplicable sense of having been on the edge of understanding while she was flying, and of having been guided and saved by some external force, fell into place and fitted in with a personal message given her by a master – the title given, Cheryl Lea explained, to the hierarchy of resurrected men and women who had evolved from lifetime to lifetime until they were, in the words of St Luke, 'equal unto the angels . . . the chidren of God, being the children of the Resurrection'.

In her determination to attend a meeting at which she was to receive the master's message Sheila drove through a severe tropical thunderstorm, wondering whether she was being fearless or foolish to continue. By continuing, she felt that she had somehow proved herself worthy to be a member of the group, which was told – but without knowing her identity – that the new disciple was

> a much sought-after celebrity with all the qualifications which make her both highly attractive and deeply interesting. Yet she remains remote, untouched by it, searching the boundless areas of the mind for the answers which it is hoped will now be revealed to her – if she surmounts the hurdles which always beset the path of a new member: it is as if the Soul tests the Personality. . . . Indications are promising . . . as far as this disciple is concerned. She has proved her courage and sensitivity.

The master's long private message to Sheila spoke of 'the need for sacrifice that is rewardless in order to clear the way to higher planes – to the mental plane of purity, truth and wisdom, or service, solitude and unity – the plane of *reality*'. 'Having explored the skies of the outer world, the disciple then soars to inner heights, penetrating the barriers and finding the sevenfold rainbow that leads him through Ashramic Consciousness into the ultimate silence – the peace and bliss of union with Life – which is God, the Father,' Sheila was told by the master, who revealed that she had from time to time been aware of his Presence: 'this Presence is not that of an individual but that of a *consciousness* – "Light" which you have attributed to other sources.'

Cheryl Lea found Sheila 'a warm, entertaining, natural, courageous person. She had great humility in spite of her worldliness, fame and experience. I was, in particular, struck by her beauty. She was not young, yet she had retained her looks and trimness. She had a mannerism of flicking her hair with a slender, manicured hand so that it shone and scintillated in the artificial light. She was gentle and appealing and I found her altogether one of the loveliest people I have known, and that is the truth. And what also struck me was the fact that she was soft-spoken and gentle, and yet she had accomplished those incredible feats which demanded not only skill and courage, but sustained perseverance.'

Spiritually fortified and physically rested, Sheila announced on her return from South Africa that she was planning to leave England again in December, for the flight over the South Pole. 'I need £100,000, and with luck I will achieve it,' she told reporters optimistically, although she took no specific action to find the money.

In May, she was invited by the Girls' Venture Corps to christen their new aircraft during a celebration near Scarborough to mark the forty-fifth anniversary of Amy Johnson's flight to Australia. 'Our Cadets really enjoyed meeting you and appreciate your friendly interest in their activities,' their director, Hazel Prosper, wrote.

By July, depression had again taken hold of her, as she revealed in a letter to Kaye Maclean. She was about to leave for Idaho, where she was to attend a 99s' convention and to discuss the possibility of Britain hosting their 1978 international get-together, and told Kaye that she was relieved that two representatives of the British Tourist Board were to share 'presenting the bid': 'I am almost too depressed to sell it by myself, and the thought of having to organize all these women from all over the world terrifies me. . . . I had better make the most of this trip though as I cannot see myself ever returning so I had better shut up and be grateful for small mercies.'

American hospitality soon banished her gloom, and led to a new friendship with balloonist 99er Rosemary Longmire and her husband Tom, who invited her to stay with them for a fortnight in Southern California. Rosemary liked and admired Sheila, and wished that she had 'her fantastic ability'.

Instead of setting off for the South Pole in December Sheila went again to South Africa, as a British representative at an International Convention of Women. *Monument*, a newsletter for South African settlers, gave a glowing account of the five-day 'convention of women from different countries and from different walks of life' who

met 'for enlightenment and discussion in an effort to promote goodwill
and understanding'. It was opened by Mrs Tini Vorster, described as
the Prime Minister's wife and a pioneer graduate welfare worker, and
was, according to American anthropologist Margaret Mead, 'a
spiritual experience . . . a victory of understanding'.

There were, *Monument* reported,

> Whites, English and Afrikaans-speaking; Coloureds; Indians and
> Blacks – Zulu, Xhosa and Swazi. There were the women who
> came from S.W. Africa, Rhodesia, Great Britain, Europe, the
> United States and the Far East. . . . There were conflicting views,
> . . . heated debates, . . . confrontation. . . . As the Rev. Unez
> Smuts said: 'We did not always agree on many issues, but at least
> we knew why we disagreed. Knowing this we can begin to build
> bridges.'

Sheila's comment, among those of several dozen other women, was
published: '. . . wonderful convention in living monument . . . you
have achieved something few have been able to do.'

On a less serious note, Sheila's 'slender, manicured' hands were
the subject of a long article by a palmist, Mary Anderson, published
in a magazine called *Prediction* in January 1976. They revealed
among other qualities sensitivity, a dynamic personality and a
tough, resilient character, an explosive nature when anyone disagreed with her reasoning, and a need and ability to face challenge.
From the end of her forties Sheila's life should, according to the
palmist's reading, have been 'far more settled and successful'.

Whether or not Sheila believed this – she was well past the end of
her forties, and feeling far from settled or successful – she submitted
her handwriting to a further personality probe, reported in an
undated, anonymous two-page report which was typed entirely in
capital letters:

> Although reason dominates impulse as a rule underlying her
> poise and notwithstanding the stamina associated with her
> smooth nervo-muscular co-ordination, she is not only aware of
> powerful imaginative forces, but is subject to an intense excit-
> ability related to her not wholly admitted desire to prove her
> worth in the scheme of things . . . although she is secretive about
> her private projects . . . and tends to resent interference in her

plans, the overall balance of her lively graphic expression indicates that her feminine sensitivity would not permit her thoughtlessly to sacrifice other people's feelings to her own needs. . . .

On at least one occasion Sheila visited a fortune teller, whom she invited to one of her own parties. At each of these gatherings there was a different collection of people, as one after another acquaintances either faded away or became associated in her mind with some imagined plot against her.

Although in public she kept up a rational front, Sheila's behaviour in private was becoming, as Jeanette Dexter put it, 'odder than usual': 'her speech was strange. It was more than just depression. She seemed mentally unstable, and could be irrational and unconnected. Often she did not make sense – but yet she could. If she was uptight she would go round in circles, nothing linked and so one couldn't find out what was wrong.' At such times she was again convinced that she was being followed; Jeanette put this down to attention-seeking: 'Sheila no longer flew, had written two books, had given everyone who wanted to hear them her set speeches – there was nothing left for her to do. She was incapable of finding anything else to do, because she was not interested: her flying past was her be-all and end-all.'

Nancy Wise, who had made a television film about *Myth Too* and was a close friend of Sheila's during the 1960s, also found her conversation increasingly disjointed, but felt unable to help her because of her 'elusive personality'. She summed Sheila up as 'basically a really nice person, but with just one cog missing – she was generous, had humour, told a good story, had a good appearance and party manners; but she was so far removed from reality.'

Towards the end of May 1976, Sheila's grasp on reality became seriously distorted by her deepening depression. On 27 May she made a partially illegible entry in her diary – the legible part of which claimed 'set up starts in earnest, i.e. car – deliberate & remembered'. Quite what she thought was being set up, or by whom or why, I have no idea, but the next night, after writing several telephone numbers on a piece of paper which she left on a table, with that of Gwen Bellew prominently displayed for emergenices, she made another suicide attempt. At two in the morning she slashed her wrists with a kitchen knife. When this merely produced a surprising amount of blood, she flung on an old camel coat, rushed out of the flat, and a few minutes later drove into a lamp-post: this was probably accidental, but inevitably attracted the attention of the police. Nevertheless the incident was somehow kept out of the press.

At 4 a.m., Gwen Bellew was woken by the telephone: 'Sheila is seriously ill – please ring this number.' She rang the number given, but did not know where it was. Sheila answered. 'I can't say what I've done but I've had an accident – I hit a telegraph pole in my car. Can you clean up my flat? I have a hazy recollection of it being in an awful mess when I left.'

Next day Gwen enlisted the help of another 99er. The porter let them into the flat, which was indeed in 'an awful mess': there was blood on clothes, on the floor and walls, and on the kitchen knife which Sheila had used to cut herself. Afterwards, Sheila said to Gwen: 'I can't thank you enough.' Her only explanation was that, after being spoilt by all the fuss and praise, 'the moment you stop, no one remembers you, you know no one.'

Although the physical damage she had inflicted was not serious, she was clearly in a seriously disturbed mental state and was admitted to Horton Hospital in Epsom for psychiatric observation and treatment. When Elizabeth Overbury visited her there, she made no mention of her suicide attempt, but just said that she was depressed.

Connie Fricker, with whom Sheila had stayed on several occasions, lived a few miles from Epsom, at Ashtead. Gwen Bellew told her that Sheila was in hospital after a suicide attempt: 'We're keeping it quiet – no one at the hospital knows who she is.'

Connie rushed straight to the hospital, where she told me that she found Sheila 'in a terrible state': 'she was dishevelled, her clothes were dirty, she was lying in bed staring at the ceiling and hadn't eaten for two days. Her wrists were stitched where she'd slashed them. She was locked into her room, because she kept trying to get out and was behaving violently.'

The next day, Connie asked if she could take Sheila out in the car. This was agreed to only reluctantly, but she felt that it was the only way to stop her 'sitting staring'. They went to Bentall's in Kingston where they had a spending spree on Connie's account: she bought Sheila new underclothes and tops so that she could at least change and feel clean, and told the shop assistant that her friend had had an accident. Sheila kept trying to run out of the changing room.

In the restaurant to which Connie insisted on taking her next, Sheila reluctantly agreed to drink some coffee and eat a ham sandwich. She then, as Connie put it, 'came round a bit' and said that she would like to have her hair done: this had always been a morale booster, and afterwards she began to recover, although she was 'a bit peculiar' in the car on the way back to the hospital.

Connie obtained permission to take Sheila out again for a 99s' meeting at Gwen Bellew's house. Sheila was at the time vice-governor; Connie told Gwen that she would take on the position until Sheila was better. Everyone else was told that Sheila was ill, but not that she had tried to kill herself.

Before the meeting, Connie took Sheila to her house, where they were sitting with Connie's husband Alan on the patio after lunch when Sheila turned on them: 'This is what I ought to have, you know!' They calmed her down, but later, when she had asked if she could have a bath, Sheila ran round the house naked, to the intense embarrassment of Alan, who shut himself in his study. Sheila asked Connie if she could borrow some clothes; although they were far from the same size, Connie readily agreed, but when Sheila then ransacked her wardrobe and left everything on the floor she was far from pleased: 'It took me two hours to tidy up,' she told me.

At the 99s' meeting, Connie was elected vice-governor. Sheila looked at her with hatred. 'This is the last thing I wanted,' she said as she rushed first upstairs and then out of the house. 'We all had to go looking for Sheila in the dark,' Connie told me, 'and found her lying under a parked car. It took four of us to get her out from under it and into our car, and all the way back to the hospital I had to keep a grip on her arm.'

Sheila did not speak to Connie again for several years, and included her among those who she thought had stabbed her in the back. Nevertheless, although she was on the receiving end of Sheila's persecution complex, and certainly did not see her through rose-coloured spectacles, Connie's admiration and affection for her were undiminished. She considered her a manic depressive with tendencies to schizophrenia – a condition of which she told me, without elaborating, that she had had some personal experience – and accepted that Sheila did not want to be reminded of the help that she had needed when she was at her lowest and had shown herself at her worst.

The scars on Sheila's wrists gradually faded, but until they did she camouflaged them with powder: she did not want to admit that she had attempted to kill herself. According to the records at Horton Hospital she was admitted on 29 May, left 'on leave' on 6 June, and was discharged in her absence on 17 June.

Within a few weeks Sheila was again in America, where she showed no sign of mental instability. She stayed with the Longmires in Escondida, and then set out with Rosemary for Sacramento, near San Diego, where she was to be honorary starter for the last Powder Puff, a cross-country air race for women which had started in 1929 and had done as much as anything else to make men take women pilots seriously. They stopped on the way at a motel in Carmel; it was Rosemary's birthday, and Sheila insisted on buying her a drink. 'She had a drink too, and then several more,' Rosemary told me. 'I finally got her back to the motel room.'

Sheila told reporters in America that she was not enjoying her enforced retirement from flying. 'Just tell me where I can find the money for another aircraft,' she pleaded. She gave several lectures while she was there, concentrating on what a newspaper called 'eerier topics': her extra-sensory experiences and beliefs.

'I feel our scientific achievements are developing much more rapidly than our personal philosophies in this age of technology,' Sheila told audiences. 'Yet undoubtedly we are on the edge of a new life, which must include the Universe – not merely Planet Earth. Already in a mere generation metaphysically the earth has shrunk, and via satellite television we can communicate through most of it within microseconds. This should have given us the major advantage of the bringing closer together of all kinds of people.'

As far as her flying was concerned, she insisted that 'we went into a realm far beyond electronics'. 'Much of it was accomplished by sheer positive thought by a group of highly scientific NASA men, physically using electronics, but men who at the same time used their own magical mental potentialities and sheer willpower that I should make it safely,' she claimed. 'Some of the help was undoubtedly from an overall power, for I believe that man is wasting and has lost the use of nine-tenths of his brain, but that it is still possible to reach other levels for which we have no spoken language – and to which some people are afraid to admit for they fear being laughed at.'

Sheila was so convinced of what she said that she apparently did not fear being laughed at, although as she revealed in a letter to

Kaye Maclean after her return from America she was aware that other people sometimes thought her 'mad':

> My dear, I am so sorry that I seem so neglectful after all that you have done for me. I never dreamt that life would become so awful on the ground, if I told you the truth it is a never ending nightmare, which means one gets into ever greater and worse messes it seems. So it's better not to go on about it all but to try and find a new life, and to try and only remember better times. I do so hope you have not been hurt by my lack of communication.
>
> The hospital was a bad time, and I have not really got over the shock. Though America was good for me and gave me something new to think about even if it was only watching other people fly off!! This is not supposed to be a misery letter! In fact this is one of the reasons that I am trying to change my life a bit 'cos miseries give not so nice people a chance to call one mad, or some such thing!! This letter sounds as if I am, but you know what I mean. I spend as much time as I can staying with friends just outside London at the above address (gloating in the country air and a whole new vista of things – like squirrels in the garden, and taking the dog for a ramble, and watching things grow). I am trying to find some inspiration to start writing again, and hopefully there are a few lecture bookings later on. I am trying to let my flat for short periods to cover its expenses, but that is not easy as of course I have to know who I am letting it to, or there could be complications all round.

The letter was written from the home of Freydis and Tim Sharland, where Sheila was attempting to get to grips with a book which was to be an anthology of handy hints, favourite quotations, potted philosophy and recipes: 'the flotsam of my mind', as she called it on the provisional title page. Although she never completed it, her notes include a drawing of 'Me by Me' and two quotations, the first from T. S. Eliot:

> Time past and time present
> Allow but a little consciousness
> To be conscious is not to be in time.

The sayings of the one-time Secretary-General of the United

Nations, Dag Hammarskjold, provided the second: 'Pray that your loneliness may spur you into something to live for and great enough to die for.'

The book was one of several she discussed with her agent, Gerald Pollinger, but for none of which she wrote outlines or obtained commissions – perhaps if she had had a commission, she would have felt committed enough to finish one of them; she had always claimed that once she had said she would do something, she would do everything in her power to carry it through. Other potential titles she suggested at various times were *Growing Up, Growing Older* and *Cats* – in her letters to Kaye she occasionally mentioned 'my feline friends'. They also talked about the possibility of a book on the carving up of airline routes after the war and the suspicion that the sabotage of Comets was connected with this. Sheila later said that one of her books had been banned by the government: she was presumably referring to this one, which would certainly have been controversial.

When Freydis offered Sheila a home she assumed that, as Sheila claimed she wanted peace and quiet to write a book, she would be no trouble; but instead she found that Sheila wanted to be involved in anything that was going on, and spent little time on her writing. 'She was low, and cast an atmosphere around by being irrational and depressed, taking a glum view of everything,' Freydis explained, adding honestly that she envied Sheila's appearance and star quality: it was galling, when she had been busy preparing for guests, to be outshone.

It would not be fair to give the impression that having Sheila to live with them presented the Sharlands with nothing but extra problems. 'There were many rewards,' Freydis told me, 'but . . .'. Her voice tailed off as she remembered the traumas. Her children liked Sheila, although only the youngest, Angie, was at home all the time. Angie was seventeen, and according to Freydis 'realized that Sheila needed fun and gaiety'.

Several weeks after my first conversation with Freydis, she wrote to me about Sheila's 'sparkle and gaiety': 'I think she gave herself most generously. I'm forever noticing snippets in letters and thinking "I must tell Sheila that" – she enjoyed so many things. . . . It wasn't all bad – in fact we had a lot of good times.'

Sheila repaid Freydis by helping to look after her elderly Aunt Selina. Selina Shuttleworth-King had featured anonymously many years before in a primary school textbook as an example of 'a typical British eccentric'. She dressed in exotic clothes and hats, had been painted by the President of the Royal Academy in one of her more extraordinary outfits, had studied religion and was a British Israelite; one of her best friends was a Hindu. She had had two sons – one had been killed in the Battle of Britain; the second had died soon afterwards – and a daughter, who was an invalid.

In return for a large attic room, with a window overlooking the garden at either end, Sheila gave Freydis some respite from her aunt's need for almost constant supervision, although it was a moot point whether she was more of a help than an added burden. Until Sheila moved in with the family, Freydis had not realized how difficult her temperament could be to work with: 'Sheila was always wanting more affection, demanding recognition, always feeling that people didn't think she was good enough.' Freydis had had fifteen years as a marriage guidance counsellor, for which she had had some psychiatric training, so felt that she could understand Sheila's problems; 'but I had never met a Sheila before,' she told me. Even having Sheila to stay after her first suicide attempt had not prepared her for the long-term strain within the family of living with her for months on end.

'Sheila met her match in Selina,' Freydis told me. 'They were good sparring partners, and understood each other's pains and losses.' Sheila helped Selina with her sewing, and they shared an interest in religious and philosophical study – Sheila had friends in a commune in Wiltshire, and thought of joining them; but she could not bring herself to give up her independence. There were, however, occasional ructions between Selina and Sheila, whose attitude, as Freydis put it, 'sometimes made people so cross that they would deliberately foil her'. 'I saw this in her relationship with Selina. Both could be deeply loving people and shared many ideas, but one day I arrived back to find Sheila furious and Selina peacefully asleep. Before she had dropped off she had said something so cruel that Sheila said it was "unforgivable", and it took her a long time to get back to her normal relationship. . . . Selina was renowned for being able to get under someone's skin to devastating effect.'

'I spend most of my time just outside London at the above address, where I have a semi-permanent room (to try and write) & help Freydis occasionally with her 90-year old aunt, to earn my keep,' Sheila wrote to Kaye Maclean.

I am still trying to let my flat for short times (as cannot afford it) because have nowhere to put my sticks of furniture & personal things. None of it of value to anyone else – but invaluable to me, because I could never ever afford to replace – even if I were lucky enough to recover, which I fear is now nigh impossible. Too much went wrong for any one person to bear – or at least me to, I mean.

I do enjoy the country though, & try to get some happiness from growing things, & the animals around. There's a lovely black dog, who spends part of the night on my bed! Now we have acquired two cats – who also compete for their place! I am completely fascinated by their antics.

Am trying to build up lectures & things with some new lectures & am still trying to do my silly booklet on how to save time, money, etc – but dont know if it is any good! Everyone else seems to be doing the same things.

Without her car, Sheila would have felt isolated in the country. It gave her some independence, although she had never become an experienced enough driver for it to become second nature and would often slow down to think, oblivious of the queue of traffic building up behind her on the country lanes. But the car enabled her to keep in touch both with friends, and with her own aunts. In the spring of 1977 her Aunt Kath became ill with cancer; when Sheila saw her she was bedridden. The atmosphere in the family was such that no one talked about her illness, nor about the possibility – soon a certainty to anyone who would admit it – that she was dying. Sheila was appalled by the hypocrisy, the secrecy and the unnecessary confinement to bed: 'That's not going to happen to me,' she resolved. To his surprise, she was, according to her cousin David Hurlstone, 'a tower of strength' during the last few days of Kath's life.

During her aunt's illness, Sheila renewed her acquaintance with David, whose wife Jean she had never met although they had been married for over twenty years. Not long before Kath died, at the end of May, Jean was gardening in the drive when Sheila shot past her in her Capri, looked at her, burst into tears and rushed into the house. David's mother, who had arrived with Sheila, commented: 'I can't cope with hysterics.' 'I expected a merry weekend!' Jean told me; but Sheila had soon pulled herself together, although she was feeling the strain of almost constantly looking after either her own dying aunt, or Freydis' Aunt Selina.

The Sharlands went away for two weeks in October, leaving Sheila and Angie in charge of the house; Selina, who needed full-time attention, was in hospital. Sheila embarked on a full-scale reorganization of Freydis' kitchen, throwing out anything she considered unnecessary and rearranging everything else. 'Of course Freydis won't mind,' Sheila reassured the cleaning lady. But when Freydis returned she minded as much as anyone else would have done. The tension in the household rose.

In November Sheila drove to Norwich to visit her former hairdresser, Sandra Collins, for the first time for several years. Sandra took her to fetch Tabitha from school. Although she had dutifully sent her goddaughter Christmas and birthday presents, and occasionally postcards when she was abroad, it was so long since she had seen her that Tabitha could hardly remember her. 'I was so pleased,' Tabitha told me. 'I was desperate to see her.'

During her absence, the Sharlands decided that it was time Sheila stood on her own feet and returned to her flat in London. Freydis felt that she had enough to cope with with her husband, three children and an aged aunt. 'I really think you must find your own way back and be on your own,' she told Sheila.

Sheila seemed so distraught that Freydis suggested she should go to talk to their family doctor, which was what she expected her to do when she left the house in the evening. She was worried enough about Sheila's state of mind, and her ability to drive when she was upset, that she watched as Sheila drove off – in the opposite direction from the one she should have taken to see the doctor. A few miles further on, Sheila drove into the wall of a pub in Holmer Green; in spite of later rumours to the contrary, she had not been drinking. Her car, her only symbol of freedom once she no longer had an aircraft, was badly damaged; and she herself received serious head injuries. She came round in High Wycombe Hospital. All she could remember about the accident was a big explosion. 'My terrible luck has hit me again,' she said.

16

Sheila's accident caused a flurry of small paragraphs in the national press; although none actually stated that she was drunk, there was a strong implication that it was no coincidence that she had driven into the wall of a pub. She was adamant that she had not been drinking, and was convinced that someone had run her off the road.

The sight of her left eye was badly affected. This, and the damage to her looks from a gash above her eyelid, threw her into gloom: she was afraid both that she would never be able to fly again, and that she would be too scarred to appear in public. It was an even greater disaster than the earlier loss of her aircraft. In her more optimistic moods she had managed, however unrealistically, to look on that as no more than a temporary setback, and to persuade herself that sooner or later she would manage to make the elusive flight over the South Pole. Now the partial loss of her sight put paid to any such optimism.

After three weeks she was told that she could leave the hospital, provided she had someone to look after her. Freydis had made it clear that she did not want her; Sheila felt rejected and persecuted, and turned to her Aunt Millie. It was a measure of the gulf between her and her father and stepmother that she did not consider asking them to take care of her. It was only a few days before Christmas, which Millie was planning to spend as usual with her son David and his family in Derbyshire; Sheila seemed, however, to need her more than they did, and so she telephoned to say that she would be unable to visit them after all. 'Bring Sheila with you,' David and Jean Hurlstone said immediately.

Sheila wrote to Kaye Maclean – 'Please forgive me for not being in touch' – explaining that:

> when one goes on for so long in an unendurable unending nightmare of trouble – however much you give, or try to cure it, it

221

is better not to go on inflicting more bad news on friends, I think! I
believe you have understood that it is not selfishness on my part
that I have not written.

Please have a happy Christmas & New year with your friends.
I wish I could do something that would make it even better.

I had a car crash a few weeks back – car smashed, & me
concussed, etc. Now out of hospital walking round like a zombie
& feeling quite ghastly most of the time, but it's nothing
compared to the even worse situation I am being pushed into by
non understanding people. However I am still trying to ignore the
'Drop Dead' signals – I believe life has a way of settling these sorts
of issues in the end (as you know, or we would never have met in
the beginning!) This is not a sob story, just the bare facts – and
also the reason for not writing.

The 'drop dead' signals, and the reference to 'non understanding
people', as well as the remark about 'however much you give',
presumably referred to the Sharlands' unwillingness to cope with
her problems; Freydis had already telephoned David Hurlstone to
say, apologetically, that she could not have Sheila back. Sheila felt
hurt that her help with Selina and her general participation in their
family life had not been appreciated.

She did not enliven the Hurlstones' family Christmas: she was in
a black mood, and, as David and Jean readily admitted, was
justified in feeling sorry for herself. 'Her looks, the sight of one eye,
her chances of flying and her car had all been written off,' David
explained. She also resented his family stability, as she had envied
Freydis her family: 'You don't realize – you've always had stability,'
she told David.

When she returned to London, for the first time in months Sheila
was on her own in her flat, where Kay Bird visited her. She was still
so depressed that Kay told her to pack some things and took her
home with her for a few weeks. 'She seems very strange, very within
herself,' Kay's brother commented.

She continued to suffer from almost constant severe headaches as
the result both of her accident and of tension. Towards the end of
January she felt strong enough to write to Kaye Maclean, who had
sent her some money for Christmas:

Thank you for your marvellous present which I enjoyed spending, though the manner may surprise you as I spent it to help get rid of my headaches! A most welcome respite, and it was accomplished by my first acupuncture – and yes it positively works. I was getting more and more lackadaisical and mooning around not doing anything I did not have to, with acute fibrositis from my habitual tension, and headache whenever I woke up in the mornings. The acupuncture centre is opposite here, and so many people had been helped. Anyway I screwed up my courage ('cos I normally would not think of allowing anyone to stick indiscriminate pins or needles in me) and do you know I walked out full of pep., and without the headache (and it has not returned either) and my fibrositis is improving. . . . I hope that you do not think that I have gone crazy, but I think we are perhaps overlooking a lot that was once good because there was also so much that was backward.

The letter finished with an anonymous quotation which Sheila thought that Kaye would find comforting:

Those whom you mourn would not have it otherwise. They have gone a little way ahead – that is all – they are just out of sight behind a veil, whose lifting is the one certainty in life. In the meantime they would not have you staring at that veil. They would rather you looked around you to see that the dawn is coming fast, and that the love in your own heart is part of all that golden glory.

During the months after the accident, Sheila was so self-conscious about her appearance that she was reluctant to be seen in public even on informal occasions with close friends. She adopted a new hairstyle, with her hair draped across the left side of her forehead and half hiding her eye to conceal her scar, and wore dark glasses.

One of her few comforts was that she could keep in touch through Max Coote with *Myth Too*. When he crashed at the end of March, Sheila wrote immediately to Kaye Maclean; her letter revealed both her continuing identification with her old aircraft, and her paranoid reactions to other people:

Myth Too crashed yesterday, but I know you will be happy to know that she lived up to HER very own wonderful spirit – for she

was never a robot – and the three men who were in her came out
without a scratch. I went to see her – her cabin is intact and
sheltered the men – but bits of her are scattered over the field, and
her wings broken beside her. Her engine and propeller completely wrecked, so we cannot make her fly again. She hardly
scarred even the tree she hit. I am trying to be thankful the people
are all right – but I don't feel thankful for anything except to you
and the few people who truly tried to keep us both in the air.
There are so many monsters on this earth – its been too much to
bear with good humour – when so many reply with unkindness,
and unthinkingness.

In April, Sheila made one of her first publicity appearances since
her accident when she opened a four-bedroomed show house in
Frimley for Guildway, which she called 'a company that believes in
people': 'a house is a very special place; it's a home, a sanctuary'.
Her unbusinesslike attitude to money had clearly not improved:
instead of asking for a fee, as she felt that she was doing a favour for
friends she accepted a set of engraved glasses in payment. 'Sheila
was great fun, and did the whole thing terribly well,' Guildway's
managing director James Molyneux told me. He and his wife were
committed Christians, and once took Sheila to a prayer meeting; but
although they often discussed religion, and he felt that Sheila was
'always aware of the spiritual dimension', he admitted that 'we
didn't get far with her on this'.

At the end of the month, her father wrote to her on her birthday;
his handwriting was quavery, and letter writing clearly did not
come easily: 'My darling Sheila, To wish you a very happy birthday
and I hope your many setbacks will clear away soon and life become
more normal. There is no news of interest we are plodding on as
usual and as well as can be expected.' He signed himself 'Daddy'.
Aileen added a PS: 'A Happy Birthday from me too.' It was the only
letter from either of them which she kept – perhaps the only one she
received.

In the summer, after a further operation, Sheila went to America
and Canada; she felt that she had to take every possible opportunity
of paid travel and public appearances, and was a guest of honour
and banquet speaker at an air show in Abbotsford, British
Columbia. In America she stayed with the Longmires in Albuquerque, New Mexico, where Tom was stationed at the air base.

Rosemary arranged for Sheila to have a balloon ride – her first for many years. 'She couldn't believe that she had to get up early enough to be at the field at 4.30 a.m.,' Rosemary told me. 'That didn't give her time to get glamorous, and above all she had to look glamorous. They had a nice long ride, but the wind came up and it was a rough "Rip Out!" landing.'

'Are you all right?' Rosemary asked.

'What do you think?' Sheila snapped.

Like Sheila, Kaye Maclean had recently undergone eye surgery, possibly for cataract; she also had other recurring health problems. In November Sheila wrote to her from her aunt's house in Bredon, Gloucestershire, and told her about her trip:

I do hope you are fully recovered and seeing things as you used to!! I'm sorry not to have written before. I went into hospital to have my eye operated on further (minor compared to yours!) & felt terrible afterwards – couldn't really see straight to pack my things for my visit to the West Coast of America, but as you know I have to take any opportunities to travel as & when they arise so couldn't put it off.

I didn't enjoy it as much as I might have, but nevertheless did a few exciting things. Stayed with friends in Beverly Hills (that sounds chic doesn't it!) & saw all the old style Hollywood homes (which sadly were destroyed by fire a few weeks later). Then went to an aviation conference in Las Vegas (no I did not gamble – except a very little which I doubled, believe it or not – I expect if I had really gambled I would have lost the lot!! In my usual fashion.)

Then went to stay with friends in New Mexico, which is so lovely and warm, even in the winter. She is a balloonist so I went up in a hot air balloon (unlike the quiet hydrogen balloons I'd been up in before) and at the same time the International Balloon Fiesta was held there for a week. You cannot imagine the fabulously beautiful sight of dozens of balloons all taking off together and floating over a great city. I really enjoyed it. . . . Alas the time to come home arrived too soon, and after a horrible journey home I got back exhausted and miserable, and came to stay in Gloucestershire, near Bredon Hill, with my aunt. I really wanted to have a talk with my father – I went to see him but he was very frail, and to my utter shock, he died that night. As you know we were not very close, or very much together owing to family circumstances, and I was horrified that it happened the way it did.

Harold Hopkins died on 30 October. Although Sheila had always felt resentful that he had not given her any financial support when she lost her aircraft, it seems unlikely that he would have been in a position to do so. He left less than £2000, a third of which was to go to Sheila and the rest, with his house, to Aileen. There had always been a feeling in the family that the rift between Sheila and Aileen had been Sheila's fault; Aileen's treatment of Sheila after Harold's death to some extent changed her cousins' views. As David Hurlstone put it, 'Aileen pulled up the drawbridge for Sheila.' Sheila asked him and Jean to look for her possessions for her; but there was no sign of anything of hers in the house. It was as if she had never existed. She had nothing to remind her of her father. Although she went to his funeral, it was with John and Paddy Pimley that she stayed, not with Aileen; she was, the Pimleys told me, 'most upset that she'd been offered nothing by her stepmother or in her father's will other than the cash donation'.

Sheila was still living at Park West. Although she was often lonely and depressed when she was there, her flat was her sanctuary. She sub-let it, as she told Kaye, whenever she could – when she was in America for several weeks at a time, for instance, or staying with her aunt. There was even some discussion about her moving in permanently with Millie Hurlstone in Bredon, but both realized that this would not work – it would have been a clash of two strong personalities, each equally unwilling or unable to see the other's viewpoint. Although there was a strong bond of affection between them, they could even argue about such trivialities as how to eat a peach: Millie thought Sheila's method, with a knife and fork, was ridiculous, and Sheila over-reacted when she told her so.

She was still suffering from double vision, which, as she wrote to Kaye Maclean, could be 'a bit embarrassing'. 'People must think I'm drunk sometimes,' she admitted. She had already had three operations, and in May 1979 was to have a fourth, which she hoped would at last cure her sight: she was determined to fly again. On the thirteenth anniversary of her first flight with *Myth Too* the Fleet Air Arm acquired the aircraft for its museum in Scotland, where it was to be rebuilt. 'Good news of the greatest woman pilot in the world

("I'm Sheila Scott – fly me") and of the love of her life. Both are recovering fast,' Philip Colmore wrote in the *Daily Mail*. 'I could hardly bear the day and having to look at her,' Sheila, who was invited to be present at the hand-over, wrote to Kaye.

In 1978 Park West was sold by Peachey Properties to a company called First Cross Ltd, which promptly embarked on a refurbishment programme. New long leases started at Christmas, and many existing tenants whose rents were, like Sheila's, considerably lower than the current ones moved out. She told friends that she was under considerable pressure to do so too, and found this upsetting, especially when one after another most of her neighbours left. Her rent was apparently still being paid by Teddy Sugden; nevertheless the prospect of an increase alarmed her. She felt increasingly threatened, although this can possibly be put down as yet another symptom of her persecution complex.

By October, her sight was at last good enough again for her to think seriously – if optimistically – about flying again. As usual, there was the problem of finance. Sheila attempted to solve this by applying for a helicopter scholarship given annually by the Whirly Girls in America. Her application was supported by letters to Jean Ross Howard, the Whirly Girls' founder and president, from the chairman of the Royal Aero Club, as well as from Peter Masefield, Gwen Bellew and Margot Morse of Zonta.

'Without the scholarship, there is no doubt that Miss Scott cannot afford the financial outlay necessary to regain her helicopter licence,' Peter Masefield wrote; 'with such a rating, there will be great opportunities open to her to achieve further recognition of the abilities of women helicopter pilots.' Margot Morse's letter was enthusiastic: 'I have known Sheila personally for 15 years and during that time she has never spared herself, her time or her money in the interests of advancing aviation for women. . . . I know Sheila's hope is to use her licences as a standby pilot in emergencies in the event of disasters.' Gwen Bellew concentrated on the publicity angle: 'I feel we badly need her to show the way as only someone of her world wide standing can hope to do so.'

Although her application was unsuccessful – not surprisingly there was no shortage of younger, fitter women wanting to fly helicopters – Sheila was still determined to fly. Her licences had inevitably lapsed since her accident. In 1980 she went to Dr Ian Perry for a flying medical; because of her head injuries, he sent her to see a neuro-psychiatrist. He felt that ever since her polar flight odd things had preyed on her mind: this was, he told me, typical of a lonely person. She did not sleep well, and therefore suffered from chronic fatigue which in turn brought on worry; but other than her suspicion of everyone, which he considered schizoid rather than paranoid schizophrenic, he did not find her mentally unbalanced, and was unaware of either her suicide attempts or her psychiatric treatment in Harrow and Epsom. 'She was always up against the limits of her own ability,' he told me. 'She was not the person she would have liked to be, and felt that the world owed her more than it did.'

The world did nevertheless pay her from time to time in small ways, such as a free trip to Las Vegas in February 1980 as the first British woman helicopter pilot: at Jean Ross Howard's invitation, Sheila was to address a banquet at the Helicopter Association of America's four-day annual meeting at the Las Vegas Hilton. 'How very flattering to invite me,' Sheila replied, 'though I really am not very good at public speaking. I have only just recovered from my accident, which believe me makes one very unconfident, but I suppose in a way an interesting experience as I have been lucky. They performed miracles on my sight. . . . I still have to take things moderately easy . . . flying is hard to come by, which is why I applied for the scholarship.'

Sheila's round-the-world record had just been halved by Judith Chisholm, who after a two-year campaign for sponsorship eventually had to borrow to put up over half the cost herself, with £2000 from a national newspaper and £10,000 from a television company. Raising money for record-breaking flights – Judith's broke thirty records – was as difficult for her as it had always been for Sheila.

Sheila was gradually beginning to feel that she could at last rebuild her life. 'Sheila Scott has transcended the serious physical injuries which she suffered after her car accident, just as she transcended her sorrow when she saw her beloved aeroplane broken up,' Lady Lothian told an audience composed mainly of journalists in December 1980. 'I see in this great if not greater valour and truth than when she was the first person, man or woman, to fly over the true North Pole.' She had invited Sheila to present the Valiant for Truth Award, an honour given annually to 'a person or persons who have worked for Media . . . and have courageously used modern means of communications to convey the truth in the public interest'.

The recipient was Pat Seed, a journalist who, instead of giving in to terminal cancer, had launched a successful £2 million fund-raising scheme to buy an X-ray scanner for a Manchester hospital.

In her speech, Sheila called cancer 'violence in all its forms'. 'I have known many of its victims,' she said, 'and shared the ghastly experience of being totally inadequate, and unable to help a very gentle person, of whom I was fond, while she died. It was unendurable, a waste in an unnecessary way of dying simply because of false conventional – though loving – attitudes, as though it were an unmentionable social stigma.' Pat Seed had, Sheila continued, 'used her talents and valour as a journalist with others in the world of media to diffuse the amount of help that can be made available. But in spite of her great fame as a result of her work, she has remained of herself – a real executive of truth.'

Lady Lothian called Pat Seed and Sheila Scott 'two Champions of Courage'. Courage was perhaps the quality which Sheila most sought in herself and most admired in others. She saw it in the ex-resistance fighters and commandos of the Special Forces Club, of which she had been made an honorary member and which increasingly dominated her social life. She felt that through youth training and adventure schemes young people could learn to be courageous, and so she was delighted to be the guest of honour at a festival organized in the summer of 1981 by the Girls' Venture Corps to celebrate the twenty-fifth anniversary of the Duke of Edinburgh Award scheme. She was equally enthusiastic in her support for the Poole and Dorset Adventure Centre, with which she had close associations over several years.

When her own courage was, however, unexpectedly put to the test in September 1981, it was in a way which threw her again into a nightmare of fear, depression and paranoia. 'BOSS plot to implicate Sheila Scott', a *Daily Telegraph* headline announced. Gordon Winter, in a public display of professed guilt about his role as a BOSS spy, had written a detailed confession in a book called *Inside BOSS*. This revealed not only his own duplicity in the Mandela rescue plot – among other deceptions – but also gave the names and addresses of almost everyone who had been involved, including Sheila's. She was appalled. So was Marianne Borman, who had been cruelly taken in by Winter and had been a full member of the plan.

Marianne Borman told me she was staggered to find that there was so much financial support for undercover government organizations; she was sure that the book was Sheila's first insight into how far-reaching and awful a regime could be, and into its 'utter ruthlessness'. She had known of Sheila's intended role, although they had never met, but had not been surprised that she backed out, and confirmed that Winter's version of the story, and of the role Sheila had been intended to have, was accurate. 'Had the plan gone through, none of us would be here,' she said.

Norman Lonsdale was shaken to see his telephone conversation with Sheila reproduced; her room had been bugged after all, as she had claimed. He began to wonder if there was more substance to other occasions when Sheila thought that 'they' had been after her than he had previously been inclined to believe. Marianne Borman told me that she considered it quite feasible that Sheila might have been kept under surveillance: 'It would have been strange if Winter's expenditure had been allowed to be dissipated – therefore there was a possible reason to keep people under surveillance.'

It seems unlikely that, twelve years later, Sheila would still have been under surveillance; but she became convinced that this was the case. 'They' became BOSS agents. She saw them everywhere, and was never again able to escape from them for long. Anything which went wrong was blamed on them, and she spoke in a whisper whenever she thought they might be listening. Her old CSE friend Tom Carpenter took her out for dinner one evening, and although neither of them drank excessively, afterwards he felt dreadful: Sheila insisted that 'they' had given him a 'Mickey Finn' because he was with her.

'They' were waiting for her at the Kronfeld Club when she arrived with Gwen Bellew and her husband for a balloon meeting. 'They' were also at an air show which she went to with the Bellews.

'I want to talk to you,' she told them. To their surprise she removed her pearl necklace, put it in her handbag and then put the handbag on the ground. 'Now I'm clear of bugs,' she told Gwen, who at first thought she meant insects. 'We must go to the middle of the field where we can't be overheard.'

'I wouldn't leave your handbag there,' Gwen said as Sheila drew them away.

'I'll keep my eye on it,' Sheila told her. 'You must keep your eye on it too.'

As soon as they were out of earshot of the handbag she explained that 'they' had bugged her necklace, and that she was waiting to see who they were when they approached the bag – although she was pretty sure they had been sent by BOSS.

She later told James Molyneux of Guildway that evil spirits were being beamed on her by South Africa. 'In an open spiritual life, that's what will happen to you,' he told her. 'With Christ you'd be protected.' He felt that she was near breaking point: 'very highly strung, not behaving as she normally did; she was het up, edgy, not rational to talk to.'

It would not be fair to give the impression that Sheila spent her entire time in a deluded and paranoid state of mind. As far as most people were concerned – people whom she did not know well enough to confide in – she was as normal as before. Even with those with whom she sometimes dropped her voice to a whisper because she suspected that 'they' were in the vicinity, her behaviour was otherwise perfectly rational. But there was no point trying to talk to her about 'them': she considered this far too dangerous other than in an obliquely worded whisper, and refused to consider that 'they' were figments of her imagination. That way lay madness, and it was only in the minds of 'not so nice people' that she thought she could be considered mad. The only thing anyone could do when 'they' entered Sheila's conversation was to ignore the subject and talk about something else.

Her friends at the Special Forces Club thought that she was merely trying to keep her end up and be interesting when she spoke in hushed tones about 'them'. As most of the men she mixed with at the club had either been involved in SOE's wartime activities, or later with equally secret SAS operations, there was no shortage of true stories which seemed almost incredible, or which involved espionage and surveillance: it was, as more than one member has told me, 'the sort of place where anything can be believed'.

Sheila was generally popular at the club, although some of the older and more staid members did not entirely approve of her. She was one of a number of women who had been invited to join it, either on their own merits or as companions to husbands or male friends, and whose presence was welcomed to add some feminine variety and spice to life. On club nights Sheila reverted to the bar propping of her youth, and postponed eating for as long as she could so that she would not waste good wine drinking time – she only ever drank white wine, or champagne when it was offered; she gained a reputation at the club as a drinker.

When she collapsed there one evening, not long after the publication of Gordon Winter's book, it was therefore assumed that she was drunk. She was taken to hospital, but escaped and returned to the club where she created a scene; she told the club manager that she wanted to be arrested rather than go back, as the nurses were working for some secret police force. She was convinced that 'they' had caught up with her.

Eventually she was admitted to the Charter Clinic, a private psychiatric hospital in London SW3. Someone from the club telephoned Margot Morse, a fellow member both of the Special Forces Club and of Zonta, and said 'unkind things': that Sheila was tight, was on drugs, had said things she should not have said. Margot went straight round to the hospital, where she found Sheila in much the state described by Connie Fricker after her second suicide attempt, and indeed by Lana Jeffers after the first. She did not, as far as Margot could tell, appear to be having any treatment, but was just lying on the bed, and had been locked in her room because she kept trying to get out – which Margot did not find surprising. Sheila told Margot that she refused to have any injections, and did not want her cousin told where she was; she had given no names of next of kin. Margot visited her there every day for a week.

Dr Colin Herridge was asked by Dr Michael a'Brook of the Charter Clinic to see Sheila there for a second opinion. He told me that he spent over an hour with her, and that for the first fifteen minutes she refused to speak to him, saying that everything was in the hands of her solicitors. 'Eventually she relaxed and told me of her terror of BOSS, which she felt was following her and whose agents were everywhere. She denied abusing drugs or drinking for some time, and this was borne out by liver function tests.' He was inclined to think that she was again in 'a severe social and financial crisis and that her illness was a function of a paranoid reaction to this'. Although he persuaded her to take some anti-psychotic drugs, he gathered that she discharged herself soon afterwards.

It was probably not long after this that Sheila wrote an undated letter to Kaye Maclean, obviously responding to some advice as well as to a weekend she had spent in Somerset before her collapse:

Please forgive me for not writing before to thank you for the lovely weekend – I am afraid I did get sick but I am fine now – or rather getting much better. It's all too silly really – but you may be right – anyway I'm trying to cut down on the smoking!! Yes really! – I know you'll never believe that one! – It was great to see you looking so much better. Keep on getting fitter and fitter and may this year be a good one.

The year 1982 was not a good one for Sheila. Teddy Sugden, who had remained in the background as a source of psychological and financial support, died at the age of eighty. Soon after his death, presumably because her rent was no longer being paid and had also gone up, Sheila moved out of Park West. In May she wrote from the Special Forces Club to Jean Ross Howard in America, where she was thinking of attempting to start a new life:

I have been through hell moving out, which broke me. Now camping out at my club. I *need* some real help! Have two professional lecture bookings, Nov. 3rd in Dallas & another in Richmond in Feb. Really do have to get some other lucrative ones Nov/Dec to merit the airfare across the Atlantic (which I pay). Usually get $500 plus travelling expenses out of Washington D.C. Please, please shop around for me. I feel caught in a cage. . . . I am quite heartsick that I am not already living over there by now. . . . Few friends left here in London, and none in the aviation world. I do not feel ready to vegetate.

Later in the year she moved into a housing association flat in Cambridge Street in Pimlico. In her last letter to Kaye Maclean she called it 'a nasty little basement flat'; Kaye found the letter upsettingly irrational. Sheila was complaining yet again about financial and physical problems, and seemed to her to be blatantly, even aggressively, begging. She did not file it with the rest of Sheila's letters.

A few months later, in 1983, Kaye, whose health had deteriorated, took her own life. She had planned her death carefully, and left Sheila £1000 in her will.

17

SHEILA SPENT CHRISTMAS 1983 at Elizabeth Overbury's cottage in Yorkshire. Although Elizabeth told me that 'she was great fun – she made the Christmas', they came nearer than ever before to a serious row when Sheila started talking about her conviction that she was being followed by secret agents. Elizabeth, who knew nothing of Winter's book about BOSS, suggested impatiently: 'If you're that frightened why the heck don't you stay with me?'

'If they want to find me, they will,' Sheila told her, 'and I don't want to put you under surveillance as well.'

On New Year's Eve, Sheila returned to London for a dinner engagement. Her escort for the evening, as he had been for many others during the three years since they had met at a party, was Hugh Collins, who had been with SOE during the war, much of which he had spent with the French Resistance in France. Although he could therefore have joined the Special Forces Club, he did not; he liked the old war and Resistance members, but not the younger SAS members – whom he told me that Sheila liked because they were 'uncompromising, positive, and doing interesting things'. Nevertheless he escorted Sheila to the club willingly enough, although he did not approve of her being known there as Scotty: it did not suit her dignity. Sheila in return often accompanied him to Free French Forces dinners at the Duke of York's Barracks, where he claimed that she was much admired for her beauty, sense of humour and expertise at the conga.

Although he clearly adored Sheila, there was never any romance between them; he was still too hurt after his wife had deserted him. Sheila felt safe and at ease with him, but considered that he was wasting his abilities. He had resigned from the insurance business at Lloyds; a business which he later attempted to set up never got off the ground, and left him in debt. During what Hugh termed 'a slight altercation' one evening – probably, although he could not remember, something to do with a taxi after Sheila had had a few drinks – she accused him of not doing enough with his life, to which he readily admitted.

'What would you like to do?' she asked.

To pacify her, Hugh said: 'Fly.'

Two days later Sheila telephoned and told him that lessons had been booked for him at Hendon: he was horrified – he needed to summon up his courage even to go on an Air France flight. 'Fortunately it was quietly forgotten,' he told me.

When I met Hugh he had a distinct limp, the result of a broken ankle. Sheila visited him almost daily when he was in hospital, and enlisted his help as a translator. She was deeply involved with the Fédération des Pilotes Européennes – FPA. Almost from the start the FPA had been beset by arguments about whether English or French should be used as its official language. Marie-Josèphe de Beauregard, who called herself 'pilot lawyer' and claimed the honour of having founded the federation, insisted time after time that it should not only use French as its main language, but should also operate according to complex French laws, which no one else understood; every report was to be lodged with the Préfecture in Paris, and no decision made by the committee could be put into effect until it had been ratified by the Préfecture, which could take months. The association's pilot lawyer founder wrote long letters in complex legal French which was incomprehensible to anyone else, but which had to be answered; all discussions held in English had to be translated into French – and vice versa.

The British Women Pilots' Association hosted the European association's 1983 annual business and social weekend meeting at the East Midlands Airport, to which many of the members – including two from Romania – flew themselves. In 1984 it was Germany's turn to provide a venue, at Baden-Baden. Sheila was elected president, and it was suggested, seconded, agreed and minuted that English should be used at meetings. A year later, in Geneva, the French disputed this decision; after 'some debate' with France about the legality of using English, it was suggested that both languages be adopted: the brevity of the minutes hid the acrimonious nature of the discussions, and did not reveal the time spent in copious letter writing and translation, nor the strain imposed on Sheila, who took her responsibilities seriously. Hugh

Collins was one of several people, myself included, who at various times helped her with translations.

As Sheila told Dina Ross of the *Sunday Times*, much of her time was spent answering letters, on various committees and at meetings of the organizations to which she belonged – FPA and BWPA, Zonta, Whirly Girls, the 99s and the Guild of Air Pilots and Navigators (GAPAN): she was particularly proud of being a GAPAN Livery-man of the City of London. Like many others who have enjoyed the limelight but then have to settle for an occasional candle glow, she was allocated a full back page in the colour magazine for a day in her life in 1984. Apart from allowing her age to be given as fifty-six when she was in fact sixty-two, it was an accurate account of the more peaceful and positive aspects of her life – of which there were still many.

Her flat in Pimlico had become home, although she alternated between finding it a sanctuary and a gloomy cage. The one advantage of having a semi-basement flat was that the kitchen door and bedroom window opened on to a minute L-shaped private courtyard which Sheila called her garden. On visits to her aunt and cousin she brought back sacks of soil, and managed to grow tomatoes, strawberries, shrubs and flowers. Potted and climbing plants grew in the gloomy narrow space between the steep steps down to her front door, as well as on the outside windowsill.

None of Sheila's book projects had been completed, although she was still intending to finish the one on pioneer women in aviation; but this was again set aside when she was asked to contribute to a publication called *Pink Line*, a collection of accounts about women's role in aviation – the result was a hotch-potch of different styles from various countries in Europe. The 'handy hints' flotsam of Sheila's mind had been abandoned when Shirley Conran beat her into print with a similar concoction. She had, however, almost completed a children's book in which Buck Tooth relived many of their joint flying adventures from a rabbit's point of view. 'Of course, Richard Adams put paid to that with *Watership Down*,' Sheila said.

It was at the Special Forces Club that Sheila found new friends, to take the place of her old friends in aviation who had, she felt, abandoned her; (social life at the club to some extent replaced the camaraderie of flying). She had a regular arrangement to meet Sadie Robinson at the bar where they were often joined by ex-air hostess Sheila Bond. Sadie was small, plump and talkative. 'We got on together because we were both sophisticated and liked clothes and drinks,' she told me. The one topic of conversation on which they disagreed was Margaret Thatcher: Sadie thought she was wonderful, whereas Sheila blamed her for everything that did not go right in Britain, particularly when she was personally affected. But when Sheila tried to needle her, Sadie refused to be drawn into an argument: 'I'm out for an evening's enjoyment,' she said.

Sheila took every possible opportunity to return to America, where she combined the business of giving lectures with the pleasure of being appreciated and entertained. She spoke in 1983 at the Smithsonian Institute in Washington, where Claudia Oakes, who ran the museum's series of aviation lectures, considered her 'a real class act – so gracious and lovely'. 'But hired killers are what sell,' she admitted, 'so Sheila only had a small audience, about a hundred to a hundred and twenty-five; but they were captivated.' Sheila received the normal Smithsonian fee of $250 and expenses.

Out of the money left to her by Kaye Maclean, she paid for twenty-three and a half hours' tuition in a Cessna 172 in California. Her instructor, Sidney Amster, told me that she received her instrument competency check and biennial flight review as required by aviation law, although it was more than two years since she had last flown. Amster, a retired shirtmaker from New York, worked for Claire Walters, whom Sheila had met at the international 99s' convention in Idaho and with whom she stayed for a month. Claire had strong feelings about both smoking and drinking: she considered that Sheila did both to excess. But she did not voice her concern as she felt it was none of her business, although she told me that she hated seeing 'a potential problem'.

Although Sheila did not drink during the daytime she made up for this in the evenings, and as she always insisted on taking her turn to pay for rounds of drinks her constant plea of poverty was not always believed. She resented the cramped conditions of her flat so much that few of her acquaintances ever saw it; many assumed that in spite of her complaints she was living in comfort, if not luxury. Her appearance, which as always was elegant, well groomed and looked as if no expense had been spared, gave the lie to any serious financial problems, and she did not seem depressed in public.

Among those who were aware both of her financial position, and of her depression, were the trustees of a fund set up by Sir Alan Cobham. Gerard Kealey, a co-trustee with Michael Cobham, began sending her money from the fund soon after she moved to Pimlico. In February 1985 she wrote to thank Kealey for the help given by the trust, without which she felt that she could scarcely have survived:

> Alas I am living in the most horrendous circumstances (though publicly pretending all is well – as there is no future in appearing miserable!!) My basement is entirely without sound proofing, & with the most evil Southern Irishwoman living above me, & supervising my every movement of the day, there is no quality of life at all. My friends, of course, cannot visit me, as they certainly do not want their lives described in detail to all & sundry! I explain all this, so that you understand why I cannot say much on the telephone. . . . I am trying to rebuild my life, but cannot afford to move from this place yet, but this is the ultimate aim!

It was later that year that I first attempted to contact Sheila. Naomi Christie, who was then president of BWPA, refused to give me her address, but agreed to forward a letter: 'She has not been at all well for the last two years,' she told me. As I discovered later, she was referring to mental rather than physical illness. Nevertheless when I met Sheila, in the autumn of 1985, she did not appear to be mentally ill, although she seemed lonely, mentioned problems with a neighbour, and hinted that she was being spied on. As I left her flat after our first meeting, she said: 'Wish me luck. I'm going away with the man I may spend the rest of my life with.' She would not tell me his name, in case the relationship did not work out as she hoped; but he was, she told me, attractive, compassionate, brave and loyal, lived in an exotic and sunny place and had been involved in secret but admirably patriotic operations in the war.

His name, I found out later, was Trevor Jones – Colonel Jones, ex-SOE and ex-managing director of Ovaltine: the man who would, or so he claimed with hindsight, have leaped at the chance of sponsoring Sheila had he not been away when Lord Erskine was looking for sponsors for her. He met Sheila at the Special Forces Club soon after the death in 1985 of his wife, whom he had looked after for eight years after she had suffered a complete stroke. Like Sheila, he saw possible long-term companionship: '. . . but it was not to be,' he wrote to me from Malta.

Sheila, like us all perhaps, had various idiosyncrasies and it soon became evident that I was unable or perhaps just not 'big' enough to handle them. The realisation was mutual, and Sheila and I remained friends. . . . I helped her as much as I was able. . . . I bought her Amstrad etc so, according to Sheila, she could save secretarial money on her correspondence for various flying associations etc.

All Sheila told me when she returned from Malta was that 'things didn't work out'; later she elaborated only with a comment that she could not live with a hypochondriac; Trevor had recently had a colostomy. When I met him, with Iain Erskine, at the Special Forces Club, he gave me a more detailed account. He had invited Sheila to visit him, envisaging that this would be the start of an arrangement whereby Sheila would keep her London flat and independence, spend a couple of months with him in Malta, and they would spend part of each year in America.

For the first few days in Malta all went well; then, although she never drank during the day, Sheila started to drink heavily in the evenings. After a few drinks she became a different person. Although Trevor soon realized that the long-term idea would not work, it was Sheila who put it into words. They remained friends, although her drinking caused some awkward moments both socially and privately. Among the most embarrassing was an episode in a restaurant, where Sheila wanted to invite some Australians – whom Trevor considered 'rather rough types' – to join them at their table: 'Why not?' she asked belligerently, then started shouting about how they had been our allies in the war. 'Even they found it over the top,' Trevor said.

During the day, he told me, she always made a lot of sense; but at night, after starting to drink, she seemed to enter a fantasy world and became verbally abusive and even physically violent. On one occasion, she smashed four wine bottles so thoroughly that they were little more than ground up glass. At some point during the night she cleared up the broken glass, and in the morning seemed to have forgotten all about it.

'In her cups, her conversation would become a series of innuendos, incomplete stories, hints about dark secrets and plots against her,' Trevor said. He thought that this was all probably fantasy, although he wondered whether it was part fact, part fiction, or fantasy based on truth – or even true. They continued to see each other whenever he was in London at the Special Forces Club, where once, he told me, she screamed that one of the members was a 'traitor': 'not the sort of accusation which goes down well there'. Nevertheless he and Iain Erskine agreed that the young SAS men loved her – they admired her courage and liked her raciness – although some of the older ones called her 'that mad girl'.

It seemed hardly surprising, in view of Trevor's account of Sheila's behaviour in Malta, that several people suggested to me that she was an alcoholic. I do not, however, think that she was dependent on alcohol; it was rather that it had a sudden and severe effect on her, and that under its influence a personality which bore little relation to her usual character was released and took over. Through his directorship of a big drug company, Trevor had had dealings with drugs for schizophrenia; he thought that Sheila was schizophrenic. 'Her eyes were no longer Sheila's,' he said, 'but staring, oblivious of anything except her own fantasy nightmare world.'

The dictionary definition of schizophrenia – mental disease characterized by dissociation, delusions and inability to distinguish reality from delusion – certainly fits Sheila's occasional irrationality during much of the 1970s and 1980s, as well as earlier in her life. Sometimes for long periods, sometimes only for a few hours at a time, the condition lay dormant, only to reassert itself when Sheila was depressed or under pressure, or to be revealed by alcohol.

Although Ian Perry, the doctor who examined her for her flying medicals, admitted that Sheila had schizoid tendencies, and perhaps showed signs of schizoid paranoia, he ruled out schizophrenia; but in 1984, when she told him that she wanted her licence back because she was 'busier than ever', with the possibility of some filming coming up, he refused to pass her on her medical unless she saw a psychiatric panel. 'She was behaving in an irrational and disturbing way,' he told me. Sheila was 'quite cross' about his decision, but he refused to back down. 'Look, you've got to see a psychiatrist,' he said. Two years later, although she had not seen a psychiatrist, her behaviour no longer struck him as irrational; in 1986 he passed her as fit to fly.

Early in 1986, Sheila advertised in *Pilot*: she was hoping to make a film in India later in the year, and wanted someone with filming and television facilities to help her. Her advertisement was answered by

Brian Field, a young man who had recently taken up flying, lived near her in Pimlico, and had his own business called Provideo. Although he was not in the production business, he offered to do film transfers for her. 'There was,' he told me, 'quite a rapport between us at once.' Sheila adopted him as her technical adviser – although the advice was needed about her telephone answering machine rather than for anything to do with filming – and they went out to dinner together a couple of times a month.

Brian was a devout Jehovah's Witness; although they had different religious viewpoints, they often talked about religion and about what Sheila termed 'other forces'. 'She never knocked my beliefs,' he told me. During their religious discussions, he always found Sheila's conversation rational and intelligent; otherwise it was often irrational and paranoid. She insisted that letters and telephone calls must be in code, even on one occasion handing him a letter which he was to read only in his office. 'I'm more scared than you can imagine,' she wrote, 'the Irish is trying to record everything.'

The obvious solution seemed to be for Sheila to move, which was indeed what she claimed to be her aim. 'How much would it cost?' Brian asked her. 'If a few thousand would do it, let's do it.'

He was prepared to give her an interest-free loan, but she refused: 'They'll follow me,' she insisted.

Her paranoia was displayed only in private – or only seen at its most extreme then – and she had a remarkable ability to rise to any public occasion. Although her idea of filming did not come to anything, in February 1986 she had to make a speech as vice-chairman of a World Aviation Education and Safety Congress organized in New Delhi by the Indian 99s and Indian Women Pilots' Association. Some of the American 99s – whom Sheila had always considered collectively and individually among her greatest friends and supporters – said anxiously to Gwen Bellew, who was then president of the British 99s: 'Sheila's giving a talk – is it going to be all right? We've heard she's not on the ball these days.' 'In fact Sheila gave a tremendous and fascinating talk,' Gwen told me. 'Afterwards no one could stop talking about it.'

It was, as Gwen put it, 'a week of lunches and dinners'; but Sheila was disappointed that she had seen little of Delhi. Gwen repeated this to the British High Commissioner, who was a personal friend of hers – she had spent much of her early life in India – and had asked her if Sheila was being properly entertained.

'Oh my God, how awful!' he exclaimed. Next day he sent a white Rolls Royce, with a Gurkha driver who took Sheila on a tour of the city.

'What an extraordinary thing to do,' Sheila commented to Gwen. She was peeved because there had been only a chauffeur and no VIP guide. Gwen did not dare report this, and said instead that Sheila had found the tour most interesting.

Sheila wrote to Gerard Kealey again in April, thanking him for further help from Sir Alan Cobham's fund, and complaining about the misery of her basement life: 'The conditions that I live in are almost unbelievable to the kind of people we know.' She was convinced that a 'jobbing painter' who lived in a top-floor flat was bugging hers and that her nearest neighbour, whom she called a very bad Southern Irish Catholic female gossip, was trying to make trouble for her with various local authorities; she told Kealey that 'they would all like to establish their own gang' in her flat, as it was a self-contained basement.

'Because of all this, I became very much iller last year than I need have been,' she went on, referring to yet another breakdown.

I really cannot afford a move . . . and frankly if I was put into a Housing Association house sandwiched between people like this, I would be terrified. Now unfortunately it's all started again, aided & abetted by the second evil Irish woman with flat here. They have been to some local authority (DHSS, I should think) telling heaven knows what tale, except I overheard, I am supposed to be a criminal! (a laugh when you consider what I was at the top!) I don't happen to be committing any great crime, & creep around my own flat to avoid harassment from above. It is frightful having to live in Soviet Union conditions in my own country, particularly when you know you are actually being 'set up' by very bad people.

I hope you now realise why I am so nervous about the telephone.

What I really wanted to say, is that I really would not have survived without the help you give me. I do have a pension now, but it is only a Social Security one, which has *many* restrictions.

Sorry this is a letter of misery, but it is important that my friends realise now that there is little that can be done, or said in privacy in my own home, without horrendous trouble making. Amazing isn't it that this country is helping these people? . . .

Talking to Sheila in her flat, or on the telephone, became increasingly frustrating as she insisted on keeping the television on to stop her neighbours eavesdropping; and she often spoke in such an oblique way, to prevent them knowing what she was talking about, that other people were confused. Her friends were expected to know what she meant, and were drawn into her side of the conspiracy, in which she appeared to think that BOSS, the IRA, all Catholics – except those whom she knew personally and liked – and especially all Irish Catholics, were in league against her. It was no use trying to persuade her of the improbability of a plot against her, or of her flat being bugged, or even, as she claimed on one occasion, of her Irish neighbours attempting to poison her through a heating vent; the only thing to do was to humour her – or at least to try to steer the conversation into more rational channels.

It was in Vienna, at the 1986 meeting of the Federation of European Women Pilots, that I first became aware of how odd Sheila could be, and suspected that she was either mentally ill, or was strangely affected by alcohol, or both. But apart from one incident of a young couple in the bar who were, she told me, spying on her, and an occasional aside that some of the other women present were out to get her, she was as rational as anyone else, even when she was again under considerable pressure from the French representative. If she had merely described the long and acrimonious committee meeting at which I had to act as interpreter, I would have thought she was exaggerating; she was not. It was sad to see her battling to keep the Federation together. In public, at dinners and at a ball which was preceded by a dressage display under the full moon and a spectacular firework display, she was at her elegant and gracious best.

Sheila spent Christmas with us that year for the first time, although at the last minute she nearly changed her mind: she was suffering from a persistent bronchial cough which she was afraid would disturb us. There was no point suggesting that it might improve if she smoked less: she could not and would not give up smoking, she said. My children immediately adopted her as an extra aunt, and she responded by treating each one sensitively as an individual. She was more relaxed, in spite of her cough, than I had ever seen her, and was a warm and witty addition to our family gathering.

In February Sheila went again to America, where she made

several public appearances and speeches. As her cough was still troubling her she went to see Bob Poole, an aviation doctor whom she had met on several occasions and who considered her 'a lady', a description used of her by many Americans. 'She was quiet and friendly – a person you met and felt you'd known a long time,' he told me. 'Although she was famous, she didn't act like it and didn't use it. She was politely strong-willed, and very warm and compassionate, very interested in her friends, but very reserved.'

In his opinion she seemed generally physically and mentally healthy, apart from her usual financial worries and a severe cold. But he wanted her to have X-rays: he thought she might have pneumonia, and treated her with antibiotics. She told him that she would rather leave the X-rays until she was back home in England.

18

When Sheila was told she had lung cancer, for ten days she stopped smoking before being admitted to hospital for, as she thought, the removal of the affected lung. Not smoking seemed the hardest challenge she had ever faced, but she told herself that it was worth it if it would keep her alive. She refused to face the possibility of death: there were too many things she still wanted to do.

Further investigation revealed that the cancer had already spread too far to be operable. Sheila was told that she probably had only a few months to live. Her first reaction was of fury: 'Why should it be me? How can it be me?' she asked. On her way back by taxi to her flat she looked at the trees and the sun, and at people playing tennis: 'I can't be going to die,' she thought. 'I am walking around and sitting in this taxi. I can't die.' She telephoned Sadie: 'They can't do anything. I think I'll just go into the garden and think.'

Gradually her rage turned to grief: 'You reach a stage when you are actually mourning for yourself because you know you are going to die, and you are crying for yourself,' she explained. Although he was not her doctor, Sheila turned for help and advice to Dr Paul MacLoughlin, whom she had known for several years through the Special Forces Club. 'She was distraught,' he told me. 'I did nothing for her medically, but encouraged her to take a positive line.' They spoke almost every day; Paul made Sheila feel that she could win. 'Life post-diagnosis was better than in the previous year or so,' as he put it. 'She had had a dreary period. When she had the cancer to fight, it provided a focus.'

Paul's first and lasting impression of Sheila was that she was amusing to be with, was very proud, had had a full life and was always ready for fun. He felt that she should have been given 'a damn sight more state recognition' – society should, in his view, reward its heroes and heroines for its own sake. 'But Sheila was a woman on her own, and she was naughty because she was not enough of a diplomat to play the establishment game. She was one of those who fell between all society's stools.'

Although Sheila was not ready to die, she had no doubt that she would; she could analyse her own changing physical condition. Many of the problems connected with her cancer which bothered her most were trivial – minor skin ailments and scabies, for instance – and were dealt with by the hospital. Although she believed in alternative medicine, and went to an acupuncturist recommended by Paul MacLoughlin, she decided to put her trust in the traditional approach of the Royal Marsden and Brompton Hospitals.

She called her cancer 'the Beast', and deliberately set out to fight it for as long and as hard as she could, never once entertaining the idea of suicide as a way out. Remembering her aunt's death, she was determined not to allow herself to be an invalid but to carry on leading as normal and active a life as possible and to retain her independence by living at home. The knowledge of impending death gave her a new lease of life and a renewed grasp on reality; after the diagnosis, her paranoia almost vanished.

In August Sheila wrote again to Gerard Kealey, thanking him as usual for the trust's financial assistance: 'It helps *very* much, & at least gives one some dignity, because as you know the circumstances I live in are far from that. . . . Alas no better news – have seen another bone specialist, but he merely says they cannot chop bits of my spine so there is no point in taking the living tumour, & that "they just have to keep my life as comfortable as possible"!!'

She was not too obsessed by her own illness to show concern for the problems of her friends, like Margot Morse, who had had a triple bypass operation, or Sheila Bond, whose husband had recently died. 'She seemed more concerned about me than she was about herself,' Sheila Bond told me. 'She was the bravest thing that ever walked, and had a fantastic concern for other people.'

In September, the Nigel Dempster column in the *Daily Mail* revealed that she was facing 'her greatest peril of all: lung cancer', and that Peter Cadbury, businessman and fellow pilot, was setting up a fund for her. Within a week, the newspaper announced that £6000 had been sent in by readers.

Sheila was by then suffering constant pain, for which she was given increasingly strong doses of morphia. Experimental pain-killing treatment at the Royal Marsden left her with a paralysed left eyelid, about which she was extremely self-conscious, and led to another stint in hospital, at the Brompton. From there she wrote to Gerard Kealey, apologising that her handwriting was 'worse as see almost double vision': she praised the teams of doctors and the treatment, which was 'nothing short of miraculous', although she complained that life in a public ward undid much of the good: 'Thank heavens, I am in a side ward this time, as the other drives you into deepest depression.'

When I spoke to Sheila before she went into the Brompton she sounded so depressed that I feared she was going there to die, although I was sure that she had not come to terms with her own life and death sufficiently to do so in peace. I wrote her a late night letter which next morning I hesitated about posting, although eventually I did so. She rang me from the hospital to ask if she could photocopy it for the Macmillan nurses who were helping her to accept and understand what was happening to her. It was by one of them that I was sent a copy:

> For God's sake – and yours – keep fighting! You aren't ready to give in yet, and you *mustn't* until you are ready both spiritually and psychologically. Never mind physically – so OK – easier said than done; but . . . I know you mustn't let yourself die until you are at peace. I like the idea of reincarnation best. . . . What'll you choose? – But you still have some of this life to lead anyway, of that I am covinced. Convince yourself – and don't die until you are ready. Then your spirit can waft undefeated until it is allocated a new body . . . we want you here for Christmas: don't let us down by giving in now. . . . If we are being a nuisance, just tell us to shut up and go away – that's what friends are for too. . . . Wait until your soul is ready to float away from your body's pain in peace, and don't you dare go a second before it is.

Sheila's life had become a succession of hospital treatment and periods spent at home when she kept to her intention of not giving in and of going out every day. Friends took her out to lunches and dinners, although she ate and drank little, or for shopping expeditions which equally tired and relaxed her. She needed something to look forward to from one week to the next, to keep her going. Each time it seemed that she would not make the next hurdle – and each time she did, and looked ahead to yet another. When she sold her flying memorabilia at auction in November, she was given press and television coverage. She revelled in the renewed limelight, and rose to every public occasion with dignity.

People she had not heard from for years rang her up and wrote to her. 'They're coming out of the woodwork,' she told me, with a hint of bitterness that many of them had stayed away when she had needed help and support before, during the years when she had lived almost in limbo. The one person who did not contact her was her stepmother, although David and Jean Hurlstone had written to tell her of Sheila's illness. 'We knew that she had Parkinson's disease, but surely she could have telephoned or asked someone else to write for her,' Jean said.

Aileen died in December. She did not mention Sheila in her will. A few months later a parcel of books which Sheila had given her father as birthday or Christmas presents was delivered by someone who declined to speak to Sheila, although she was in.

The Hurlstones offered Sheila a home with them in Derbyshire; but she did not want to leave London, where she felt in touch with her friends. For the same reason she rejected the idea of eventually going into a hospice, as the nearest one was too far out of London.

She spent Christmas with us again, although until almost the last minute we half expected her not to make it. Her participation was inevitably less active than the previous year, but she was as cheerful an addition to the family as before.

Her next objective was a benefit luncheon organized by Peter Cadbury at the May Fair Hotel in January. It was, as the *Daily Mail* put it, 'a glittering occasion to honour Sheila', who was definitely the star of the show, although protocol decreed that she should give precedence to Princess Michael. Sheila looked like royalty herself, as she stood greeting each of the guests who had paid £35 a head for their tickets. Eulogistic speeches were made about her by men eminent in the aviation world; her own speech was a brief and moving tribute to the work of the doctors and nurses, as well as to the friends, who had helped her during the first traumatic six months of her illness – which most had expected by then to have already killed her.

Sheila in her flying heyday looked down from June Mendoza's portrait as yet more of her memorabilia were sold during an auction after the luncheon. Those who could afford to do so outbid each other in an attempt to ensure, without appearing to be patronizing by offering charity, that she would be spared financial worries at the end of her life. A framed autographed photograph of the Duchess of York fetched £750. 'The room was full of love,' Sheila said afterwards. 'People are openly showing me love – people I would never have believed had anything in them.'

The following month she went to America for the last time, flying both ways on Concorde. This was arranged by an independent film company which was making a television documentary of her flying life; she had already been interviewed for it at some length by Brian Wolfe, who was a friend of Max Coote's and met her when Max bought *Myth Too*. 'We were all nearly in tears during the interview,' Brian Wolfe told me. 'She gave a very very graphic description of cancer and what it meant – very moving indeed; and she had a terrific sentimental side.'

The trip had been a milestone which Sheila was determined to pass, and gave her a chance to renew her acquaintance with the men from NASA, as well as to see other friends in Washington. They found it difficult to accept that she was dying: she had somehow drawn on hidden reserves of energy, and behaved almost as if she had nothing wrong with her.

Apart from two sightings of spies in Washington restaurants – which could, at this stage in Sheila's illness, be attributed to the cancer and the painkilling drugs which by then had been prescribed in large quantities – her time in America was a triumph of willpower. As soon as she arrived back in England she collapsed, and spent some time in hospital. Her recoveries were becoming more and more difficult.

When the film was finished, she hated it; she objected in particular to an unsubstantiated comment by Beverley Snook that she was 'a pain in the arse', and to a story that she had set an alarm clock when she was flying and slept until it woke her. The BBC apparently shared her reservations, although perhaps not for the same reasons, as they turned it down; it was, however, sold to nine other countries.

I was surprised to receive an invitation for myself and my husband from Sheila to a birthday party at the end of April; we did not think that she could either afford it, or was well enough. She explained that she wanted to repay some of the people she considered her closest friends for the help and hospitality they had given her. We met – a dozen of us – at a wine bar a few hundred yards from her flat. By the time we adjourned to the Thai restaurant next door we had run up a sizeable wine bill, which Sheila insisted on paying. Things went from good to better, or perhaps from bad to worse, at the restaurant. Sheila presided from the head of the table in a haze of cigarette smoke, egging each of us on to our pet hobby-horses and then sitting back to enjoy the ensuing heated but reasonably amicable arguments. Sadie and a retired diplomat from Laos retired at a reasonable hour, separately.

It was between two and three in the morning when the party eventually broke up. Paul MacLoughlin decreed that we should have a race down the middle of Cambridge Street, and gave us all handicaps according to what he thought our political affiliation might be. Pushing Sheila in her wheelchair, he gave himself a head start. The wife of the diplomat from Laos was last seen and heard hammering at her own front door while the rest of us continued to disturb the peace towards Sheila's flat.

Paul MacLoughlin described the evening, which he called Sheila's grand finale, in his diary: 'Sheila at her wickedest best – waving her stick and shouting abuse.' I do not remember any abuse, although she was certainly shouting us all on. But Sheila's last birthday party was certainly a memorable occasion.

Her next goal was a Fighter Meet in May, to which she was flown by helicopter and which was to be aviation's last tribute to 'brave air ace Sheila'. Arthur Gibson, one of the organizers, had had his firm's Aztec painted in her original livery, and helped her into the cockpit to watch a fly-past: she was saluted by ten aircraft in formation. The *Daily Express* had organized the presentation of a Sheila Scott trophy, to be awarded later in the year to someone considered to have achieved something outstanding in aviation; it represented a moth, the *Myth* of her various aircraft. Sheila called the day 'one of the nicest things that's ever happened to me'.

In the summer Sheila went to Malta, to visit Trevor Jones and his new wife Jackie. 'Sheila was quite happy during her last stay in Malta,' Trevor wrote to me. 'We took her around a lot and had reunions with friends she had made here. Pain of course intervened and pills helped. . . . With all her idiosyncrasies one's outstanding memory of Sheila can only be contained in COURAGE from her first flight until her death.' His wife found Sheila exhausting, but told me: 'We got on well, surprisingly enough.'

Back in Pimlico, on a sultry evening at the end of July Sheila was watching television, with both the front and the back doors open to allow some air to circulate through the flat, when she heard a noise in the hall. There was a bag on the floor: she assumed that the wind must have blown it off its hook, and put it back. Ten or fifteen minutes later she again heard something, and turned round to see a man standing in the living room doorway.

Her immediate reaction was of rage that her privacy had been invaded. 'What the hell are you doing here? Get out!' she shouted as she stood up and advanced towards the figure. She grabbed her cordless telephone. The intruder, presumably thinking she was pressing an alarm button, backed down the hall passage, taking her raincoat off the coatstand and putting it over his face, then stumbled up the steep steps to the street. After her anger had subsided she felt sorry for him, as well as alarmed by the incident. 'He had sad eyes,' she said, 'and didn't have an ugly look about him.' Although she turned the episode into an amusing story, she was clearly upset and alarmed by it.

I wondered at first whether she had either imagined or invented the intrusion; but her raincoat had dirty marks on it where it had been dropped on the pavement, and her paranoia had been less in evidence since she had had the real enemy of her illness to fight. Three days later I was with her when a young CID officer asked her to go over her story again. He took it seriously enough to promise to make sure she was given an alarm pendant which would ring straight through to the local police station.

At the beginning of August I accompanied Sheila to an out-patient's appointment at the Royal Marsden Hospital. In the taxi on the way back to her flat she cried, and apologised for doing so. 'I always felt I could control myself and not mind about physical pain,' she said, 'but I'm frightened.'

Her lifeline during the last few months was Bella Mackinnon, a tiny, plump, rosy-cheeked, bustling person who looked far younger than she was – she was older than Sheila. Bella had replaced a series of home helps whom Sheila had found unsatisfactory in some way. Without Bella, Sheila would not have been able to live alone; her housework did not always come up to Sheila's standards, but her unstinting devotion more than made up for this. She renewed Sheila's dressings every day, did her shopping, ran her bath, and took telephone messages. When she was at the receiving end of a bout of ill humour, she took no offence: 'I know it's not Sheila talking

– it's the drugs,' she told me. Whenever Sheila was in hospital Bella visited her every day, and continued to look after the flat.

Visiting Sheila in hospital always turned into a mini-party, with coffee and white wine for her guests although she no longer felt like drinking either. One of the by-products of her illness was that people from different compartments of her life met for the first time. Norman Lonsdale, of whom Sheila had often spoken to me, called briefly while I was with her in the Marsden in September, bringing flowers. Philip Howe, colonel and charity director, arrived next, with Ann Lennard; they had met Sheila as neighbours and fellow campaigners against Westminster City Council, and were almost daily visitors during the last few months of her life.

When we were alone, Sheila talked about her need to work out her beliefs about what came after death. 'I keep trying to have my Big Think,' she said, 'but somehow my mind always shies away. In the sky it all worked out.' She had been dreaming more than usual, but could not decide whether her dreams were premonitions, or whether she was 'going gaga under drugs'. Both her sleeping and her waking hours were haunted – not unpleasantly – by a grey furry animal, a large rat, or maybe a rabbit or a hare, and often a grey human shadow. While I was with her the creature came and went, curling up weightlessly on her bed and visible only to her, but the human shadow stayed away.

After taking her morphia, Sheila apologised for talking too much – it always had that effect at first, she said. Her thoughts followed each other aloud, and made sense, although she was afraid that they might not. 'At least I've done what I wanted to do – not many woman have that,' she told me. 'But I do miss having a live-in partner, and the high of sex and romance.'

Summoning more willpower and self-control than most people would have had at such an advanced stage of cancer and pain, Sheila returned from the hospital to spend several more weeks of limited independence in her flat. We sat together on a warm autumn afternoon in her tiny enclosed garden. Although her feet and ankles were painfully swollen and purple, and her face puffy, there was little else to betray that she was terminally ill and that the end could not be far away.

Her courage and determination over the last year and a half of her life were heroic, and revealed the stamina and willpower which had taken her to the top of the world. Before she became ill, I had often wondered how someone with no particular physical strength and who was so easily depressed could have managed to make such gruelling long-distance flights of endurance; her illness revitalized the mental strength which had been in abeyance during the depression and the paranoia of the limbo years.

That sunny afternoon Sheila made what seemed to me at the time a very strange remark: 'I've got all these drugs in the flat – they trust me with them.' Her pride in being trusted to take the drugs as they were prescribed made sense only much later, when I realized that she had once been addicted to heroin.

It was the last time I saw her at home. The following Monday morning, Bella telephoned to tell me that Sheila had been taken into the Royal Marsden. Visitors poured in to see her: Bella was with her almost constantly, and Brian Field spent a couple of hours with her every lunchtime. They talked about dying; Sheila had said to Brian a few months earlier, as she had said to me, 'I know I'm going to die – I'm not ready – I haven't had my Big Think.' I visited her with my youngest daughter on the Sunday; she was cheerful, relaxed, and as usual fun to be with.

At the beginning of the week Brian told her: 'We'll go for a walk, kick up the leaves, see the autumn.' She promised she would. On Monday she told Margot Morse: 'You know, you and I have fought it out. I know we've all got to go some time, but it's nice to be here.' 'I've had enough,' she told Sadie later. On Wednesday, she asked Brian to give her a hug: 'I haven't had a hug for so long.' They had a good hug, and talked of walking in the woods. 'I'm ready to die now,' Sheila told him.

In the middle of Wednesday night, I was woken by the telephone. 'Judy, it's Bella. The hospital has just rung me to say that Sheila is very ill. They don't expect her to wake up. If we want to see her. . . .'

Sheila would probably have ascribed the dreams which filled the rest of my sleep to extra-sensory perception. I dreamt that she was already dead. She looked serene, and I and a group of friends who had arrived too late to say goodbye drank champagne as that was what we thought she would have wanted us to do. As I held out my glass to have it filled, Sheila turned her head, very slowly, and gave me an enormous conspiratorial wink. I had seen that wink many times before, when she wanted to share a joke or hint at something which struck her as ridiculous.

Bella had already been at the hospital for several hours by the

time I arrived. Sheila was asleep; she had not been fully conscious since the previous evening. I was pleased to see that the nurses had done her hair: she would not have liked to die looking dishevelled. Bella and I sat with her for a couple of hours, sometimes talking quietly, sometimes silent. At midday, a basket of flowers was delivered from Hugh Collins. Not long afterwards, Sheila's laboured breathing became slower and quieter, and then stopped. She looked peaceful, as serene as she had been in my dream. Her death at the age of sixty-two was announced on the six o'clock news; she was in fact sixty-seven.

Sheila was cremated at Golders Green; her funeral was arranged according to her wishes by David and Jean Hurlstone. 'What shall we do about food?' Jean had asked her. 'Oh, go to the pub,' Sheila had replied.

The Reverend David Burton Evans, chaplain of the Guild of Air Pilots and Navigators, said that Sheila had felt the touch of God while she was flying, and had 'always felt that someone had taken care of her in all the stupid things that she had occasionally done', although she would not be pressed about her deepest beliefs. 'She could also be bloody-minded,' he added, remembering Sheila the person; there was to be a memorial service for Sheila the pilot – although, as he pointed out, the two were indivisible.

A year after her death, her ashes were scattered from a light aircraft by Fred Stringer, master of the Guild of Air Pilots and Navigators, over Thruxton, where they had both learnt to fly.

Dancing the Skies

John Gillespie Magee

(read at Sheila Scott's funeral and memorial services)

Oh! I have slipped the surly bonds of earth
   And danced the skies on laughter-silvered wings;
Sunward I've climbed, and joined the tumbling mirth
   Of sun-split clouds – and done a hundred things
You have not dreamed of – wheeled and soared and swung
   Hung in the sunlit silence. Hov'ring there
I've chased the shouting wind along, and flung
   My eager craft through footless halls of air.

Up, up the long, delirious, burning blue
   I've topped the wind-swept heights with easy grace
Where never lark, nor even eagle flew –
   And while with silent, lifting mind I've trod
The high, untrespassed sanctity of space,
   Put out my hand and touched the face of God.

Index

Abbotsford, British Columbia, 224
a' Brook, Dr Michael, 232
Adelaide, 152ff
aerobatics, 47, 56
  world championships, Hungary, 49
Aero Club *see* Royal Aero Club
  Austrian, 4
  Munster (Ireland), 89
aircraft: Beagle, 70
  Beechcraft Queen Air, 97
  Concorde, 128, 203, 249
  Cessna, 49, 54, 237
  Condor, 61
  Hunter jet, 113
  Jackaroo, converted Tiger Moth, 42, 45, 49, 53f,
    57, 93
  Jodel, 54
  Machetti, 143, 150f
  Mosquito, 57
  Mustang, 57
  Myth, Myth Sunpip, Myth Too, Mythre, see separate
    entries
  Piper, 59, 99, 100, 103
  Piper Aztec, 161, 164, 192, 205 (*see also Mythre*)
  Piper Cherokee, 99
  Piper Comanche, 48, 49, 54, 58, 60, 62, 68ff (*see*
    also Myth)
  Navajo, 189
  Tiger Moth, 42, 57 (*see also* Jackaroo)
  Vickers Vimy, 117
Adelaide, 152ff
Adelaide News, 154
Alice Springs, 153
Adventurer's Club, New York, 110
Airfix Ltd, 117
air races: 49
  Australian race, 141ff
  Daily Mail transatlantic 'Top of the Towers' race,
    122, 129ff, 134–5
  King's Cup Air Race, 47, 99, 104
  Manx Air Derby, 61
  National Air Races, 45ff, 61, 89, 99
  Sicily, 54
air shows: Abbotsford, British Columbia, 224
  Biggin Hill, 192–3
  Fighter Meet, 250
Air Tours, 67

Akai video camera, 172
Alaska, 178, 182
Alberta, 206
Albuquerque, 224f
Alcock, Sir John William, 74, 117
Aldrin, Edwin, 105
Alexandra, Princess, 105, 108, 207
Allen, Lt Chris, 168
Allen, Sir Peter, 108
Allen, Jack, 27
Alps, 75
America, 50ff, 54f, 62, 79, 102, 123, 194ff, 198,
    215–16, 224, 233, 237, 243, 249
  Air Force, 110
  aviation, 50ff
Ames, Simon, 43, 50, 57, 60, 67, 85, 104
Amster, Sidney, 237
Anchorage, 184
Andersen, Mary, 211
Anderson, J. R. L. (John), 120–21, 122–3
Anrite, Aviation, 77
Andoya, 174–5
Antarctic, planned flight over, 191, 192–3, 198,
    210
Apollo, American space launch, 163–4
appeal funds, 90–91, 201–2
Aquascutum, 103
Arctic Circle, 173
  clothing, 174
  Ocean, 174
  Research Station, 184
  Antarctic flight, plans for, 191, 192f, 198, 210
Arrowsmith, Clive, 110
Ashford Airport, 136
Aston Martin, 130, 132, 134
Athens, 75, 143, 185
Atlantic, 79, 84, 107, 111, 117, 130, 132, 133ff, 158,
    198; *see also* Records
Australia, 45, 57, 60, 62, 71, 77ff, 141ff, 157, 185,
    191
Australia race, 141ff
Austria, 50, 243
Austrian Aero Club, 3–4
Azores, 84
Aztec, *see* aircraft, Piper *and Mythre*

BAC, 128

Bach, Richard, 197
Baden-Baden, 235
Baffin Island, 205
Bahamas, 111
Bahamian Tourist Board, 111, 116
Bahrein, 185
Bald Eagles, 197
Bali, 77, 78, 152
Barbour, Joyce, 26
Barefoot in the Sky, 202
Barrow, 178, 182
Barter Island, 182
Bartlett, Valerie, 90
Baston, Les, 148–9, 161
Batten, Jean, 79, 111, 144
Batten, John, 79
Battersea heliport, 130
BBC, 58, 114, 117, 132, 134, 150, 249
Baxter, Raymond, 135
BEA, 75, 173
Beauregard, Marie-Joseph de, 235
Bedford, Massachusetts, 205
Belfast, 61
Bellamy, Rupert Leaman, 21ff, 24, 25, 26, 28, 29
Bellamy, Frederick, 25
Bellew, Lady Gwen, 212ff, 227, 241
Benghazi, 97, 100, 138, 169–70
Benjamin, Benjie, 53
Bianchi, Angie, 97
Bianchi, Doug, 95ff, 104–6, 132
Bianchi, Edna, 96
Biggin Hill, 192, 193
biomedical tests, on Polar flight, 166, 169ff
Bird, Kay, 204–5, 206, 208, 222
Bird, Nancy Bird Walton, 90, 156
Bird, Richard (Dickie), 26f
Blake, John, 49f, 57, 73, 135, 142, 154, 204
Blyth, Chay, 121, 190–91
BOAC, 69, 78, 79, 105, 138
Board of Trade, 162, 167
Bodo, 173ff, 178
Bond, Sheila, 246
Bormann, Marianne, 229–30
BOSS, 173–4, 139–40, 229, 230, 232, 234, 243
Boston, 134
Bowden House psychiatric clinic, 200
BP, 58, 64
Brabazon, Lord, 47
Brabazon, Lady, 45
Brantly helicopter factory, 54
Bredon, 225f
Brighton, 198ff
Brisbane, 78
British Balloon and Airship Club, 65
British Columbia, 224
British Committee for Exports to Canada, 102
British Embassy, 22, 110
British Executive Air Services Ltd, 48

British Leyland, 191
British Racing and Sports Car Club, 202
British School of Motoring, 190
British Skydiving Ltd, 53
British Week (Canada), 105, 107ff
British Women Pilots' Association (BWPA), 43, 52, 55, 61, 89, 90, 120, 129, 204, 235–6, 238
Brompton Hospital, 246–7
Brown, Sir Arthur Whitten, 74, 117
Brussels, 60
BUA, 138, 145, 159
Buck Tooth (mascot), 74, 76, 134, 176, 180, 194, 204, 236
Bruce, Gordon, 137, 139
Buddhism, 30, 35, 208
Burbeck, Rodney, 70ff
Burton Evans, Rev. David, 254

Cadbury, Peter, 246, 248
Calcutta, 76
California, 237
Campbell, Donald, 65, 71–2
Canada, 6, 93, 102, 103, 123, 134, 135, 194, 205, 224
Canadian Expo, 93, 102
Canton, 80, 185
Cape Canaveral, 161ff
Cape Town, 98, 99f, 101, 139
Mayor of, 99f, 102
Capri, 54
Cardiff, 45
Carpenter, Tom, 168, 230
Catholics, 243
Catlin Aviation, 201
CBS, 92, 163, 166
Cessna aircraft, 40, 49, 54, 150, 172, 175, 237
Sales Week, 50
Chad, 97
Champion Spark Plugs, 58, 63
Trophy, 61
Chapman, Phil, 163ff, 169, 180, 186, 188, 198, 205, 206
Charter Clinic, psychiatric hospital, 232
Chile, 198
Chipmunk, 49
Chichester, Sir Francis, 89, 96, 115, 117, 121
Chisholm, Judith, 228
Christianity, 10, 208, 224
Christie, Naomi, 238
Churchill, Alberta, 206
circumnavigation, 62; *see* record flights
Clarkson Aviation, 196
Claridge's, 19
clubs: Adventurer's, 330
Austrian Aero Club, 110
Durban Country Club,
flying clubs, 42, 43, 47
Munster Aero Club, 89

Special Forces Club, 160, 229, 231–2, 236–7, 238–9, 243
Tiger Club, 43, 47, 53, 74
Variety Club of Great Britain, 90, 124
Zonta, 81, 83, 89, 201–2, 227, 232
see also Royal Aero Club
Coachair Services, 136
Cobham, (Sir) Alan, 8, 44, 47, 53, 62–3, 68–9, 73, 84, 91ff, 103, 105, 113, 125
Achievement Award, 63
Air Circus, 8
trust fund, 237, 242
Cobham, Michael, 237
Cochrane, John, 128
Collins, Hugh, 234–5, 254
Collins (publishers), 113
Collins, Sandra, 108, 119, 132, 158, 220
Collins, Tabitha, 158, 220
Colmore, Philip, 226
Comanche, *see* aircraft, *Piper and Myth Too*
Commons, House of, 106
Conrad. Max, 81, 110
Conran, Shirley, 236
Coote, Max, 189, 193, 194, 223–4, 249
Copenhagen, 135
Cote, Chuck, 164, 171, 178, 180
Coulson, Alan, 139
CSE Aviation, 48, 59, 68, 138, 145, 148, 161, 166, 168, 230
Cuban crisis, 51–2
Cussen, Dr Denis, 187

Daily Express, 250
Daily Mail, 58, 93, 116, 122, 129–30, 150, 193, 248
Air Race, 122, 129ff, 134f
Daily Mirror, 85–6, 89, 90, 190
Daily Telegraph, 229
Dakar, 111
Dallas, 233
Damascus, 75
Dan Air, 56, 191
Darwin, 77–8, 144, 150, 152, 154, 185
Aero Club, 152
Davies, Alison, 202
Day, John, 78
de Havilland, National Air Racing Trophy, 47
Delhi, 76
Dempster, Nigel, 246
Denham Studios, 20
Desert Island Discs, 90
Dexter, Jeanette, 190, 207, 212
Donegall, Lord, 130f
Doolittle, Gen. James, 110
Dublin, 61
Duffy, Jean, 194
Duke-Woolley, Hilary, 36ff, 41
Duke of Edinburgh, 89, 135
Award scheme, 229
Dunkerley, Fred, 57

Durban, 99f, 208

Earhart, Amelia, 52, 56, 80, 111, 147, 192
East Midlands Airport, 235
Edwards, Geoffrey, 141, 145, 186
Effner, Jack, 171
Eggleston, June, 158, 164, 194
El Adem, 101
El Paso, 83
Elstree, 40, 41, 43, 67, 189, 204
Equator, 110, 185, 196, 198
Erskine, Lord (Iain), 159–60, 238ff
European records, 57ff
European Women Pilots' Association, 3, 235–6, 243
Eustace, Jane, 122
Evans, Pete, 143
Expo 67, 102

FAA, 81
Academy, Oklahoma, 55
FAI, 161
Farnborough, Institute of Aviation Medicine, 76, 166–7
Fédération des Pilotes Europeennes (FPE), 3, 235, 243
Field Aviation, 173
Fields, Brian, 241, 253
Field, Lee, 178
Fighter Meet, 250
Fiji, 80, 157, 185, 191
Fijian chief, 204
Firestone Tyres, 58, 60, 61
First Cross Ltd, 227
First World War, 6–7, 91
Fleet Air Arm, 113f, 138, 142, 226
Flight magazine, 61
Flores, 151
Flying Treasure Hunt, 111
Flying 'W' Ranch, 51f
Forbes, Ian, 58, 60, 75
Ford, 191, 193
Presentation of Capri at Biggin Hill Air Show, 193
prize, Australia race, 154
Foyles, 121
Free French Forces, 234
French Resistance, 234
Fricker, Alan, 214
Fricker, Connie, 129, 213f, 232
Friede, Eleanor, 197

GAPAN *see* Guild of Air Pilots and Air Navigators
Gander, 84, 107, 134
Garrick Theatre, 27
Gatwick, 70, 142, 158, 169, 191
Geneva, 58, 61, 65, 75
Gibson, Admiral Donald, 114
Gibson, Arthur, 143, 150ff, 250

Gielgud, Sir John, 124
Gilbert and Ellice Islands, 158
Girls' Venture Corps, 210, 229
Globe and Mail, Toronto, 108
Gloucester, Prince William, Duke of, 157f
Goddard Space Center, 169ff, 178ff, 192, 194
Goodchild, Bert, 106, 133
Good Morning, (naval wartime mag.), 19f
Goose Bay, 135
Gosport, naval hospital, 16f
Gray, Elizabeth, 71
Graylin Hotel, 195, 197
Greenland, 177ff
Green Room Club, 124
Griffith, 155
Guild of Air Pilots and Air Navigators, 53, 74, 89, 128, 236, 254
   Silver Award of Merit, 89
Guildway, 224, 231

The Hague, 60
Harley Street, 18f, 27
Harmon Trophy, 79, 104f, 107, 109
Harper, Aileen, 8, 9; *see* Hopkins, Aileen
Harrods, 39, 122
Hawkes, Ted, 64
Heath, Edward, 136
Heathrow Airport, 73, 84ff, 97, 133, 173, 186
Heaton, John, 41, 42, 45f, 53
Helicopter Association of America, 228
Hendon, 234
Herridge, Dr Colin, 200, 232
Hewitt, Bill, 69, 74, 77, 95, 105
Heyerdahl, Thor, 121
High Altitude Course, 55–6
   certificate, 113
High Wycombe Hospital, 220
Hilton Hotel, 159
Hoagland, Dick, 163ff, 184, 186f
Hodder and Stoughton, 113, 115, 120, 122, 197
Holland, 64
Honolulu, 80, 82, 158, 185
Hope, Bob, 83
Hopeline, 27
Hopkins, Aileen (stepmother), 9, 10, 11, 13ff, 19, 23, 25, 26, 221, 224, 248
Hopkins, Edyth (mother), *see* Kenward
Hopkins, Harold (father), 6, 7, 8, 9, 19, 23, 25, 26, 85, 221, 224, 225, 226
Hopkins, Sheila Christine, 6ff
Hopkins, William, 6
Hopkins, W.H. and Co., 7
Horton Hospital, Epsom, 213ff
hospitals, 33
   Bowden House, 200f
   Brompton, 246f
   Charter Clinic, 232
   Dudley Road, Birmingham, 16

High Wycombe, 220
Horton, 213ff
   National Temperance, 27
   naval, Gosport, 16
   Roehampton, 37
   Royal Marsden, 246, 251ff
   St Stephens, 38
Housing Association, 242
Howard, Jean Ross, 55, 227, 233
Howe, Col Philip, 252
Hughes, Christine, 61
Hull, 206
Hunter jet, 113
Huntly, Lady Pamela, 61f, 73, 85
Hurlstone, David, 219, 221f, 226, 248, 254
Hurlstone, Jean, 219, 221f, 226, 248, 254
Hurlstone, Peter, 11
Hurlstone, Millie, 219, 221, 226
Hurricane Agnes, 195
   victims fund, 201
Hussein, King of Jordan, 89

Iceland, 192, 194
Idaho, 210, 237
I Must Fly, 115, 117, 121f, 125
India, 240, 241f
Indian Women Pilot's Association, 241
Indonesia, 77, 147ff, 151ff
   Air Force, 150, 152
International Convention of Women, 210f
International Tour of Britain (motor), 202
International Wool Secretariat (IWS), 141f, 150
Institute of Sports Medicine, 166
IRA, 243
IRLS (Interrogation Recording and Locating System), 164ff, 198
Isabella d'Este Award, 90
Isle of Man, 61
Isle of Wight, 129
Italy, 143

Jackaroo, *see* aircraft
Jacobs, David, 190
Jaipur, 76
Jamaica, 111, 127
Jason, 60
Jeffers, Lana, 118ff, 122, 124, 127f, 130ff, 135, 148f, 150, 158f, 197, 199f, 232
Jersey, 45
   Tourist Board, 89f
Jet Ranger helicopter, 133
Johannesburg, 139, 208f
Johnson, Amy, 44, 57, 60, 71f, 77, 94, 97, 98, 111, 120, 130f, 206
Jones, Jackie, 250
Jones, Margaret, 58
Jones, (Col.) Trevor, 159f, 238ff, 250
Jordan, King Hussein of, 89

Journal of Aerospace Medicine, 187
Juba, 171

Kansas, 50f
Karachi, 76, 143, 185
Kealey, Gerard, 237f, 242, 246f
Kent, Princess Michael of, 248
Kentley, Margaret/Peter, 155
Kenward, Edyth (mother), 7, 8, 12, 14, 16
Kenwood, 94, 97ff
Kenya, 100, 169, 208
Kerr, Deborah, 20, 24
Khartoum, 138, 170f
Kidlington, 59 (*see also* Oxford, CSE)
Kildare, Lord, 59
Kimberley, Lord, 30ff
King's Cup (Air Race, trophy), 47, 54, 104
Kingsley, Terry, 143, 156
Knapman, Dr William, 200
Knox-Johnson, Robin, 121
Korda, Alexander, 17, 19, 20, 23
Korda, Peter, 17ff, 21, 23
Kronfeld Club 230
Kupang, 151

Las Vegas, 228
Lea, Cheryl, 208ff
Leavesden, 70, 86
Lennard, Ann, 252
Lewis, David, 122
Libya, 97, 101, 138, 169ff
    pollution over Libyan desert, 171
licences, *see under* Scott, Sheila, flying
Lindbergh, Charles, 192
Loyd, Peter, 152ff
Lloyds, 201, 234
Lockhaven, 110, 194, 205
Lodge Flying Group, 189
Lombank, 92, 168, 193, 197, 201
London, Lord Mayor of, 99, 102
Longmire, Rosemary and Tom, 210, 215, 224f
Lonsdale, Norman, 65ff, 68f, 71, 73, 76f, 85, 91ff,
    97, 112, 116, 124, 128, 139f, 172, 230, 252
Lothian, Lady, 228f
Lovell, James, 105
Luanda, 98
Luton, 86
Lympne, 136

McAlpine, Sir Robert and Sons, aviation division,
    86
Macdonald, Captain Peter, 60
McDonald, 'Mac', 75
McGinley, Fiona, 167, 172
Machetti, 143, 150f
Mackinnon, Bella, 215ff
Maclean, Archie, 91, 111, 112, 124

Maclean, Kaye, 91ff, 103, 105, 107, 108, 110, 111,
    112, 115, 117, 123ff, 129, 145, 157, 161ff, 195f,
    207, 208, 210, 216, 218f, 221ff, 232f, 237;
    suicide, 233
MacLoughlin, Dr Paul, 245f, 250
Macmillan publishers, 197
Macmillan nurses, 247
Madras, 185
Maitland Smith, Geoffrey, 112
Makassar, 147ff
Malta, 97, 101, 138, 172, 238ff, 250
Mandela, Nelson, 137f, 229f, 237
Mansion House, 102, 105, 128
Manx Air Derby, 61
Markham, Beryl, 208
Masefield, Peter, 70, 78, 227
Masefield, Charles, 78
Massachusetts, 206
Matthews, Stanley, 191
Mayfair Hotel, 248
Mayne, Philip, 60
Mead, Margaret, 211
Meccano Ltd, 117
Mediterranean, 169
Mendoza, June, 120, 121, 248
Metterlink, Charles, 137
Miller, Arnold, 186
Minimodels Ltd, 117
Ministry of Aviation, 165
Mock, Gerry, 71
Molyneux, James, 224, 231
Monument, 210f
Monkton, Bryan, 156
Montreal, 102
Morgan, Henry, 137
Morse code, 145ff
Morse, Margot, 227, 232, 246, 253
Moscow, 116
Mulchrone, Vincent, 193
Mosquito, 57
Murphy, Terry, 171
Myth, 42, 45ff, 48, 53f, 250
Myth Too, 70, 74ff, 85f, 89, 90, 91, 94, 95, 99, 101,
    107, 109, 111, 112f, 117, 124, 133ff, 138f, 144ff,
    157, 160f, 166, 168, 189, 193, 204, 212, 223f,
    226, 249
Myth Sunpip, 59, 61, 62, 65, 68
Mythre, 166ff, 168ff, 189, 191, 194ff, 205, 206

Nairobi, 138, 169, 171, 184
NASA, 80, 163ff, 173ff, 180ff, 184, 187, 198, 215,
    249
    Satellite tracking experiment and, 164ff
Nassau, 111, 112, 116
Natal, 111
National Geographic magazine, 166
National Portrait Gallery, 120
National Temperance Hospital, 27

Nestlé, 63f
Newfoundland, 106, 134
New Mexico, 224
New York, 51, 52, 83f, 92, 105, 109, 110, 117, 132,
    134f, 158, 164
New Zealand, 79f
Nice, 3
Nimbus satellite, 164, 184, 198
Ninety Nines (99s), 52f, 61, 74, 83, 99, 112, 127,
    129, 155, 158, 207, 210, 213f, 237, 241
Nord, Greenland, 177ff, 187
North Atlantic, 192
North Pole, 159ff, 174ff, 180ff, 186, 196, 228
North Sea, 127f
Northolt, 59f
Norwegian Air Force, 175
Norway, 168, 172ff
November, Pacific weather station, 83
Nubian, HMS, 134, 142

Oakes, Claudia, 237
Oakley, Vaughan, 194
Oakley, Vaughan and Clarkson, 193, 196
Observer, 109
O'Donnell, Mrs, 34
Ogilvie, David, 41
Oklahoma, 83f
On Top of the World, 188, 202
Ouis, Mrs, 36
Overbury, Elizabeth, 5, 43, 49, 61, 68, 73, 112, 115,
    128f, 136, 145, 148, 167, 206, 234
Ovaltine, 159
Oxford, 48, 128, 138; *see also* CSE, Kidlington

Pacific Ocean, 68, 79, 82f, 106, 157, 185, 198
Pacific Flight Services, 81f
Palace Theatre, 27
Paris, 101
Pawle, Gerald, 27
Peachey Properties Ltd, 227
Percival Gull, 97
Perring, Sir Ralph, 102, 107f
Perry, Dr Ian, 227, 240
Peterson, Phil, 75
Pheonix, Arizona, 83
Pilot magazine, 240
Pimley, John, 14f, 18, 34, 226
Pimley, Paddy, 226
Pimlico, 233, 236, 238, 241, 251
Pink Line, 236
Piper aircraft, 59, 99, 100, 103
    Aircraft Corporation of America, 91
    Aircraft Factory, USA, 110, 161, 194f
    Aircraft International, 58, 68, 81
    engineers, 69ff
    Aztec, Cherokee, Comanche, Navajo, *see* aircraft
Plumley, Roy, 90
Pole, North and South, 91, 111, 116, 168, 189, 196
    see also North Pole, South Pole

Pollinger, Gerald, 113, 115, 117f, 122, 125, 217
Poole and Dorset Adventure Centre, 229
Poole, Dr Bob, 244
Pooley, Bob, 67
Port Barrow, 178, 182
Portugal, 84
Post Office Tower, 117, 130, 132
Prediction magazine, 211
press, 65, 97
    conferences in Australia, 152ff
    coverage, 74, 75, 84f, 93, 97, 99
        of Australia race, 143
        of *Daily Mail* race, 134f
    relationship with, 69, 75, 86, 124
Preston, Dr Frank, 187
Prestwick, 135
Prosper, Hazel, 210
Proops, Marjorie, 58
publications, autobiographical *I Must Fly*, 115, 117,
    121f, 125
    On Top of the World, 188, 202
    Barefoot in the Sky, 202
    others in which SS is mentioned:
    Anderson, J. R. L., *The Ulysses Factor*, 120f
    Cussen, Denis and Preston, Frank, 'Sleep
        Patterns in a lone global pilot', *Journal of
        Aerospace Medicine*, 187
    Lewis, Pater, *British Racing and Record Breaking
        Aircraft*, 122
    Winter, Gordon, *Inside Boss*, 229
Punta Arenas, 198

Queen Elizabeth, 89, 100
Queensland, 185

Rangoon, 76
Reitsch, Hanna, 2, 3
René (hairdresser), 59, 131
Ridgway, John, 121
Robinson, Bill (Robbie), 105, 106f, 250
Robinson, Sadie, 236f, 245, 253
Robosch, Zsuzsi, 131
Rolls-Royce, 242
Rome, 75
Romney, Paul, 37
Ross, Dina, 236
Royal Aero Club (RAeC), 43, 49, 50, 58, 60, 67, 73,
    85, 99, 104, 127, 128, 134, 227
    Air Racing and Competitions Committee, 99
Royal Air Force, 60, 77, 101, 138, 174, 187; *see also*
    Fleet Air Arm
    Institute of Aviation Medicine, 166
    Manby, 167
    Red Arrows, 143, 150ff, 156
Royal Army Ordnance Corps, 22
Royal Flying Corps, 91
Royal Marines, 133
    School of Music, 138

Royal Navy, 19f, 142, 144; *see also* Fleet Air Arm
Royal Tournament, 207
RSPCA, 207

Sahara, 98
San Francisco, 81ff, 184
Sarbe beacon, 144
SAS, 231
Saunders, Beryl, 54, 56
Saward and Baker Ltd, 159
Scarborough, 210
Schneider Trophy, 91
Scott, Michael, 21f
Scott, Peter, 122
Scott, Sheila
  acting career, 13, 20–21, 24, 26ff, 30, 33, 35;
    Equity card, 25; lessons, 24
  acupuncture and, 223, 246
  aerobatics and, 47, 49, 56
  alcoholism, 27, 35, 37, 124, 231–2, 237, 238–9,
    243
  awards: first aviation award, in Jersey, 45
    Sir Alan Cobham Achievement Award, 63
    Amelia Earhart Award, 56
    de Havilland National Air Racing trophy, 47
    Guild of Air Pilots Silver Award of Merit, 89
    Harmon Trophy, 105–7
    Isabella d'Este Award, 90
    Jean Lennox Bird Trophy, 49
  ballooning in Holland, 64
  birth, 7; childhood, 8–15
  cancer, 219, 229, 245ff
  car accident, 220–21
  charity appearances, lectures, speeches, 91, 117,
    198ff, 207, 215, 228, 229, 237, 241, 244
  charter, plans for *Mythre*, 191–2
  Commercial Licence, 48, 51, 53
  company, establishment of, 94ff, 103, 112
  comparison of self with Amy Johnson, 44–5
  courage 3, 64, 65, 72, 87, 106, 121, 158, 229, 250
  death of 254; reactions to imminence of, 245ff
  debts, financial problems, 11, 71, 86, 88, 91–2,
    189ff, 193, 227
  diary of, 26, 32, 34, 40, 41, 42, 45ff
  divorce *see under* marriage
  driving lessons, 40–41, 190
  drug addiction, 19, 25, 27–8, 33, 35ff; overdose 19
  extra-sensory perception and, 71, 205, 215, 254
  family, *see entries under* Kenward, Hopkins,
    Hurlstone, Turner
  father, *see* Hopkins, Harold R.
  flying: clubs, 42, 43, 47
    cost of, 43f, 48, 58
    lessons and tuition, 40, 41, 47
    licences: PPL (Private Pilot's Licence), 41, 42
    instrument and night flying ratings, 48
    refused British commercial licence, 48
    American commercial licence and instrument
      rating, 53

    American helicopter licence, multi-engine and
      seaplanes ratings, 54
    American civilian high altitude ratings, 55
  funeral, memorial service, 254
  fortune teller and, 35, 212
  graphology and, 211
  helicopter: application for helicopter scholarship,
    227
    Brantly helicopters, 54
    Jet Ranger, 133
    training and licence, 54f
  heroin and, 16, 25, 35, 37
  Hurricane Agnes and, 195, 201
  insurance problems, 193ff
  marriage to Rupert L. Bellamy, 21–3, 26, 29;
    divorce, 26, 28; hopes of marriage to Teddy
    Sugden, 32, 35ff
  memorabilia, sale of, 248
  modelling career, 30, 35; course, 24
  mother, *see* Kenward, Edyth
  music and, 15, 32, 66, 76
  NASA, satellite tracking experiment and, 164ff
  nursing training, 13, 1–16; as VAD, 16ff, 20, 37
  Order of the British Empire awarded, 111, 115
  palmistry and, 211
  paranoia, persecution complex, 4, 31–2, 34, 35,
    38, 43, 66ff, 96–7, 140, 228, 230ff, 238, 241–2,
    246
  patriotism of, 2–3, 65, 71
  portraits of, 106, 120, 131
  pregnancy, abortion, 18–19
  Private Pilot's Licence, 41–2
  psychiatric treatment, 27, 31ff, 201–2, 228
  radio and, 96, 98ff, 114; problems with, 59–60,
    74–6, 78, 101, 142ff, 150ff
  records: Darwin–London, 186
    European inter-capital, 57ff
    Jean Batten's, 144
    polar, *see* North Pole
    transatlantic, 106, 135
    South African, 98, 101, 104
    see also solo flights
  religion and, 10, 48, 208–9
  sabotage, suspicion of, 148ff
  sailing and, 40, 156, 191
  Scott surname, assumption of, 24
  schizophrenia, 228, 240
  schooling, 9, 12, 13, 14
  secretaries, 66, 86, *see also* Jeffers, Lana
  sleep loss and, 87, 184ff
  smoking and, 15, 114, 124, 157, 233, 237, 245
  solo flights: European inter-capital records, 57ff
    (chapter 5)
    polar flight, 169ff
    round the world flights, 73ff, 142ff, 157f, 169ff
    South Africa, 95ff, 138
    transatlantic, 106ff, 111ff, 132ff, 135, 193f

sponsors, sponsorship, 58, 62ff, 71, 86, 94ff, 103–4, 110, 115, 119, 122, 125, 135, 139–40, 141, 192; Bahamian Tourist Board and, 111–12, 116; *see also* Maclean, Kaye
stepmother, *see* Hopkins, Aileen
suicide: attempts, 199, 212ff; threats of 124
telepathy and, 149
television and, 74, 75, 84, 96, 99; *This is your Life*, subject of, 204–5
theft of trophies, 172, 251
World Unity Trust and, 208ff
world aerobatic championships (Hungary), 49
  see also aircraft; air races; air shows; clubs; hospitals; *Myth; Myth Two; Myth Sunpip; Mythre*; press.
Second World War, 12, 17ff
Seed, Pat, 229
Shannon, 106f, 133
Sharland, Angie, 217, 220
Sharland, Freydis, 53, 55, 201, 216ff, 222
Sharland, Tim, 55, 201, 216ff
Sheila Scott Flying Enterprises, 112, 168, 198, 201
Shipton, Eric, 121
Shuttleworth-King, Selina, 217ff
Sicily, 54
Singapore, 76f, 142, 144, 185
  Aero Club, 144
Skouras, Spyros, 27
Smith, Anthony, 66
Smithsonian Institute, 111, 237
Snook, Beverley, 43, 47, 101, 104, 153, 249
Snoxell, Robert, 138
SOE, 231, 234
South Africa, 94ff, 98ff, 103, 111, 135, 136ff, 139f, 158, 208ff, 231
South Pole, 194, 198, 210
Spain, 45
Special Forces Club, 160, 229, 231f, 236f, 238ff, 243
Spencer, Fred, 82
Sperry autogyro compass, 173
Spicer, Roy, 190
Stafford, Flt Lt Eric, 174f
Steering Wheel Club, 204
stepmother – *see* Hopkins, Aileen
Stewart, Angus, 141
Stockwell, Bunty, 39
Stonehouse, John, 55
Stringer, Fred, 254
Sudan, 100, 138
  customs of, 171
Sugden, Catherine, 44
Sugden, Dr Edward (Teddy), 32ff, 35ff, 39, 40, 44, 58, 66, 73, 148, 158, 199, 227, 233
Sumba, 144
Sumbawa, 151f
Sun newspaper, 58f
Sunday Times, 236
Sutton, Joan, 205

Sydney, 78, 154ff

Tangier, 45
Tarawa, 198
Tateman, Jocelyn, 22
Thatcher, Margaret, 237
theatre, tour, 33
theatres: Garrick, Palace, Southsea, 27
Theta Sensors, 186
Thornton, Frank, 27
Thruxton, 41ff, 49, 51, 53, 254
Tiger Club, 43, 47, 53, 74
Tiger Rag, 56
Tiger Moth, *see* aircraft, *also Myth*
Tilman, Bill, 121
Times, 27
Timor, 144, 151
  Sea, 77
This Is Your Life, 204f
Toronto Sun, 205
Transpo 72 (Washington), 192, 194
Trinidad, 111, 198
Trollope, Bill, 60
Tripoli, 98
Trubshaw, Brian, 128, 203
Tupperware, 141
Turner, John, 10, 12, 34
Turner, Kathleen, 10, 219

Uganda, 171
United States, see America
  Navy, 178
Utevik, 184

Valiant for Truth Award, 228f
van den Bergh, General, 137, 139
Variety Club of Great Britain, 90, 124
Vickers Vimy, 117
Vienna, 3, 50, 243
Vorster, Mrs Tini, 211

Wagstaff, Elsie, 24
Walters, Claire, 237
Walton, Nancy Bird, 90, 156
Washington DC, 51, 110, 111, 192, 194f, 233, 237, 249
Waterpark, Lord, 59
Watford, 28
West, Ernest Waldron, 106, 120
Westminster City Council, 252
Whirly Girls, 55, 227
Whitbread's brewery, 108f, 125f, 127, 132, 135
Whitbread, Colonel, 125
  and family, 160, 191
White, Alvin, 105
White, Ann, 100
White Waltham, 45
Whittingham, Dr Peter, 187

Whitsell, Bill and Lee, 51f, 83
Wichita, 45
Wilken Aviation, 171
Williams, Jackie, 167
Wings Club, New York, 84
Winter, Gordon, 136ff, 139f, 232
Wise, Nancy, 212
Wolfe, Brian, 249
Wodehouse, Johnny, 30ff, 38
Wood, Ken, 94, 96ff, 101, 116
Woolley, Hilary Duke, 36ff, 41
Worcester, 6, 7ff, 17, 18, 22, 106
　Association, 23
　Playhouse, 7

race course, 10
Wordsworth, William, 131
World Aviation Education and Safety Congress,
　241
World Record Club, 65, 78
World Unity Trust, 208ff
Wyckoff, Charles, 163, 166, 186
Wycombe Air Park, 96
Wynne-Morgan, David, 85, 87

Young, Dottie, 54f
York, Duchess of, 249

Zonta, 81, 83, 89, 201f, 227, 232

SP 11/04

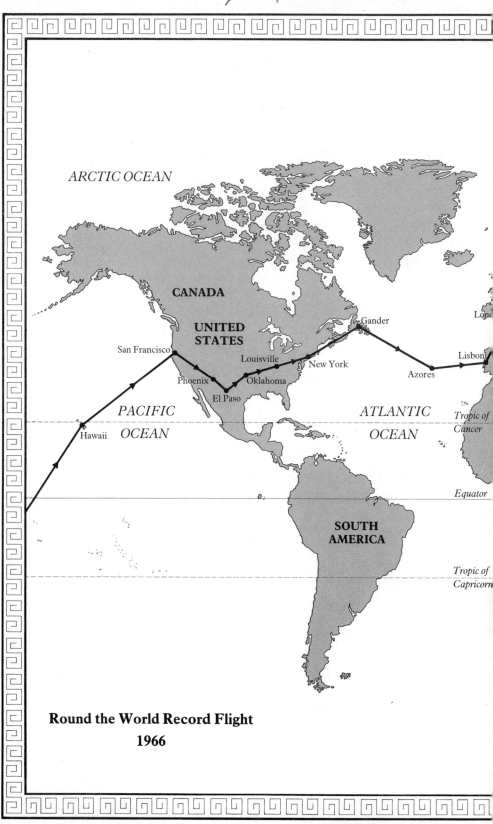

Round the World Record Flight
1966